Nicholas Murray is a biographer, poet, novelist and critic, and the author of the biographies *Bruce Chatwin*; *A Life of Matthew Arnold*; *World Enough and Time: The Life of Andrew Marvell*; *Aldous Huxley: An English Intellectual*; and *Kafka*. His most recent book with Abacus is *A Corkscrew is Most Useful: The Travellers of Empire*. He lives in Wales and London.

The
Red Sweet Wine
of Youth

*The Brave and Brief Lives
of the War Poets*

NICHOLAS MURRAY

(ABACUS)

LITTLE, BROWN

First published in Great Britain in 2010 by Little, Brown
This paperback edition published in 2012 by Abacus

A CIP catalogue record for this book
is available from the British Library.

ISBN 978-0-349-12143-7

Typeset in Caslon by M Rules
Printed and bound in Great Britain by
Clays Ltd, St Ives plc

Papers used by Abacus are from well-managed forests
and other responsible sources.

MIX
Paper from
responsible sources
FSC® C104740

Abacus
An imprint of
Little, Brown Book Group
100 Victoria Embankment
London EC4Y 0DY

An Hachette UK Company
www.hachette.co.uk

www.littlebrown.co.uk

Out of my sorrow have I made these songs

IVOR GURNEY, 'SONG AND PAIN', *COLLECTED POEMS*

Contents

Memory and Truth

In the small Welsh village of New Radnor on the border of England and Wales, by the side of the steep path leading up to the church, a stone war memorial shows a soldier in conventional pose, tin hat on his bowed head, his hands before him clasping the muzzle of a rifle whose stock is set on the ground. Grey and undistinguished, it is nonetheless representative of the seventy-five thousand similar memorials scattered across the towns and villages of Britain. Running one's finger over the lichen-spotted stone one reads the names of families still busy about the Radnor valley. A handful of names among the three-quarters of a million British soldiers who died in the war of 1914–18.

I lived in this village in the late 1980s and my next-door neighbour, a very elderly Radnorshire woman, still expressed anger at 'the Germans' who had taken all three of her brothers in the two world wars of the twentieth century. These country boys, farmworkers, labourers, tradesmen, went off to fight, calling to mind the haunting line from Wilfred Owen's poem 'Anthem for Doomed Youth':

And bugles calling for them from sad shires.

This book, however, is not primarily about those millions of ordinary young men who fought and those who died. It is about what must inevitably be a relatively small group of combatants. These were poets – some also artists and musicians – who wrote about the experience of war. It is not a book about military strategy, nor the detail of particular battles. The literature on those topics is vast and readily available. It is about poets and war, about the impact of that war on the sensibility of the artist. It is about the way poets struggled to bear witness, to speak the truth, but above all to practise their art – to live as fully as possible as writers and artists in the infernal conditions of trench warfare.

In contrast to the wars of today in Iraq and Afghanistan, the soldiery was entirely male and therefore women must often seem excluded from much of what follows. 'History has gendered the Great War as male,'[1] a recent critic wrote, and the feminist Christabel Pankhurst, writing only weeks before the War began in August 1914, saw what it entailed for her as a radical and a woman:

> As I write a dreadful war-cloud seems about to burst and deluge the peoples of Europe with fire-slaughter, ruin – this then is the World as men have made it, life as men have ordered it.
>
> A man-made civilisation, hideous and cruel enough in time of peace, is to be destroyed.
>
> A civilisation made by men only is a civilisation which defies the law of nature, which defies the law of right Government.
>
> This great war, whether it comes now, or by some miracle is deferred till later, is Nature's vengeance – is God's vengeance upon people who held women in subjection, and by doing that have destroyed the perfect human balance . . .
>
> Women of the W.S.P.U. [Women's Social and Political

Union], there will be much suffering for women in this war. The price of war as of all tragedy is mainly paid by women.[2]

Though the renowned war poets of the anthologies were predominantly male, there were of course many women writers. Women also played a vital part in the War. They were nurses in the field most obviously, and as a result women lie in many of the British military cemeteries of Flanders, but they also entered the factories, unleashing a social revolution. They sustained families, morally and materially, eking out their 'separation allowance' and taking their share of the suffering. The poet Hilda Doolittle, who wrote as 'H.D.' and was married to the poet Richard Aldington, whose powerful novel *Death of a Hero* (1929) is one of the most searing fictional accounts of trench experience, wrote her own very autobiographical novel around the same time as her ex-husband, though it was not published until 1960. *Bid Me to Live*, a finer, more intricate and subtle work of art than Aldington's, records the distant impact of the War on separated lives. Alone in Bloomsbury, while her husband is at the Western Front, the novel's heroine reflects on the emotional damage, the dislocations, and the pain of a relationship sustained in wartime:

Beauty is truth, truth beauty. But could this truth be beautiful? Maybe it was. They had shouted of honour and sacrifice for two years, three years now. This was winter or early spring [1917] but seasons revolved around horrors until one was numb and the posters that screamed at one on street corners had no more reality, not as much, as the remembered Flemish gallery of the Louvre and the abstract painted horror of a flayed saint – they were past feeling anything; she was. He was right, then, maybe, when he said 'You don't feel anything.'[3]

Very early in the research for this book I encountered at a social occasion a prominent British military historian of the First World War who, on learning of my new project, observed sardonically: 'Teachers of English have a lot to answer for.' I was taken aback. What could he possibly mean? As the subsequent weeks and months of research went by, however, I gradually came to see his point. Like most British schoolchildren I was fed large portions of the poets of the Great War during English lessons. These texts were eminently teachable, and unlike that rather offputting Modernist stuff, they were, to us schoolboys, vivid and arresting and palpably About Something. A central poem, perhaps *the* war poem of the First World War, was Wilfred Owen's 'Dulce et Decorum Est', drafted at Craiglockhart War Hospital in the first half of October 1917 and revised early in the following year. I recall it well from an English lesson at my Liverpool grammar school at the end of the 1960s. Once the Latin had been explained to us – 'it is sweet and fitting to die for one's country' from the third book of Horace's *Odes* – we relished the scarifying detail, rising to its easy-to-understand sententious conclusion.

Here was a poem about 'the horror of war', its futility, its absurdity, its senseless slaughter of the innocent, sent to their deaths by 'fools in old style coats and hats',[4] to borrow Philip Larkin's phrase, or 'lions led by donkeys' in another popular cliché about incompetent generals in the field. If ever there was a resounding 'anti-war' poem, this was it. Surely? But within weeks of completing its revision Owen had rejoined his regiment, the 5th Manchesters, and was preparing to go back to the Front. At the end of September 1918 he was awarded the Military Cross for his performance in the successful assault on the Beaurevoir–Fonsomme line. On 4 November, precisely one week before the Armistice was signed, he was killed on the bank of the Oise–Sambre Canal, near the village of Ors in northern France. Siegfried Sassoon was likewise famous for his protest against the War, read out in the House of Commons on 30 July 1917, but no sooner had he made this protest – which it should always be remembered was about the effectiveness of the War at that stage of the conflict, an expression of his feeling that it had lost its sense of direction, not a philosophical questioning of its original moral legitimacy – than he was to be found colluding with the plan cooked up by his alarmed friends to send him to the Craiglockhart War Hospital under the pretence that he was shell-shocked, but actually to get him off the hook and out of the way. He arrived at the hospital, which he immediately dubbed facetiously 'Dottyville', in remarkably good spirits and his only thought became to get back to the Front and share the sufferings of his men.

In short, the British poets of the First World War, widely perceived as being 'anti-war', were far from being pacifists of the kind Sassoon had encountered on Lady Ottoline Morrell's lawn at Garsington in Oxfordshire and whom he didn't much care for, even though he agreed to accept their support in making his protest. Bertrand Russell was one of these, who objected to war on philosophical grounds and who went to prison for that belief. The only poet who had anything like a rooted philosophical objection to war was Isaac Rosenberg. This was influenced by his Jewish background, his father having come to England in exile from Lithuania rather than serve in the Czar's army. Rosenberg hated war and militarism, and was a sloppy and incompetent soldier, who joined up without daring to tell his family so that he could support them. It was a way of alleviating their East End poverty. He wrote: 'I never joined the army for patriotic reasons. Nothing can justify war.' But he immediately added: 'I suppose we must all fight to get the trouble over.'[5]

This pragmatic response was typical of the war poets. Aside

from the early 'heroic' poetry of Rupert Brooke – whose patriotic rhetoric Rosenberg loathed – and his myriad imitators, the
poets were fighting because, whatever they thought of its ends
and means, they saw it as their duty to do so. Some, like T. E.
Hulme, were firm about the War's necessity: 'What is being settled in the present war is the political, intellectual, and ethical
configuration of Europe for the coming century. All who can see
an inch in front of their nose must realise it. The future is being
created now.'[6] He had no truck with pacifists and sarcastically
proposed bundling them all together into a special battalion:
'Call them the "No Conscription" Battalion, 55th Royal
Fusiliers . . . I would not send them into the trenches, for their
overweening vanity, leading them to look at their own cessation
of existence as not only a personal but a world catastrophe,
would be an undue handicap to the courageous facing of
death.'[7] Rupert Brooke, though writing in the early phase of the
War before the horrors of the Somme, and with very limited
experience of actual battle, nonetheless remembered when
writing to his friends that he was a socialist and an internation-
alist and that if war could be avoided it should be: 'I hope you
don't think me very reactionary and callous for taking up this
function of England,' he wrote from the Royal Naval Barracks
at Chatham to his friend Lowes Dickinson in October 1914.
'There shouldn't be war – but what's to be done, but fight
Prussia? I've seen the half million refugees in the night outside
Antwerp: and I want, more than before, to go on, till Prussia's
destroyed. I wish everyone I know were fighting.'[8]

    It is the argument of this book that the British poets of the
First World War were not anti-war but 'anti-heroic'. They did
not think, for the most part, that modern trench warfare was a
chivalric pursuit, full of high nobility and exalted emotion, and
martial heroism like something out of Malory's *Morte d'Arthur*.
Unsparingly, they painted vivid and sometimes terrifying
pictures of 'the horror of war' (and we wrote enthusiastically

about this in our O-level English examination papers) because this is what they experienced and this is what they knew. They satirised the pomposity of those who could not see the reality of the trenches and they did indeed believe that it was a 'lie' to call the carnage of the Western Front 'sweet and fitting'. But they also saw no alternative and so they went to war and, when they were wounded, then healed, went back again to the war to join their comrades.

In the famous preface to his posthumously collected poems Wilfred Owen said that his subject was 'the pity of war', that is to say, its tragic reality:

> This book is not about heroes. English poetry is not yet fit
>   to speak of them.
> Nor is it about deeds or lands, nor anything about glory,
>   honour, dominions or power, except War.
> Above all, this book is not concerned with Poetry.
> The subject of it is War, and the pity of War.
> The Poetry is in the pity.
> Yet these elegies are not to this generation,
> This is in no sense consolatory.
> They may be to the next.
> All the poet can do to-day is to warn.
> That is why the true Poets must be truthful.[9]

Owen was claiming the writer's true role: to be an authentic witness. 'Pity', or tragic acceptance, was preferred to the righteous anger of those who were root-and-branch anti-war (in the way that many of us were, and remain, in relation to the war in Iraq). He knew that there were better solutions and that future generations should seek them – even if his generation was too late for 'consolatory' comfort. There had to be a better way, but in the meantime he and others had no choice but to go on fighting. But also to warn.

Today the British poets of the First World War have never been more popular. New anthologies regularly erupt in the publishing calendar like Verey lights. Websites dedicated to them proliferate and the former Poet Laureate, Andrew Motion, has referred to this body of work as 'a sacred national text'.[10] If one visits the website of the War Poets Association one finds war poetry defined and valued in a way that recruits the poets for that elusive intellectual task of defining the essential meaning of 'Englishness': 'War poetry is currently studied in every school in Britain. It has become part of the mythology of nationhood, and an expression of both historical consciousness and political conscience. The way we read – and perhaps revere – war poetry says something about what we are, and what we want to be, as a nation.'

One can make of this rather abstract passage what one will. What exactly are we, and what do we want to be, 'as a nation'? Who can possibly answer this? And who are 'we'? Different parts of Britain, different communities and faiths, different political and cultural traditions, will have different answers. But the idea that the First World War and its literature are really about the nature of Englishness could be seen, from one point of view, as more than a little perplexing, for this was a European war, the product of European causes and with profound European consequences, and it was fought out largely on continental European soil.[11] When the War was declared in August 1914 a writer who earned his living as a lawyer in an insurance company in Prague, Dr Franz Kafka, was a citizen of the Austro-Hungarian Empire. When the treaties that followed the peace were concluded and signed he found himself a citizen of the Czech Republic. Although it would be simplistic to argue that the War alone was the cause of the dismantling of empires – history moves in more mysterious ways – the conflict was thoroughly European and indeed global, a truly world war. But it is certainly true to say that each nation that fought retained its own individual sense of what the conflict meant to it. The idea of memory that is so central to the way in which the First World War is talked and written about in Britain – powerful emotions are still released on the annual Remembrance Day – finds a natural language in poetry, part of whose role has always been to commemorate and record. It is also a medium of truth.

The poets here discussed were united by that conviction, that their words had meaning and value even when the hells whose gates were thrown open by modern warfare seemed to exhibit the destructive unreason of nightmare.

The twelve poets I have focused on have been chosen solely on grounds of poetic merit, for I do not intend this as a contribution to the military history of the First World War. It is a book about poets, about the lives they led before and after the War as well as their period of service, and about how the creative imagination survives in extreme conditions, how poetry fares in time of war, and how it gives expression to that shattering human experience, both in the heat of battle and, for those who survived, in long retrospect.

I

The West End Front

We are young, we are experimentalists, but we ask to be judged by our own standards, not by those which have governed other men at other times.[1]

RICHARD ALDINGTON, 1916

I am still in my teens and when this ridiculous war is over, I will write Chapter II at the top of the new sheet and with the help of other young Georgians . . . will try to root out more effectively the obnoxious survivals of Victorianism.[2]

ROBERT GRAVES, 1915

Certain of our Georgian singers . . . are so haunted by a dread of smoothness that they have very nearly erected cacophony into a cult. They pursue it as an end in itself laudable . . .[3]

WILLIAM WATSON, 1916

What imbeciles the Imagistes are![4]

EDWARD THOMAS, 1915

Entrenched in the anthologies of First World War poetry, in a landscape of trench, duck-board and engulfing mud, the night sky lit up with unearthly flares and loud with exploding shells, whistling bullets and terrifying whizz-bangs, promiscuous trench-rats scuttling across the waste expanse of No Man's Land, and somewhere the iconic nodding poppy, it can sometimes seem that the war poets emerged fully formed from that Flanders mud with no prior poetic life. It is certainly true that the war actually made certain poets, like Wilfred Owen, bringing them into voice, sharpening their aesthetic, launching their careers, but most had already begun to practise their art in prewar literary England. Many of the great war poems were not scribbled out in trench notebooks but composed in tranquillity, in hospitals, training camps, at home on leave in country houses, or in quiet rooms in Bloomsbury salons. If the War was a shattering, epochal event it also occurred in the midst of a time of extraordinary artistic ferment. The first two decades of the twentieth century saw an explosion of innovation and experiment in all the arts. Poetry, like music, painting, sculpture and dance, shared in this heady atmosphere of revolution and fertile innovation. 'It was a time of isms,'[5] wrote H.D.

Yet the picture is complicated. Picking up a recent study of this period, Helen Carr's *The Verse Revolutionaries* (2009), I found no mention in its nine hundred pages of Owen or Gurney and hardly any of the other poets who are discussed in the present book. Many of the British war poets were simply absent from the Modernist party. To trace the causes and consequences of this line of separate development is not easy and requires care in negotiating the personalities, the colourful artistic impresarios, the manifestos, the polemical anthologies and, it must be said, the critical stereotypes that have often clouded the issue and fostered mutual incomprehension. One way of picking one's path through the maze is to look at the rival anthologies produced by the different schools, the two most prominent of which were the Georgians and the Imagists. The Georgians, in particular, have suffered from a bad press, branded as reactionary English weekend pastoralists cut off from the avant-garde European mainstream, yet in their day they saw themselves as cutting-edge innovators, setting poetry free from dead and sterile conventions, inaugurating a new and vital movement every bit as significant as the Imagists' more colourfully launched polemics.

One of the most acute critics of the new early-twentieth-century movement in poetry, C. K. Stead, in his classic *The New Poetic* (1964), argued that the new poetry which needed to emerge from the exhausted late-nineteenth-century English tradition was provided by the work of Eliot and Yeats. He cited Yeats's 'Easter 1916' as the representative example of a poem that addressed the modern world and the modern audience in terms that transformed personal experience into 'universal image'.[6] Stead argued that the British war poets, though humane and honest in their poetry of personal experience, a vast improvement on the bad poetry still being written at the time in England, failed this test. They simply didn't possess the major transforming imagination, the universalising gift, the aesthetic grandeur of Yeats:

> The particularization of experience in the work of the new war poets was an immense improvement over the generalizing facility of their imperialist predecessors. But their poems still fall short of the yardstick we have taken – Yeats's 'Easter 1916'. The relationship between the poet and his experience of life is now an honest relationship: here is the poet, and here his experience which he faces without preconceptions. It remained yet for other poets – or for at least one other poet – to approach what Yeats had achieved: the transformation of his personal experience into a universal image.

Stead's judgement is severe and challenging. To some it will seem unfair, to others irrelevant. The body of work produced by the war poets is of such intrinsic poetic value and human resonance that such academic ranking and placing, they would argue, is beside the point. And, as ever, there is a gap between mandarin critical pronouncement and popular taste.

Such a gap existed also in the immediate pre-war years. There was much more agreement, however, with the contention that poetry had lost its way and become irrelevant, that there was simply too much vapid poeticising. Poets like Rupert Brooke and Robert Graves saw themselves as being in revolt against the real enemy: fag-end Victorianism and its pallid Edwardian imitators, still fluting their wan tunes as the new century dawned. T. S. Eliot would later write: 'The situation of poetry in 1909 or 1910 was stagnant to a degree difficult for any young poet of today to imagine.'[7] Virginia Woolf wrote that the world changed in 1910,[8] the year not just when the Edwardian era ended (in May George V succeeded to the throne) but of the first post-Impressionist exhibition in London. The Victorians and Edwardians, the young writers hoped, were about to be put to flight. Before considering in turn the Georgians and the Imagists, their rival manifestos and claims, it is worth trying to establish what was supposed to be wrong with English poetry in the years immediately before the outbreak of war in 1914.

Five years before the War, in 1909, the senior poets George Meredith and Algernon Swinburne died (and Eliot started to draft 'The Love Song of J. Alfred Prufrock'). A lively, if partisan, critic, Harold Monro, founder of the Poetry Bookshop, wrote a couple of years after the War his own retrospective diagnosis: 'About 1890 literary language had passed into a condition of the utmost stultification. A century filled with poets of every denomination and of extreme productiveness had drained our poetic vocabulary to its lees ... New poets of originality were little sought, and their prospects were not good, for the public was still satisfied with the achievements of the immediate past, and was tired and conservative.'9

Monro judged the first decade of the twentieth century an 'extraordinarily barren' period for English poetry redeemed only by the appearance of Thomas Hardy's *The Dynasts* in 1904. But gradually things started to change: 'By 1910 the numbing effect of the Victorian period seems finally to have relaxed its pressure on the brain of the rising generation. The new movement which then began was related neither to the Tennysonian era, nor to the brief epoch of reaction generally known as the "nineties", nor, indeed, to the comparatively barren decade noted above ... In 1910 the expression *free verse* had hardly been used.' One of the problems with the conventional verse of the day was its fondness for antique poetic diction but also its removal from life, its air of effeteness. Some poets were beginning to look across at the success of the new dramatists like Galsworthy who brought a bracing whiff of social realism into their plays. One poet who thought poetry could do the same was John Masefield and in 1911 the *English Review* brought out his long poem, *The Everlasting Mercy*. For Monro this lively, vigorously written narrative of a drunken, brawling poacher who eventually sees the light and reforms himself was the signal of something new, so new in its use of swear-words that it was banned from some station bookstalls: 'Here was stuff that the general public could appreciate without straining its intelligence. People who thought that English poetry had died with Tennyson suddenly recognised their error. The blank verse of Stephen Phillips was a mere echo of the Victorian manner, but the rapid free doggerel of "The Everlasting Mercy", its modernity, its bold colloquialism, and its narrative interest awakened the curiosity of the public of 1911, and a revival of the dormant interest in poetry was at once assured.'

Clever young poets like Rupert Brooke immediately grasped the significance of what was happening and, the following year, 1912, the Georgian movement was launched. To understand it, one needs to understand the unusual and influential figure of Edward Marsh, not himself a poet but a man who understood poetry, within the limits of his taste, and who was the midwife and financial backer of the new movement. Marsh was born in 1872, the maternal grandson of Spencer Perceval, the prime minister who was assassinated in 1812 in the lobby of the House of Commons. The Perceval family was paid substantial compensation by the government and in 1903, on the death of an uncle, Marsh inherited a sixth of what he called his 'murder money'. It enabled him to become a wealthy and influential patron of the visual arts and, more importantly, literature. At Cambridge he had been a member of the exclusive 'Society' more popularly known as the 'Apostles', and mixed with the philosophers G. E. Moore and Bertrand Russell, and afterwards he moved effortlessly in elite London literary circles while pursuing a career as a senior civil servant, becoming Winston Churchill's private secretary when the latter became Parliamentary Under-secretary for the Colonies in 1905. A twenty-three-year association with Churchill began, including the crucial period when Churchill was First Lord of the Admiralty in the early part of the war, responsible for the Dardanelles campaign and the fiasco of Gallipoli.

Marsh had started collecting pictures as early as 1896 but it was not until 1911 when he bought a painting by Duncan Grant that he began to be a patron of the new painters at the Slade School of Fine Art, including Mark Gertler. He also supported John and Paul Nash and Stanley Spencer, to create the most important and valuable collection of modern art in private hands. The walls of his apartments at 5 Raymond Buildings, Gray's Inn, were obliterated by paintings and it was here that painters and poets would gather, the most significant for the future of English poetry being Rupert Brooke, who treated Raymond Buildings as a second home when in London and who introduced Marsh to another poetic cell around the corner in Gray's Inn Road, the editors of the magazine *Rhythm*, John Middleton Murry and Katherine Mansfield.

It was on 19 September 1912 that Edward Marsh returned home late from the Admiralty to find his flat full of poets and Rupert Brooke in high flight on the subject of the lack of public interest in poetry – a topic which united all the poetic factions of the day, conservative or avant-garde. Marsh's biographer, Christopher Hassall, takes up the story:

Brooke suggested that he might try playing a practical joke on the public which would at least draw attention to poetry. He would write a book himself under twelve pseudonyms and issue it as an anthology selected from the poems of a dozen promising writers. Marsh's view was that there was no need to go to all that trouble when there must be twelve representative flesh-and-blood poets with material ready to hand. They began to count. As well as Masefield and Brooke himself there were of course Gibson, [W. H.] Davies, de la Mare, and [Gordon] Bottomley. They included A. E. Housman and Ezra Pound, and Brooke added his Cambridge friend Elroy Flecker, who had shown some promise. Marsh came out with the idea that Brooke should compile his anthology from the work of these writers, but he declined. It needed someone older and of more authority – but what could it be called? They believed that Victorianism in literature was gone for good and that a new era had begun. Marsh pointed out that the natural thing was to name eras after reigning sovereigns, the new reign itself as new and hopeful as the renaissance in poetry, which train of thought led him to come out with what he afterwards described as 'my proud

ambiguous adjective – *Georgian*'. But Brooke didn't like it.
He thought it sounded too staid for a volume designed as the
herald of a revolutionary dawn.'[10]

The eclectic poets in Brooke's list, mingling old and new, conservative and experimental, didn't survive this first excited talk,
but Marsh nonetheless realised that they had hit on an idea that
might work and he accepted Brooke's idea that he himself
should be the editor – anonymously of course because his position as Churchill's private secretary 'might strike the uninitiated
as absurd and so damage the cause'. The next thing to think
about was who would publish the anthology and also how it
would be financed. The most obvious candidate was yet
another Holborn-based poetry organ, *Poetry Review*, edited by
Harold Monro from 43 Chancery Lane and printed, like *Rhythm*,
at St Catherine's Press in the Strand. The world of poetry, then
as now, however intense its rivalries, was very small. At this
point Marsh mentioned his 'murder money', currently being
spent almost exclusively on contemporary art, and promised
that if Monro would carry the initial expense of publication of
what would be the first of the famous Georgian anthologies, he
would personally underwrite any losses.

The next day Marsh threw a lunch party at Raymond
Buildings at which Brooke, Monro and others gathered to refine
the plan. Initially, there was a certain amount of opposition to
the proposed title, *Georgian Poetry*, Marsh's 'proud ambiguous
adjective',[11] but, since nothing better could be thought of, it
stayed. According to one contemporary, the critic Frank
Swinnerton, it was an excellent title:

Georgian Poetry was another 'generation piece'. It seemed to
put the younger writers in a class apart from Victorians and
Edwardians, and for that reason was cleverly named . . . by
1912 Victorian and Edwardian poets, less fortunate than

Victorian and Edwardian novelists, were being found
wordy ... Their mellifluousness and verbosity, pleasant to
older readers, revolted men impatient of Wordsworthian prat-
tle or Tennysonian memorial surveys; for the Georgian poets
were 'new', as moving pictures and aeroplanes were 'new'.
John Masefield's poetic narrative, *The Everlasting Mercy*, published at the end of 1911, and carrying the vernacular to an
oathful extreme, was the most widely read verse of the 'new'
age.'[12]

Monro modestly concealed the fact that it was he who had
invented the term 'Georgian Poets' fifteen months earlier in
June 1911, when he returned to England from abroad and went
for lunch with his friend A. K. Sabin at Harrods' new 'Georgian
Restaurant' on the fourth floor, oak-panelled and oak-beamed,
with gas chandeliers. The ascent to the throne of a new sover-
eign had caused the management of Harrods to change the title
of the new restaurant at the last minute from the Tudor
Restaurant (to which its decor should properly have consigned
it). Sabin later recollected this lunch at Knightsbridge:

We walked along the Brompton Road to Harrods, and went
up in the lift to their newly decorated refreshment rooms.
'Georgian Restaurant,' shouted the lift-boy as we reached the
top floor. Hundreds of people were seated at lunch. 'It ought
to be called the *Gorgean* Restaurant,' said Harold, with one of
his rare touches of slightly sardonic humour. As we followed
an attendant to a vacant table, he continued reflectively:
'This is the first time since my return that I have been
reminded we are living in a new Georgian era – and, by Jove,
Arthur, we are the new Georgian poets.'[13]

Although Monro kept Marsh at a little distance – perhaps
because he was not entirely sure about his poetic taste and

because he would probably have preferred to edit the anthology himself – his knowledge of printing and publishing was invaluable to Marsh and in turn the runaway success of the first annual *Georgian Poetry* in 1912 was a great boost to Monro's own venture, the Poetry Bookshop in Devonshire Street, which was just about to open. Half the profits of the anthology went to the Bookshop and the other half was divided up among the contributors, an arrangement that would be the envy of twenty-first-century anthologised poets. Walter de la Mare later told Edward Marsh that he had made more out of his appearances in *Georgian Poetry* than from all other publications of his verse put together.[14] Monro was an independent spirit who published both *Georgian Poetry* and, as we shall shortly see, the Imagist anthology, seemingly able to rise above the poetic factions – in the same way that some of the contributors, like D. H. Lawrence, managed to move comfortably between the two camps. Nonetheless, one can see that his aesthetic was not wholly in accord with that of Marsh, who had little time for the avant-garde and took a specific dislike to Ezra Pound, even if he tried, unsuccessfully as it turned out, to find a Pound poem for the anthology that poet and editor were happy with. On the other hand, some of the older generation felt that *Georgian Poetry* was too new and fashionable for them. 'I do not really belong to your "new era",' A. E. Housman announced rather sniffily.[15] The Poet Laureate, Robert Bridges, struggled manfully to be a little more positive, saying that he found it 'really rich in thought and diction' and that he was glad to have made the acquaintance of Lawrence's poetry. Trying to be nice about the fact that the volume was dedicated to him, he went on:

I think I am mainly sympathetic with the psychological tendency of the 'school', which is generally, I suppose, a reaction against intellectualism. As far as a new moral position is deduced from this, I feel that the necessity of its being subordinated to aesthetic beauty is in danger of being lost sight of. I feel sometimes as if I were reminded of the Post-Impressionists' pictures. You know however that I am not offended by novelties and that I welcome any revolt against dull conventional bondage.[16]

In his later memoirs, published in 1939 just before the outbreak of another world war, Marsh looked back at his aims for the *Georgian Poetry* annuals:

My sole and simple object was to provide a means by which writers whose work seemed to be beautiful and neglected might find a hearing from the reading public – to get the light out from under the bushel. This, and this only, was the 'definite aim' of which I spoke in my first preface. I had no smallest intention of founding a school, or of tracing a course for Poetry to follow; for such enterprises I was ill-equipped, in knowledge, in leisure, and in self-esteem ... I was, of course, guided by the preferences which instinct and training had formed in my mind; and these can be easily, if roughly, set forth. I liked poetry to be all three (or if not all three, at least two; or if the worst came to the worst at least one) of the following things: intelligible, musical, and racy; and I was happier with it if it was written on some formal principle which I could discern, and from which it departed, if at all, only for the sake of some special effect, and not because the lazy or too impetuous writer had found observance difficult or irksome. I liked poetry that I wanted to know by heart, and *could* learn by heart if I had time.

'Intelligibility' is a relative term, and I naturally don't use it so as to exclude the poetry of suggestion; but I hold strongly that poetry is communication, and that it is the poet's duty, to the best of his ability, to let the reader know what he is driving at. Some of the moderns seem to think that to be understood is to be damned (and so far as they are speaking for themselves, they may indeed be right); but this is an ungenerous attitude.[17]

The first annual anthology, *Georgian Poetry 1911–1912*, dated 12 October, actually appeared in December with that strategically prudent dedication to the Poet Laureate, Robert Bridges, and with the editor's name given merely as 'E.M', which everyone in the know in literary London would instantly have recognised. Marsh attached a brief 'Prefatory Note', which announced the principles behind the anthology:

> This volume is issued in the belief that English poetry is now once again putting on a new strength and beauty. Few readers have the leisure or the zeal to investigate each volume as it appears; and the process of recognition is often slow. This collection, drawn entirely from the publications of the last two years, may if it is fortunate help the lovers of poetry to realize that we are at the beginning of another 'Georgian period' which may rank in due time with the several great poetic ages of the past. It has no pretension to cover the field . . . Two years ago some of the writers represented had published nothing; and only a very few of the others were known except to the eagerest 'watchers of the skies'.[18]

The anthology would not strike anyone now as being in any way revolutionary, launched as it was in the era of Eliot and Pound. The young Brooke was present with 'The Old Vicarage, Grantchester' and Lawrence's 'Snapdragon' sat alongside the work of older poets like G. K. Chesterton, Walter de la Mare, John Masefield, W. H. Davies and James Stephens. Many of the new names of this new Georgian era are now no longer read – Gordon Bottomley (much admired, however, by Isaac Rosenberg), Wilfrid Gibson, and Ronald Ross – and it is noticeable that many of the poems chosen by Marsh were long or dramatic ones. Marsh sent out a hundred copies of the anthology to significant people in the literary world and it was an immediate commercial success, selling nine thousand copies in the first year. A second volume appeared in 1915: *Georgian Poetry 1913–1915*, but it had the sad dedication 'In Memoriam' to two previous contributors. 'Two of the poets,' wrote Marsh, '– I think the youngest, and certainly not the least gifted – are dead. Rupert Brooke, who seemed to have everything that is worth having, died last April in the service of his country. James Elroy Flecker, to whom life and death were less generous, died in January after a long and disabling illness.'[19]

This time the selection opened with Bottomley's forty-five-page verse play *King Lear's Wife* and ended with Lascelle Abercrombie's play *The End of the World*, of the same length. Brooke was represented by 'The Great Lover', 'The Soldier', and others. Many of the original contributors returned and there were two new voices: Ralph Hodgson and the Irish war poet Francis Ledwidge. The third volume, *Georgian Poetry 1916–1917*, appeared in September 1917 and contained work from the new war poets: Siegfried Sassoon, Robert Graves, Isaac Rosenberg, Robert Nichols and others alongside the old faithfuls like Masefield, John Drinkwater, and de la Mare. And in November 1919 the fourth volume, *Georgian Poetry 1918–1919*, enabled Marsh to say in his customary Prefatory Note that the new book 'may be thought to show that what for want of a better word is called Peace has not interfered with the writing of good poetry'.[20] There was now a long gap before the publication of the final volume in the series in November 1922 (the year of Eliot's *The Waste Land* and Joyce's *Ulysses*), and Marsh's Prefatory Note to *Georgian Poetry 1920–1922* had a newly defensive ring which reflected the palpable resistance to its dominance on the poetry scene which would lead in subsequent decades to a growing criticism of its aesthetic values:

When the fourth volume of this series was published three years ago, many of the critics who had up to then, as Horace Walpole said of God, been the dearest creatures in the world to me, took another turn. Not only did they very properly disapprove of my choice of poems: they went on to write as if the Editor of *Georgian Poetry* were a kind of public functionary, like the President of the Royal Academy; and they asked – again, on the assumption, very properly – who was E.M. that he should bestow and withhold crowns and sceptres, and decide that this or that poet was or was not to count.

This, in the words of Pirate Smee, was *a kind of a compliment*, but it was also, to quote the same hero, *galling*; and I have wished for an opportunity of disowning the pretension which I found attributed to me of setting up as a pundit, or a pontiff, or a Petronius Arbiter; for I have neither the sure taste, nor the exhaustive reading, nor the ample leisure which would be necessary in any such role.

The origin of these books, which is set forth in the memoir of Rupert Brooke, was simple and humble. I found, ten years ago, that there were a number of writers doing good work which appeared to me extremely good, but which was narrowly known; and I thought that anyone, however unprofessional and meagrely gifted, who presented a conspectus of it in a challenging and manageable form might be doing a good turn both to the poets and the reading public. So, I think I may claim, it proved to be. The first volume seemed to supply a want. It was eagerly bought . . . there has been no break in demand for the successive books.[21]

Marsh then added what he called:

. . . a mild protest against a further charge that *Georgian Poetry* has merely encouraged a small clique of mutually indistinguishable poetasters to abound in their own and each other's sense and nonsense. It is natural that the poets of a generation should have points in common; but to my fond eye those who have graced these collections look as diverse as sheep to their shepherd, or the members of a Chinese family to their uncle; and if there is an allegation which I would *deny with both hands*, it is this: that an insipid sameness is the chief characteristic of an anthology which offers – to name almost a random seven only out of forty (oh ominous academic number!) – the work of Messrs. Abercrombie, Davies, de la Mare, Graves, Lawrence, Nichols and J. C. Squire.

The ideal *Georgian Poetry* – a book which would err neither by omission nor by inclusion, and would contain the best, and only the best poems of the best, and only the best poets of the day – could only be achieved, if at all, by dint of a Royal Commission. The present volume is nothing of the kind.

I may add one word bearing on my aim in selection. Much admired modern work seems to me, in its lack of inspiration and its disregard of form, like gravy imitating lava. Its upholders may retort that much of the work which I prefer seems to them, in its lack of inspiration and its comparative finish, like tapioca imitating pearls. Either view – possibly both – may be right. I will only say that with an occasional exception for some piece of rebelliousness or even levity which may have taken my fancy, I have tried to choose no verse but such as in Wordsworth's phrase

The high and tender Muses shall accept
With gracious smile, deliberately pleased.

With these words, Marsh retired from the fray and Georgian poetry retreated into literary history, from which it has emerged all too often in cartoon form as a symbol of timid English aesthetic conservatism. The radical poets of the 1930s, in particular, were contemptuous. 'The Georgian poets,' wrote Cecil Day Lewis as late as 1944, 'a sadly pedestrian rabble, flocked along the road their fathers had built, pointing out to each other the beauty spots and ostentatiously drinking small-beer in a desperate attempt to prove their virility.'[22] The American poet and editor Harriet Monroe had already complained in 1920 of 'King George's Poets' in the following terms: 'The "Georgians" live in the twentieth century, no doubt, but their subjects, ideals and methods follow the old standards of English song . . . almost nothing in the book reminds us of the age we live in.'[23]

The forward spirits in poetry in the 1920s and 1930s continued to mock. Peter Quennell, writing of the Sitwells, notes how Edith and Osbert 'were apt to laugh at the rustic Georgian Poets, who seemed to pass their time sauntering and botanising around the muddy landscape that enclosed their country cottages, picking a celandine here, and there, over a five-barred gate, holding despondent conversations "with a lonely lamb"'.[24] And Stephen Spender accused them of reducing poetry to 'a minor art like embroidery, to be done of a week-end in a country cottage'.[25] To an extent these comments are part of the merry dance of literary politics and all these critics had personal and poetic agendas. But it is probably fair to say that the Georgians strike us now as being of mixed quality. There was certainly work that is hard to read today with any interest but, equally, much of it has endured and this includes some of the significant poets who will be discussed later. A good judicial assessment of what the Georgians saw themselves to be about and what made poets like Graves and Owen and Sassoon keen to be identified with them, is given by a recent historian of the movement:

The Georgian movement was rebellious rather than conformist. It was a revolt against Romantic and Victorian

conceptions of poetry and the contemporary representatives
of those conceptions: against 'public' poetry, on the one hand,
and 'pure' poetry, on the other; against the moralist and the
aesthete. Relatedly, it was a revolt against poetic mannerism,
against the continuing fashionability – in the first decade of
the twentieth century – of archaic and heavily 'poetic' language. It rebelled against poetry written by rhetoricians,
sentimentalists, and sensualists. Thus, the Georgians were
hardly the docile and fatigued legatees of nineteenth-century
poetic tradition. That distinction fell rather to poets like
William Watson, Stephen Phillips, and Alfred Austin, whom
the Georgians thought fully representative of the low state
into which English poetry had fallen in the first decade of the
new century.[26]

The poetic 'old guard' certainly saw the Georgians as young
revolutionaries and Marsh as a dangerous poetic radical.
William Watson deplored the modernity and 'harshness' of
diction that seemed to trample on the sonorous sweetnesses
of his post-Tennysonian ideal poetry: 'Certain of our Georgian
singers, and even one or two poets whose roots go down into
late Victorian antiquity, are so haunted by a dread of smoothness that they have very nearly erected cacophony into a cult.
They pursue it as an end in itself laudable,'[27] he wrote in a
fustily titled polemic written in the middle of the War:
Pencraft: A Plea for the Older Ways (1916). It was that challenge
offered to the older poetic establishment by the new movement that explains the relative lack of tension between the
Georgians and the Imagists and others at the time. Perhaps
most significant is what Wilfred Owen wrote to his mother on
New Year's Eve, 1917, when he had become aware that he was
being recognised as a poet by Sassoon and others. He knew
where, for him, the standard of value and reputation was being
set:

I go out of this year a Poet, my dear Mother, as which I did not enter it. I am held peer by the Georgians; I am a poet's poet.

I am started. The tugs have left me; I feel the great swelling of the open sea taking my galleon.[28]

For the young war poets there was absolutely no doubt about what the Georgian movement meant. It was the future of English poetry, and they wanted to be a part of it.

Visiting the printers of *Georgian Poetry* in Norfolk Street off the Strand, Marsh and Monro would have noticed stacks of another poetry magazine, launched in the summer of 1911. *Rhythm* described itself as an 'Art Music Literature Quarterly' and its rather windy and vague opening editorial declared: 'We have all become futurists.'[29] The first issue also carried a statement of its 'Aims and Ideals':

Rhythm is a magazine with a purpose. Its title is the ideal of a new art, to which it will endeavour to give expression in England. Aestheticism has had its day and done its work. Based on a reaction, on a foundation essentially negative, it could not endure . . . We need an art that strikes deeper, that touches a profounder reality, that passes outside the bounds of a narrow aestheticism, cramping and choking itself, drawing its inspiration from aversion, to a humaner and broader field. Humanity in art in the true sense needs humanity in criticism. To treat what is being done to-day as something vital in the progress of art, which cannot fix its eyes on yesterday and live; to see that the present is pregnant for the future, rather than a revolt against the past; in creation to give expression to art that seeks out the strong things of life; in criticism to seek out the strong things of that art – such is the aim of *RHYTHM* . . .

There was much more in the same vein, but what made it interesting was less the manifesto prose than the striking drawings by Picasso, S. J. Peploe, and Gaudier-Brzeska. By June 1912 it had moved to monthly publication which enabled the editors, John Middleton Murry and Katherine Mansfield, to claim that 'a unique attempt will be made to unite within one magazine all the parallel manifestations of the modern spirit in every province of Art, Education and Philosophy'. This would secure its position as 'the organ of Living Art and Living Thought'.[30] The following March it published a review of the first *Georgian Poetry* anthology, headed 'The Georgian Renaissance', by D. H. Lawrence, who seemed unperturbed by the fact that he was one of the contributors to the volume under review. It was Lawrence at his vatic best:

> This collection is like a big breath taken when we are waking up after a night of oppressive dreams. The nihilists, the intellectual, hopeless people – Ibsen, Flaubert, Thomas Hardy – represent the dream we are waking from. It was a dream of demolition. Nothing was, but nothing. Everything was taken from us. And now our lungs are full of new air, and our eyes see it is morning, but we have not forgotten the terror of the night. We dreamed we were falling through space into nothingness, and the anguish of it leaves us rather eager . . . But we are awake again, our lungs are full of new air, our eyes of morning. The first song is nearly a cry, fear and the pain of remembrance sharpening away the pure music. And that is this book.[31]

There is rather more on the same lines but this open welcome, in a seemingly avant-garde context, of the new anthology seemed to suggest that it was not seen as a reactionary or conservative project. But, during the five years leading up to the declaration of war, a poetic movement had been building which, unlike that of the Georgians, had a powerful and sharply defined aesthetic creed, a manifesto all its members sought to live by. It was called Imagism.

In March 1914, what had begun on 25 March 1909 as a regular series of meetings of poets at the Eiffel Tower restaurant in Soho – 1909 being also the year of Marinetti's *Futurist Manifesto* and Schoenberg's *Five Orchestral Pieces* – bore fruit in the publication of a small green-covered volume with, in gilt, the title *Imagistes*. Inside, the book was more fully titled *Des Imagistes: an anthology* and none of the contributors had appeared in *Georgian Poetry*. The new names were Ezra Pound, James Joyce, William Carlos Williams, Amy Lowell, Richard Aldington, H.D., F. S. Flint, Skipwith Cannell, Ford Madox Hueffer (later to style himself Ford Madox Ford), Allen Upward, and John Cournos. There was no preface or manifesto but the poems themselves. Though London was the place where the new movement was launched most of the poets were American or Irish and the book was published by Harold Monro's Poetry Bookshop, the same imprint which had brought out, at the end of 1912, the first *Georgian Poetry*. It was not a success and many unhappy readers sent their copies back to the Bookshop.[32] But it was the climax of a decade or more of avant-garde enthusiasm in London. In these heady years of the post-Impressionist exhibitions in 1910 and 1912, the arrival in London of Diaghilev's Russian Ballet in 1911 and the explosive impact the following year of his production of Stravinsky's *Le Sacre du Printemps*, then the exhibition of Italian Futurists at the Sackville Gallery in March 1912, had all conspired to make London seem like a place of revolutionary artistic ferment. On 8 January 1913 Harold Monro's Poetry Bookshop was officially opened by Sir Henry Newbolt, this choice of a leading representative of the poetry establishment a characteristically canny move by Monro, and it rapidly established at its Bloomsbury base in Devonshire Street a centre for the new poetry.

The Bookshop was to become the epicentre of both the Imagist and the Georgian poetic movements. Monro was an evangelical promoter of poetry of all kinds and the Bookshop, through its publishing activities and readings, became the centre of the early-twentieth-century poetry scene in London.

In 1913, Devonshire Street was a nondescript area for Monro to choose. No. 35 – a faded elegant eighteenth-century house destroyed in the Blitz which today is the site of Cecil House, a hostel for single homeless women – looks attractive enough from the drawings, with its flat-fronted, pedimented façade, but the area was distinctly seedy if not an actual slum district. Police took the precaution of patrolling it in pairs. Sir Osbert Sitwell described it as 'a narrow street . . . rather dark, but given over to screaming children, lusty small boys armed with catapults, and to leaping flights of cats'. When he sailed down the road to perform his poetry at the Bookshop, he acquired a tail of hooting, derisive urchins who mocked his elegant suit and canary-yellow waistcoat. Rupert Brooke, in his trademark broad-brimmed hat, attracted a similar crowd of young people who chanted: 'Buffalo Bill! Buffalo Bill!'[33]

Monro actually chose the shop deliberately because it was within easy reach of literary Bloomsbury, the university, and the art schools. The house next door was occupied by a large, noisy woman who kept a flower stall at Piccadilly Circus and whose two rather rough sons allowed their children to express their gratitude for a gift of some of the Poetry Bookshop illustrated children's books by tearing them into small pieces and stamping them into the ground. On the other side was a gold-beaters' workshop. Browsers in the Bookshop could hear the regular thump, thump of the goldbeaters' hammers coming through the wall as they read the latest publications. On the upper floors were some rooms that Monro let out to deserving artists and poets like the sculptor Jacob Epstein and the poet T. E. Hulme. Wilfred Owen, after he had just signed up to fight, hoped to get digs here while training, but was disappointed and had to rent a room above the coffee shop opposite.

The Poetry Bookshop readings were held in a sort of annexe behind the house (another former goldbeaters' workshop), dimly and theatrically lit, and the performers included T. S. Eliot, Robert Graves, Ezra Pound, Walter de la Mare, and just about every significant poet of the era. When W. B. Yeats performed he was such a draw that the reading was staged instead at the Artificers' Guild Hall (today's Art Workers' Guild), a hundred yards away in Queen Square. As well as being a poetry bookshop and a publishing house and a centre for lovers of poetry, 35 Devonshire Street was also a kind of missionary outpost for the avant-garde. On the night of 11 July 1913, after the first London performance of Stravinsky's *Le Sacre du Printemps*, the Philistines in noisy retreat, 35 Devonshire Street was packed with an impromptu gathering of excited intellectuals and artists still reeling from the thrill of this modernist explosion.[34]

There were other signs of artistic and intellectual excitement in the air. The first translation of Freud's *The Interpretation of Dreams* appeared in 1913 and the same year saw the publication of Einstein's *Theory of Relativity*, Proust's *Du Côté de chez Swann*, and Thomas Mann's *Death in Venice*. On New Year's Day, 1914, the first issue of a new magazine designed to capture and reflect all these new trends, *The Egoist*, appeared. The magazine grew out of a feminist publication called the *New Freewoman* whose editor, Dora Marsden, remained in the chair while the cuckoo in her nest, assistant editor Richard Aldington, proceeded to turn it into the major voice of the early-twentieth-century avant-garde. The first issue had an article by Percy Wyndham Lewis on Cubism, a poem by D. H. Lawrence, and an essay by Ezra Pound, and very soon *The Egoist* started to serialise James Joyce's *A Portrait of the Artist as a Young Man*, instalments continuing throughout the War. In April an advertisement appeared for the first number of the Vorticist movement's organ *Blast*, which left readers in little doubt of *that* new movement's explosive aims:

Discussion of Cubism, Futurism, Imagisme and all Vital
Forms of Modern Art.
THE CUBE   THE PYRAMID
Putrefaction of Guffaws Slain by Appearance of
BLAST
NO Pornography   NO Old Pulp
END OF THE CHRISTIAN ERA.[35]

On 1 June, only weeks before the outbreak of war, Richard Aldington wrote in *The Egoist* an 'Introductory Essay' entitled 'Modern Poetry and the Imagists'. It reflected his trenchant and pugnacious approach to life and art and he began by trying to answer the question that is always put when poetry is discussed in England: 'Why don't people read poetry?' His answer was that the poetry they were offered was not much good. 'When a poem does get immediately down to the people,' he declared (giving the instance of Masefield's supposedly ground-breaking *The Everlasting Mercy*), 'it is usually doggerel.'[36] His article consisted initially of a review of some new poetry books whose sheer awfulness 'accounts for the terrible indifference of many educated people towards poetry', but soon he moved on to his main focus which was to review the new anthology, *Des Imagistes*. In an echo of Lawrence reviewing the Georgian anthology in which he appeared, Aldington, claiming that no one competent could be found to do the job, said that, though a contributor himself, he must 'try and explain the aims and common sympathies and theories which have bound us together between two violent green covers'. In his very best insouciant style Aldington jumped in:

Why do we call ourselves 'Imagists'? Well, why not? People say, 'Oh, because it looks so silly, and everyone is some sort of an "ist", and why give yourselves a tag, and what on earth does it mean, and it's dam [*sic*] cheek anyway.' Well, I think it a very good and descriptive title, and it serves to enunciate some of the principles we most firmly believe in. It cuts us away from the 'cosmic' crowd and it equally bars us off from the 'abstract art' gang, and it annoys quite a lot of fools. So there you are.

In spite of the provocative tone Aldington's article is a good primer and draws explicitly on two very useful documents: a piece from *Poetry* written by F. S. Flint for its March 1913 issue defining 'Imagisme' and Ezra Pound's famous aesthetic manifesto in the same issue, 'A Few Don'ts by an Imagiste'.[37] Aldington summed up the core Imagist philosophy:

1. Direct treatment of the subject . . . 2. As few adjectives as possible . . . 3. A hardness, as of cut stone. No slop, no sentimentality. When people say that Imagist poems are 'too hard', 'like a white marble monument', we chuckle; we know that we have done something good. 4. Individuality of rhythm. We make new fashions instead of cutting our clothes on old models. Mr. Hueffer says that the unit of our rhythms is the unit of conversation. I daresay he is right. 5. A whole lot of don'ts, which are mostly technical . . . 6. The exact word. We make quite a heavy stress on that. It is most important. All great poetry is exact. All the dreariness of nineteenth century poets comes from their not quite knowing what they wanted to say and filling up the gaps with portentous adjectives and idiotic similes . . . 7. I know there are a lot more but I can't remember them now . . .

Aldington conceded that this hard, spare, clear, unadorned poetry was an acquired taste and one that implied a familiarity with 'the other poetry' of the tradition, 'but when you do come to like it there is greater emotional pleasure than in any other sort of writing . . . It is to me the justification of my years-long plaintive defence of poetry – that there was more in six lines of real poetry than in 350 pages of fiction.' With the exception of T. E. Hulme (an important exception because he was the movement's most interesting thinker) none of the war poets considered in this book appeared in the Imagist anthology and, at a time when this glittering Hellenic hardness (exemplified so well in the poetry of H.D.) was the touchstone of the *Egoist* poets' practice, poets like the emerging Wilfred Owen were deep in the lusher pastures of the sub-Keatsian. Very few of the trench poets had much time for the aesthetics of the avant-garde. Siegfried Sassoon and Edward Thomas, in particular, thought it a lot of nonsense.

And then, that summer of 1914, after the arrival in splendour at the Berkeley Hotel in Mayfair of the rich American Imagist poet Amy Lowell, and her hosting of the 'Imagist Dinner' on 17 July at the Dieu Donne Restaurant, war was declared. A new kind of experience would now temper and make 'hard' and 'objective' the poetics of the trench poets. Days after the declaration of war on 4 August, Aldington was back in his *Egoist* pulpit to offer readers some 'Notes on the Present Situation'. The tone will strike some as arrogant and this disposition to *épater* was part of the act, but there was some native shrewdness in his assessment and prediction:

There seems now to be only one subject exercising everyone's mental and physical activities – the War . . . The state of mind of the individual in a case like the present is undoubtedly influenced by the mob psychology . . . A great war like the present tends towards the creation of type as opposed to the creation of individuals . . . This kind of feeling [patriotism] does not produce art – for proof of this

consult the war poems in the papers. The impulse is too
vague, too general; the impulse of art is always clear and particular . . . The truth is that we are all too much engulfed in
the 'group psychology' to be artists . . . I see at least two good
results in this war – two good results I mean from a somewhat
narrow and personal standpoint. First of all, numbers of the
hangers-on of the arts, those dirty little vultures which hang
around merely looking for carrion, will be done away with . . .
The second result will be that art will be practised for its own
sake and will be more sincere: in London I know of only two
artists who are not either charlatans, poseurs or 'vaniteux' . . .
Think of the appalling number of tedious periodicals and
books which will be produced during the war and after – all
on the same subject! . . . we shall have endless sentimental
novels, novelettes, stories, pictures and patriotic music, all
warlike and all damned . . . Notice that this is the war of the
bourgeois, rather rare in history. The aristocracy of all the
nations engaged have no real hostility towards each other; the
cosmopolitanism of practically all the artists and scientists
rules them out; the people – except in France – have no particular feeling against the other races.[38]

The gap, between the views of the advanced critics and
poets and the taste of the general public, is a gap that is still
with us. The poetry preferred by the man and woman in the
street, a poll in the *Journal of Education* in 1913 confirmed, was
not to be found in any of these rival anthologies but in the work
of Rudyard Kipling, William Watson, Robert Bridges, and
Alfred Noyes who topped the poll. There were those indeed
who saw the War as potentially a new aesthetic broom that
would sweep away all this avant-garde rot and steady poets'
minds. Five months into the War, the *Times Literary Supplement*
concluded that the conflict was exerting a beneficial effect on
British verse because it had made poetry 'more impassioned

and more manful'.[39] The first weeks and months of the War saw the floodgates open and torrents of bad poetry washing over the land, mostly in newspapers, but often in privately published collections from serving soldiers, those who had lost their lives finding thus a memorial and an access of appreciative emotion in the reader. In the phase from August 1914 to the death of Rupert Brooke in April 1915 (the latter event marking another surge of mass verse production) the serious poets and critics stood back and watched the verses multiply. As Harold Monro put it: 'On the very morrow of the declaration an uproar of song burst from the throats of our lyrical poets.'[40] He had in mind the senior figures like the Poet Laureate, Bridges ('an expected but unfortunate poem ['Wake up England!']'), Newbolt (whose poem appeared in *The Times* on 5 August), and William Watson (who 'panted through a series of preposterous threats and ejaculations').

The best of these senior poems was Thomas Hardy's 'Men Who March Away' which appeared in *The Times* on 9 September – though a young poet, Charles Sorley, called its refrain, 'Victory crowns the just', which he thought was filched from a leading article in the *Morning Post*, 'the worst line he ever wrote'.[41] In the view of critics like Monro: 'Many young authors acquired spurious reputations under the cloak of Patriotism: these might, in fact, be called War Profiteers. The danger of writing verse to fulfil a demand is well known.' Another contemporary critic, Frank Swinnerton, later looked back on this period with dismay: 'One curious and disgusting phenomenon of the first war-months was a flood of jubilant articles by professors, near-professors, and literary romantics who detested Realism, Futurism, *Blast*, and tranquillity. They said, with one accord, that the war would prove the salvation of English letters. It would purge us of evil humours, and release the stream of pure poetry which had been too long muddied by science, meticulousness, and nonsense.'[42]

Soon, the anthologies of this new wave of patriotic poetry would start to appear, but many of the poems that have come to form the corpus of the former Poet Laureate's 'sacred text' did not emerge until later and many were not published in their authors' lifetimes. Time has decided which poems endured.

2

The First Phase, 1914 to the Somme: Rupert Brooke, Julian Grenfell and Charles Hamilton Sorley

Come and die. It'll be great fun.[1]

RUPERT BROOKE

I hate the growing tendency to think that every man drops overboard his individuality between Folkestone and Boulogne, and becomes on landing either 'Tommy' with a character like a nice big fighting pet bear and an incurable yearning and whining for mouth-organs and cheap cigarettes: or the Young Officer with a face like a hero and a silly habit of giggling in the face of death.[2]

CHARLES HAMILTON SORLEY

The declaration of war on 4 August 1914 came at the height of a long, hot summer. 'During this exceptionally hot season river parties were in great vogue,' wrote a foreign observer, Count Constantine Benckendorff, son of the Russian Ambassador.[3] There were Zeppelin raids on London and a theatre in the Strand was hit:

I was told that the audience had behaved in a very distinguished way, either by keeping their seats in an orderly
fashion, singing patriotic songs, or walking out of the theatre
ditto . . . all the main thoroughfares visible from our height
[the roof of the Admiralty], full of traffic during the raid,
became quite empty after it was over and stayed so for the
rest of the night . . . For the rest, dimmed-out London
seemed to carry on in a fairly normal way, with, as yet, comparatively few uniforms visible, not enough, in any case, to
change its outward appearance – it was, of course, early days.

The famous propaganda slogan was 'business as usual', but the
calm was deceptive and the War had in fact long been predicted.

In those early days there was no conscription but volunteers
were plentiful, and much has been written about the spirit
in which young men joined up – the idealism, the public
school ethos,[4] the conscious emulation of heroic models from
the classical studies which dominated English middle- and
upper-class educational curricula. There was a sense that it
was something of an exciting adventure, and would probably
be over by Christmas (though Kitchener warned very early on
that it would last at least three years). 'There was something
almost idyllic about those early weeks of the War,'[5] Siegfried
Sassoon later reminisced, of a time when training camps and
barracks in the Home Counties rather than the realities of
the Western Front were young men's first taste of service. The
poets were not tardy in signing up: in August 1914 Julian
Grenfell, already in the Army since 1910, was sent to France
with the Royal Dragoons and was soon awarded the DSO.
Charles Hamilton Sorley enlisted in the same month in the
7th Battalion of the Suffolk Regiment, as did T. E. Hulme as
a private in the Honourable Artillery Company, his friend Richard
Aldington, who went with him to sign up, being rejected. Siegfried

Sassoon joined the Sussex Yeomanry and Ivor Gurney made an initially unsuccessful attempt to volunteer. Another poet rejected in the first weeks was David Jones, who tried to enlist in the Artists' Rifles. At this stage, in the first month of the War, the selectors could afford to be choosy. In December, Rupert Brooke was drafted into the Hood Battalion, 2nd Naval Brigade, Royal Naval Division, and was sent to Blandford Camp in Dorset, and in the same month T. E. Hulme arrived in France.

On 2 September a secret meeting – whose minutes, if kept, have still not been located in any national archive – took place in London under the chairmanship of Charles Masterman who headed the War Propaganda Department based in a block of flats at Buckingham Gate known as Wellington House. Masterman had summoned a group of very senior writers – all far too old to fight – to find out what they could offer to the war effort. Around the table at Wellington House were William Archer, J. M. Barrie, A. C. Benson, Mgr Hugh Benson, Arnold Bennett, Robert Bridges, Hall Caine, G. K. Chesterton, Arthur Conan Doyle, John Galsworthy, Thomas Hardy, Anthony Hope Hawkins, Maurice Hewlett, W. J. Locke, E. V. Lucas, J. W. Mackail, John Masefield, A. E. W. Mason, Gilbert Murray, Henry Newbolt, Owen Seaman, G. M. Trevelyan, H. G. Wells, and Israel Zangwill. Arthur Quiller-Couch and Rudyard Kipling sent their apologies. The average age of those present was over fifty, the youngest, at thirty-four, being Masefield and the oldest, at eighty-four, Hardy. 'It is practically impossible to exaggerate the literary power which was thus assembled in one room,'[6] one historian has commented. Since no transcript of the meeting has survived, what happened has to be pieced together from assorted memoirs of those present, most notably Thomas Hardy who wrote: 'The yellow September sun shone in from the dusty street with a tragic cast upon them as they sat around the large blue table, full of misgivings, yet unforeseeing in all their completeness the tremendous events that were to follow.'[7] Arnold Bennett noted in his diary: 'The sense was talked by Wells and Chesterton.'[8] The immediate outcome of the meeting was a letter to *The Times* published on 18 September and signed by fifty-two authors, this time including four women (gentlemen only having been summoned to sit around the blue table), one of whom was the novelist Mrs Humphry Ward. They were replying to a manifesto of support for the attack on Belgium that had been issued by a group of prominent German academics.

Two striking aspects of this letter were the determination of the very broad church of literary opinion gathered together as signatories to make the moral case for war, and the almost pained sense of regret that it was to be with Germany. For most English literary intellectuals of the nineteenth and early twentieth centuries German literature and culture were to be revered, and many of the young poets who would die loved Germany. As the signatories put it: 'The undersigned writers, comprising amongst them men and women of the most divergent political and social views, some of them having been for years ardent champions of good will towards Germany, and many of them extreme advocates of peace, are nevertheless agreed that Great Britain could not without dishonour have refused to take part in the present war.'[9] They went on to argue that the seeming German conviction that it was 'the destiny of Germany to be the dominating force in Europe and the world' could not be tolerated, given its actions in violating Belgian neutrality. They went on:

> These views, inculcated upon the present generation of Germans by many celebrated historians and teachers, seem to us both dangerous and insane. Many of us have dear friends in Germany, many of us regard German culture with the highest respect and gratitude; but we cannot admit that

any nation has the right by brute force to impose its culture upon other nations, nor that the iron military bureaucracy of Prussia represents a higher form of human society than the free constitutions of Western Europe.

And so they opposed 'the domination of the whole Continent by a military caste'. Among the poets, of an established older generation, who signed were Laurence Binyon, Robert Bridges, Thomas Hardy, Rudyard Kipling, John Masefield, and Henry Newbolt.

More indirect results of this mass mobilisation of established authors were the poems that were published in newspapers in the late summer and autumn, including Hardy's 'Men Who March Away'.

Not everyone, as we have already seen, was impressed by this mass outbreak of verse, and at the start of November 1914 the poet John Gould Fletcher in a review essay entitled 'War Poetry' in the new number of *The Egoist* lambasted the first of the patriotic-poetic cullings published by Chatto & Windus as *Poems of the Great War*. This was to be the first of many such anthologies of non-professional verse that would appear throughout the War. After quoting some ineffable William Watson lines, Gould Fletcher attempted to skewer the Poet Laureate and his recent patriotic effort 'Wake up England!' He declared: 'Parliament ought surely to vote an increase of sack to the Laureate's doubtless exiguous salary. Mr Bridges has made his niche in English literature secure . . . Unless indeed it turns out that these verses are not really by Mr. Bridges but are of the Kaiser's own manufacture, and were written to discredit, demoralise, and utterly metagrabolise poor England. Let it be looked into.'[10] He mocked the senior poet's turgid and clichéd diction but sarcastically urged everyone to buy the book because the shilling cover price would contribute to the National Relief Fund:

Those who are incapacitated by its reading will doubtless obtain their share of this fund later on. Those who are not, can do still another and a greater service to England by posting their copies to 'The Kaiser, Potsdam, for Free Distribution to the German Army'. If any such copies reach their destination, we may all sleep secure in our beds, as Lord Rosebery long ago exhorted us to do. The German Army will explode with laughter, and everyone will see that 'poetry, or at any rate verse . . . is of some use after all'.

Two weeks later Gould Fletcher was back on the warpath, having encountered another clutch of opportunist anthologies including John Lane's selection of *Songs and Sonnets for England in War Time*, which he dismissed as 'fifty soul-stirring ditties for England in this war'.[11] Once again, it was the poetic diction that became the object of his scorn and he asked, in a dig at Lloyd George's notorious sale of peerages, 'whether a "storied scutcheon" . . . is an adequate description of a knighthood obtained through subscription to the Secret Party Funds'. He also dismissed a Methuen anthology called *Remember Louvain!* as 'a yellow-hued concoction', and concluded that while another called *Lord God of Battles* was printed on good paper the verse, alas, had 'a periwigged manner'. And in the December issue, the magazine ended its opening critical salvo against war poetry with a satirical squib by Herbert Blenheim:

'Song: in War-Time'
At the sound of the drum,
Out of their dens they come, they come,
The little poets we hoped were dumb,
The little poets we thought were dead,
The poets who certainly haven't been read
Since Heaven knows when, they come, they come

At the sound of the drum, of the drum, drum, drum . . .
It isn't the horrors of war we fear,
The horrors of war, we've got 'em here,
When the poets come on like waves, and come
At the sound etc etc[12]

One young poet who was not so cynical was Rupert Brooke. In a short piece published in the *New Statesman* on 29 August 1914 he tried to fictionalise the confused patriotic sentiment of a young alter ego at the declaration of war. The young man loved Germany, as Brooke and several other young poets did, yet he was 'sickened' by the possibility of an invasion. He let rip a strange and ecstatic vision of Edwardian England:

His astonishment grew as the full flood of 'England' swept over him, on from thought to thought. He felt the triumphant helplessness of a lover. Grey, uneven little fields, and small, ancient hedges rushed before him, wild flowers, elms and beeches, gentleness, sedate houses of red brick, proudly unassuming, a countryside of rambling hills and friendly copses. He seemed to be raised high, looking down on a landscape compounded of the western view from the Cotswolds, and the Weald, and the high land in Wiltshire, and the Midlands seen from the hills above Prince's Risborough. And all this to the accompaniment of tunes heard long ago, an intolerable number of them being hymns. There was, in his mind, a confused multitude of faces, to most of which he could not put a name. At one moment he was on an Atlantic liner, sick for home, making Plymouth at nightfall; and at another, diving into a little rocky pool through which the Teign flows, north of Bovey; and again, waking, stiff with dew, to see the dawn come up over Royston plain. And continually he seemed to see the set of a mouth he knew to be his mother's, and A—'s face, and, inexplicably, the face of an old man he had once passed in a

Warwickshire village. To his great disgust, the most commonplace sentiments found utterance in him. At the same
time he was extraordinarily happy.[13]

Rupert Brooke was to become the type of the young poet
sacrificed heroically to war and his death had profound consequences for the national mood, letting the sluices discharge
more patriotic verse, and becoming a symbol of heroic endeavour when, before the Battle of the Somme, the War was still
susceptible of that kind of exalted presentation.

Brooke was dashingly handsome, his premature death making
the halo of glamour around his image shine more intensely, and
this aspect was most famously captured in the lines of the poet
Frances Cornford:

A young Apollo, golden-haired,
Stands dreaming on the verge of strife,
Magnificently unprepared
For the long littleness of life.

The poet W. B. Yeats called him 'the most handsome man in
England', a view from which few would have dissented. He was
attracted by and to men and women and his intellectual gifts
and academic success made him always an admiring centre of
attention. His innate sense of theatricality and love of drama,
both practical and scholarly, ensured that he always performed
with panache.

Brooke was born on 3 August 1887 in Rugby, where his father
was a classics tutor and housemaster and where he first learned
to juggle conventional success in the eyes of the world with a
less orthodox sensibility. Between 1906 and 1909 he read classics at King's College, Cambridge, and threw himself into the
life of the university, his attractive and charismatic presence –
defined in Cornford's poem 'Youth' – making him an under-

graduate success. He joined the Apostles but also the Fabian Society and the Marlowe Dramatic Society where he met women for the first time, having moved previously in more homosexual circles. He was also a keen participator in the activities branded by Virginia Woolf as 'neo-paganism' – hiking, nude bathing, vegetarianism.[14] His passion for drama both as an undergraduate actor and as a scholar of Jacobean drama was intense. He lived at Grantchester from 1909 to 1912, and while continuing to write poems, publishing his first volume in 1911, he pursued the academic study of drama with a particular interest in Webster. He won several academic prizes and his dissertation on 'John Webster and the Elizabethan Drama' won him a Fellowship at King's in 1913. His amatory and sexual entanglements remained complicated and contradictory until his death and were the cause of a nervous breakdown early in 1912. He seems in particular to have experienced psychological problems to do with revulsion with his own body and its desires.

In May 1913 Brooke tried to resolve his problems through travel and visited for a year Canada, the United States, and the South Seas where he had a relationship with a Tahitian woman, Taatamata, but this seems to have had little impact on his unresolved tensions. In America he met the theatre manager Maurice Browne who later recalled his astounding beauty: 'Every woman who passes – and every other man – stops, turns round, to look at that lithe and radiant figure.'[15] Brooke returned to England in 1914 at the age of twenty-six ready to begin more complicated amatory manoeuvres, when the War intervened. Staying at Rugby at the end of June he wrote to Stanley Spencer: 'But this damned war business . . . If fighting starts, I shall have to enlist, or go as a correspondent. I don't know. It will be Hell to be in it; and Hell to be out of it. At present I'm so depressed about the war, that I can't talk, think, or write coherently.'[16] He complained to his friend, the painter Jacques Raverat:

Everyone in the governing classes seems to think we shall be at war. Everything's just the wrong way round. *I* want Germany to smash Russia to fragments, and then France to break Germany. Instead of which I'm afraid Germany will badly smash France, and then be wiped out by Russia. France and England are the only countries that ought to have any power. Prussia is a devil. And Russia means the end of Europe and any decency. I suppose the future is a Slav Empire, world-wide, despotic, and insane.[17]

Brooke was in London on the day war was declared and went to a music-hall performance at the Coliseum. He reported to his lover, the actress Cathleen Nesbitt: 'Nearly everyone sat silent. Then a scribbled message was thrown: "War declared with Austria. 11.9." There was a volley of quick low hand-clapping – more a signal of recognition than anything else. Then we dispersed into Trafalgar Square, and bought midnight war editions, special. All these days I have not been so near tears. There was such tragedy, and such dignity, in the people.'[18]

But the War was yet to perform its function of steadying his mind and quelling his internal turbulence of spirit. He was still confused about it, as he explained to another of his women friends, Lady Eileen Wellesley:

It's not so easy as you think – for a person who has no military training or knowledge, save the faint, almost prenatal, remembrance of some khaki drilling at Rugby – to get to the 'front'. I'm one of a band who've been offering themselves, with a vague persistence, to their country, in various quarters of London for some days, and being continually refused. In time, one of the various doors we tap at will be opened. Meanwhile, I wander.

One grows introspective. I find in myself two natures –

not necessarily conflicting, but – different. There's half my heart which is normal & English – what's the word, not quite 'good' or 'honourable' – '*straight*', I think. But the other half is a wanderer and a solitary, selfish, unbound, and doubtful. Half my heart is of England, the rest is looking for some home I haven't yet found. So, when this war broke, there was part of my nature and desires that said 'Let me alone. What's all this bother? I want to work, I've got ends I desire to reach. If I'd wanted to be a soldier I should have been one. But I've found myself other dreams.' It was that part, I suppose, which, when the tumult & unrest in me became too strong, sent me seeking for a correspondentship. At least, it was some individualist part in me which said 'It's the biggest thing in your seventy years. You'd better see as much of it as you can. Go, for some paper, immediately.' Base thoughts, those: when decent people are offering their lives for their country, not for their curiosity. You're quite right. It's a rotten trade, war-correspondent.

I came to London a few days ago to see what I could do that would be most use. I had a resentment – or the individualist part in me had – against becoming a mere part of a machine. I wanted to use my intelligence. I can't help feeling I've got a brain. I thought there *must* be some organizing work that demanded intelligence. But, on investigation, there isn't. At least, not for ages.

I feel so damnably incapable. I can't fly or drive a car or ride a horse sufficiently well.[19]

So Brooke continued restlessly in London, 'dodging the young ladies who are in love with me'[20] and trying to find a role for himself in the War, not helped by his meetings with the progressive intellectuals who had been his pre-war friends: 'I hover on their fringes yet: dehumanized, disgusting people. They are mostly pacifists and pro-Germans. I quarrel with them twice a day.'[21]

Not all young ladies, however, were being 'dodged' and he suggested to Lady Wellesley: 'We can have fun together, can't we? And supposing I go off & get blown to pieces – what fools we should feel if we hadn't had fun – if we'd forgone our opportunities – shouldn't we?'[22] And there was even time for lunch with Edward Marsh's boss Winston Churchill at which secret gossip was heard and at which, so he told a friend, Churchill had personally offered him the commission which made him a sub-lieutenant RNVR. Brooke was happier in the Navy, the only principal war poet in this book in that service: 'I rather despise the Army. Britannia rules the waves.'[23] The poet John Drinkwater later recalled Brooke's mood as war broke out: 'In the last week of July we lunched twice together in a Soho restaurant. War was threatening. If it broke, he must go; I think it was said in so many words; it certainly was clear. He was still eager about his new fellowship work at Cambridge, but, as one feels now, there was already in the eagerness the note of foreboding, calm and indeed wholly contented, that seemed to touch all his words thereafter till the end.'[24]

Brooke was initially sent to the Navy's Betteshanger Camp at Walmer in Kent, where he was put in charge of fifty men whose Scottish and Irish accents he found challenging. In an ambiguous letter to Lady Wellesley he reported how he had been impressed by 'the rows of naked, superb, men bathing in a September sun' but quickly added: 'When I *do* think of anything, I think of how lovely it was with you.'[25]

In October 1914 Brooke finally saw active service in the Antwerp expedition. The aim – not in the end realised – was to relieve the siege of the city by the German Army. When the Anson Battalion left Dover, he reported to Cathleen Nesbitt: 'Old ladies waved handkerchiefs, young ladies gave us apples, and old men and children cheered, and we cheered back, and

I felt very elderly and sombre and full of thoughts of how human life was like a flash between darknesses, and that x per cent of those who cheered would be blown into another world within a few months; and they all seemed to me so innocent and patriotic and noble, and my eyes grew round and tear-stained.'[26] They sailed that night, and shortly afterwards were informed that they were going to Antwerp and the train was certain to be attacked: 'So we all sat under lights writing last letters: a very tragic and amusing affair.'[27] Brooke was touched by one of the men, a father of fourteen, who asked him what he should do with the money he was carrying. He wanted to avoid the Germans getting their hands on it if he were killed. He was advised to give it to the parson. In the event they were not attacked and arrived at Antwerp in triumph to be greeted by the local people with apples and chocolate and flags and kisses, and cries of *Vivent les Anglais!* The battalion was then marched through an old gate in the immense, wild garden of a recently deserted villa-château: 'There we had to sleep. The rather dirty and wild-looking sailors trudged over lawns, through orchards and across pleasaunces. Little pools glimmered through the trees, and deserted fountains: and round corners one saw, faintly, occasional Cupids and Venuses . . . gleaming quietly . . . It seemed infinitely peaceful and remote. I was officer on guard till the middle of the night.'[28] This was Brooke's first (and it would turn out last) experience of actual warfare and it left him thrilled and confused:

For when I think back on it, my mind is filled with various disconnected images and feelings . . . There's the excitement in the trenches – we weren't attacked seriously in our part – with people losing their heads and fussing and snapping. It's queer to see the people who *do* break under the strain of danger and responsibility. It's always the rotten ones. Highly sensitive people don't, queerly enough. 'Nuts' do. I was relieved to find I was incredibly brave! I don't know how I should behave if shrapnel was bursting on me and knocking the men round me to pieces. But for risks and nerves and fatigue I was all right. That's cheering.

And there's the empty blue sky and the peaceful village and country scenery, and nothing of the war to see except occasional bursts of white smoke, very lazy and quiet, in the distance. But to hear incessant thunder, shaking buildings and ground and you and everything; and, above, recurrent wailings, very shrill and queer, like lost souls, crossing and recrossing in the emptiness – nothing to be seen. Once or twice a lovely glittering aeroplane, very high up, would go over us; and then the shrapnel would be turned on it, and a dozen quiet little curls of white smoke would appear round the creature – the whole thing like a German wood-cut, very quaint and graceful and unreal.[29]

Next evening the battalion was suddenly ordered to leave their trenches and move across Antwerp and the Scheldt and catch a train at 7.30 the next morning, narrowly missing a German ambush. The Belgians set fire to petrol tanks so that the sky was full of flame and smoke:

It lit up houses wrecked by shells, dead horses, demolished railway stations, engines that had been taken up with their lines and signals, and all twisted round and pulled out, as a bad child spoils a toy. And there we joined the refugees, with all their goods on barrows and carts, in a double line, moving forward about a hundred yards an hour, white and drawn and beyond emotion. The glare was like hell. We passed on, out of that, across a pontoon bridge, built on boats. Two German spies tried to blow it up while we were on it. They were caught and shot. We went on through the dark. The refugees and motor-buses and transport and Belgian troops grew

thicker. After about a thousand years it was dawn. The motor-
buses indicated that we were bound for Hammersmith and
Fleet Street and such places and might be allowed to see
Potash and Perlmutter [a contemporary comedy made into a
highly successful movie in 1923 by Sam Goldwyn]. Women
gave us apples.[30]

Descriptions like these suggest that Brooke might have proved
a very vivid war reporter had he indeed chosen that course as he
planned.

After the excitement of Antwerp it was back to camp in
Dorset and then the Royal Naval Barracks at Chatham.
Brooke's Antwerp experience had galvanised him. He now
knew that he was committed to this war and what it was for. As
he explained to a friend:

In the room where I write are some twenty men. All but one
or two have risked their lives a dozen times in the last month.
More than half have gone down in torpedoed ships and been
saved *sans* their best friends. They're waiting for another
ship. I feel very small among them. But that, and the sight of
Belgium, and one or two other things makes me realize more
keenly than most people in England do – to judge from the
papers – what we're in for, and what great sacrifices – active
or passive – everyone must make. I couldn't bear it if
England daren't face or bear what Germany is facing and
bearing.[31]

Brooke was increasingly coming to feel that the British public
did not realise the gravity of the situation and how much other
nations were suffering. He found his own experience of military
life, certainly in training camp, to be very soft for officers, echo-
ing the view of Siegfried Sassoon.[32] He observed that for
someone who had endured public school conditions it was no

physical hardship. He complained to Cathleen Nesbitt that until some atrocity happened on English soil people would not wake up: 'I'm rather disturbed, my dear one, about the way people in general don't realize we're at war. It's – even yet – such a picnic for us – for the nation – and so different for France and Belgium. The millions France is sacrificing to our thousands. I think – I know – that *everyone* ought to go in. I pray that there'll be a raid, or, at least, a score of civilians killed.'33 He felt, too, the gulf between combatants and non-combatants: 'It's the withdrawal of combatants into a special seclusion and reserve. We're under a curse or a blessing or a vow to be different. The currents of our lives are interrupted – what is it? – *I* know. Yes. The central purpose of my life, the aim and end of it, now, the thing God wants of me, is to get good at beating Germans. That's sure. But that isn't what it was. What it was, I never knew, and God knows I never found. But it reached out deeply for other things than my present need.' He told Cathleen: 'There was some beauty and holiness it should have taken hold of. Perhaps you were near, or were, that beauty and holiness.'34

Most of his friends were training or serving, some had been killed and others wounded, yet were going back. He felt acutely the dislocation of values that war brings in its train, hearing about the death of figures on the European cultural scene:

The best Greek scholar of the younger generation at Cambridge, Cornford [Francis Cornford; his wife was Frances (née Darwin)], is a musketry instructor at Aldershot. Among my fellow officers are one of the best young English pianists, and a brilliant young composer. Gilbert Murray gets up every morning to line a hedgerow, gun in hand, before dawn. What a world! Yet I'm still half ashamed of England, when I hear of the holocaust of the young poets, painters and scholars of France and Belgium – and Germany . . . It hurts me, this war. Because I was fond of Germany. There are such good things in her, and I'd always hoped she'd get away from Prussia and the oligarchy in time. If it had been a mere war between us and them I'd have hated fighting. But I'm glad to be doing it for Belgium. That's what breaks the heart to see and hear of. I marched through Antwerp, deserted, shelled, and burning, one night, and saw ruined houses, dead men and horses . . . That was like hell, a Dantesque Hell, terrible. But there – and later – I saw what was a truer Hell. Hundreds of thousands of refugees, their goods on barrows and hand-carts and perambulators and waggons, moving with infinite slowness out into the night, two unending lines of them, the old men mostly weeping, the women with hard white drawn faces, the children playing or crying or sleeping. That's what Belgium is now: the country where three civilians have been killed to every one soldier . . . It's queer to think one has been a witness of one of the greatest crimes of history. Has ever nation been . . . Well, we're doing our best . . . It's a great life, fighting, while it lasts. The eye grows clearer and the heart. But it's a bloody thing, half the youth of Europe blown through pain to nothingness, in the incessant mechanical slaughter of these modern battles. I can only marvel at human endurance.[35]

What is additionally significant about this passage is that it recognises the way that 'mechanical slaughter' was going to define this War just three months after the declaration, and that it calls the invasion of Belgium 'one of the greatest crimes of history' – where Sassoon would later call the War itself 'a crime against humanity'.[36]

But if Brooke's ideas about the conflict were maturing, his personal life was just as chaotic emotionally. Those who read his posthumous letters can see what his lovers did not: that there were many of them and that he could not decide between them:

I spend my odd moments in a grave perplexity, about marriage . . . If it's true the war'll last two years more, there's very little chance of anyone who goes out in January 1915 returning. Now, if I *knew* I'd be shot, I'd marry in a flash – oh any of two or three ladies – and do my best to leave a son. How comforting it would be to *know*: and what delicious snatches of domesticity I could steal before January 20! But, oh, if I came back in a year, and found myself caught. It's easy to select a wife for a month: but for a lifetime – one must be a little more certain.[37]

As Brooke prepared to go overseas again in January 1915 his impatience with British home opinion grew and he repeated his wish that something would shock it into realisation of what must be done: 'I'm largely dissatisfied with the English, just now. The good ones are all right. And it's curiously far away from us (if we haven't the Belgians in memory, as I have). But there's a ghastly sort of apathy over half the country. And I really think large numbers of male people don't want to die; which is odd . . . I've been praying for a German raid.'[38] On a personal level he was suffering the after-effects of a preparatory typhoid inoculation but claimed that he was happy in his new battalion, the Hood Battalion. He described his fellow officers to Cathleen, concluding: 'And finally there's a very hard bitter man, a poet, very strong and silent, called Rupert Brooke.'[39] The bitterness kept breaking in:

I sludge through mud all the day: and am continually too ill to think . . . I want to see somebody. I love no woman and very few men . . . The large part of my fellow officers I rather hate, and wholly despise. They are very doggish, and tell dirty stories at breakfast: and their noses curve greasily and they lend money . . . My mind's gone stupid with drill and arranging about the men's food. It's all good fun . . . I'm rather happy. I've a restful feeling that all's going well, and I'm not harming anyone, and probably even doing good. A queer new feeling. The only horror is, that I want to marry in a hurry and get a child, before I vanish. Oh, oh! But *whom?*'[40]

Even though he was now told to expect 75 per cent casualties in the Naval Division in the first three months, he claimed that he had never felt happier or better in his life than in the days in Belgium. 'And now I've the feeling of anger at a seen wrong – Belgium – to make me happier and more resolved in my work. I know that whatever happens I'll be doing some good, fighting to prevent *that*. And I've got a lot of friends in Germany: good people. That's bitter . . . it may be a long job.'[41]

Brooke rejoined his battalion on 8 January 1915 after Christmas leave (during which he had a meal with Edward Marsh that he thought might have been his last such luxury on earth) and prepared to sail. He told his clergyman uncle, Alan Brooke, that the word from General Staff at the Front was that they predicted 'a sudden cracking on the part of the Germans, & peace in April. But I think we should do it by August.'[42] It was now frustrating to discover that they would not be sailing until at least mid-March and he was stuck at Blandford Camp in Dorset: 'But it's TOO bloody, to have THREE more months of life, when one hoped for three weeks.'[43] Reading Brooke's letters for the last few months of his life at the start of 1915 it can almost seem that he had either a death-wish or at least a premonition. Or was it only a young man's romantic hyperbole and self-dramatisation? He told John Drinkwater:

The days go by. I plough through mud: march: drill: eat and sleep: and do not question more . . . Still it's the only life for me, just now. The training is a bloody bore. But on service one has a great feeling of fellowship, and a fine thrill, like nothing else in the world. And I'd not be able to exist, for torment, if I weren't doing it. Not a bad place and time to die, Belgium, 1915? I want to kill my Prussian first. Better than coughing out a civilian soul amid bedclothes and disinfectant and gulping medicines in 1950. The world'll be tame enough after the war, for those that see it. I had hopes that England'll get on her legs again, achieve youth and merriment, and slough the things I loathe – capitalism and feminism and hermaphroditism and the rest. But on maturer consideration, pursued over muddy miles of Dorset, I think there'll not be much change. What there is [is] for the better, though. Certain sleepers have awoken in the heart . . . Come and die. It'll be great fun. And there's great health in the preparation.[44]

Hearing that several French poets such as Charles Péguy had been killed in action he declared: 'I want to mix a few sacred and Apollonian English ashes with theirs, lest England be shamed.'[45] He told his American friend Maurice Browne: 'England's slowly waking and purging herself of evil things. It's rather a wonderful sight . . . we march through thousand year old English villages. England! England! I'm very happy.'[46]

Brooke was happy but had a bad cold and was allowed to recover from it at Marsh's chambers in Raymond Buildings in London. This entailed a dinner at Admiralty House at which, Brooke told Violet Asquith, 'I thought I *might* be able to collar W[inston]'s ear for five minutes, and drip sense into it: for which it would be patriotic to sacrifice my health.'[47] He gave a fuller report of the occasion to his mother: 'I spent an amusing evening with Winston, who was too tired for work, after preparing his speech (a good speech). He was rather sad about Russia, who he thinks is going to get her "paws burned", and disposed to think the war *might* last two years, if Russia got at all badly smashed. But he was very confident about the Navy and our side of Europe.'[48]

Finally, at the end of February, the good news came that they were shortly to sail for the Dardanelles and Brooke was very excited, telling his mother:

> We are going to be part of a landing force to help the fleet break through the Hellespont and the Bosphorus and take Constantinople, and open up the Black Sea. It's going to be one of the important things of the war, if it comes off. We take 14–16 days to get there. We shall be fighting for anything from 2 to 6 weeks. And back (they reckon) in May. We may just lie with the Fleet off there and do nothing . . . We are only taking 15 days' provisions (beyond what we have on the boats); so we obviously aren't expected to have a long campaign! . . . We fight from the boats – i.e. we can always get taken off if we have to retreat, so we're pretty safe![49]

To his friends he showed an almost manic excitement mixed with facetious allusions to a sort of second Crusade: 'I've never been quite so happy in my life, I think. Not quite so *pervasively* happy; like a stream flowing entirely to one end. I suddenly realize that the ambition of my life has been – since I was two – to go on a military expedition against Constantinople.'[50] To another lover, Katherine 'Ka' Laird Cox, he declared: 'Briefly, we're the best job of the war. We're to take Constantinople. Isn't it luck? I've never been so happy. 80, or 100 thousand of us altogether. And I shall attend the first Mass in St. Sophia since 1453 . . . We're to be back in May; and it's a very unrisky job.'[51] These correspondents were all sworn to the greatest secrecy because he should not have been revealing details of the operation to civilians.

The Hood Battalion sailed on 1 March on a requisitioned Union Castle liner, the *Grantully Castle*, and by 8 March they were lying off Carthage. 'War seems infinitely remote,'[52] Brooke reported languidly from on board in the Mediterranean spring sunshine.

The Dardanelles campaign had been launched by Churchill to take the Gallipoli Peninsula as the first step towards taking Constantinople and supporting the Russians in removing Turkey from the war. The first naval attack had taken place on 19 February before Brooke's battalion had arrived but had not gone well, and by the time troops landed on 25 April the Turks had been able to dig in. The result was one of the famous disasters of the War with around 214,000 Allied casualties by the time the campaign was called off in December 1915.

In 1916 John Masefield, one of Charles Masterman's loyal propagandists, published an account of the campaign, *Gallipoli*, designed to refute the widespread criticism of British commanders, and to charge the critics with aiding and abetting the enemy. He provided a vivid description of the horrifying landings on the peninsula under fire, addressed to critics at home: 'Let them imagine themselves driven mad by heat and toil and thirst by day, shaken by frost at midnight, weakened by disease and broken by pestilence, yet rising on the word with a shout and going forward to die in exultation in a cause foredoomed and almost hopeless.'[53] All Masefield's literary skill could not make this look like a victory but he tried to make it seem heroic, drawing on past images and punctuating his narrative with passages from the heroic medieval poem *The Song of Roland*. 'They were, however, the finest body of young men ever brought together in modern times,' he wrote. 'For physical beauty and nobility of bearing they surpassed any men I have ever seen; they walked and looked like the kings in old poems, and reminded me of the line in Shakespeare: "Baited like eagles having lately bathed".' When the troops left their base at Moudros on the Aegean island of Lemnos on 23 April, 'All that they felt was a gladness of exultation that their young courage was to be used. They went like kings in a pageant to the imminent death . . . their feeling that they had done with life . . . All was beautiful in that gladness of men about to die.'

When Brooke arrived in the area he was full of that heroism and believed that it was going to be one of the important passages of the war. The fact that only fifteen days' provisions were on board seemed to confirm his prediction in letters to friends of a short engagement. 'We're in the dreamiest, most utter, most trustful ignorance of what's to come,' he wrote to Violet Asquith. Some even say it'll all be over before we get there . . . I rather figure us scrapping forlornly in some corner of the Troad for years and years. Everyone will forget all about us. We shan't even be told when peace is declared . . .'[54] But some of this may have been bravado because, sounding again that note of foreboding, he confessed to Violet: 'Do not care much what happens to me or what I do. When I give thought to it at all, I hate people – people I like – to care for me. I'm selfish. And nothing but harm ever seems to have come from it, in the past . . . somewhere, I think, there's bad luck about me.'[55] And to Edward Marsh he wrote: 'You are to be my literary executor . . . You must decide everything about publication. Don't print much bad stuff . . . I've been such a failure.'[56] He then told Ka Cox that after his mother's death she was to have his papers: 'I suppose you're about the best I can do in the way of a widow . . . They *may* want to write a biography! How am I to know if I shan't be eminent? . . . You were the best thing I found in life . . . It's a good thing I die.'[57]

Suddenly the breeziness, the Crusader jokes, the sunny indifference, had gone and he was thinking of death. He asked for some of his love letters to be destroyed: 'I don't much care what goes . . . Indeed, why keep anything? Well, I *might* turn out to be eminent and biographiable. If so, let them know the poor truths. Rather pathetic this . . . It's odd, being dead. I'm afraid it'll finish off the Ranee [his nickname for his mother] . . . But the realization of failure makes me *unpleasantly* melancholy.'[58] He explained to Jacques Raverat: 'I've only two reasons for being sorry for dying – (several against) – I want to destroy some evils, and to cherish some goods.'[59]

Brooke was still not engaged in action and the ship now sailed to Egypt for a break, during which he got a touch of sunstroke. Since he was Rupert Brooke he was visited on his sickbed by no less a person than General Sir Ian Hamilton: 'A notable meeting: it was generally felt: our greatest poet-soldier and our greatest soldier-poet. We talked blank verse.'[60] He complained that, in spite of the now almost intolerable idleness and waiting, he had written nothing, though he was contemplating a poem about the essence of England that, he said, would contain the line: 'In Avons of the heart her rivers run.'[61]

While recovering from his sunstroke at the Casino Palace Hotel in Port Said Brooke complained about a little sore on the right side of his lip which seems to have developed from a mosquito bite which then caused septicaemia. He was not at all well when his ship anchored off the Greek island of Skyros on 17 April in Tres Boukes Bay. Exercises took place over the next few days but Brooke, a keen swimmer, was seen to decline a swimming race back to the ship and, normally the centre of any company, he went early to bed, pleading tiredness. Yet the gravity of his condition was still not obvious until, after he had complained of further pains, the Divisional doctor was called and he found the patient had a temperature of 101. Hot compresses were applied to Brooke's swollen lip, but by the morning of 22 April back and chest pains suggested that a more serious bacterial infection had taken hold and the urgency of the situation was now admitted. Several other doctors were called in for a conference and they concluded that the blood-poisoning was likely to be fatal. Everything happened very quickly, and accounts of Brooke's death inevitably seem rushed and abrupt because that is what it was like. He was transferred to a nearby French hospital ship but no one any longer believed that he would survive. Cables were sent to General Hamilton at Lemnos and the Admiralty in London – evidence if any more were needed of the fame and reputation of the golden-haired Apollo and the extent of his important Establishment connections. Eddie Marsh telegrammed Brooke's mother as soon as he read the telegram at the Admiralty and Churchill himself cabled his cousin, Major John Churchill, who was in the Aegean, asking him to attend Brooke's funeral on his behalf. 'We shall not see his like again,'[62] Churchill added.

The next day, 23 April, Shakespeare's birthday, his friend, the musician William Denis Browne, sat with the dying Brooke: 'At 4 o'clock he became weaker, and at 4.46 he died, with the sun shining all round his cabin, and the cool sea-breeze blowing through the door and the shaded windows. No one could have wished for a quieter or a calmer end than in that lovely bay, shielded by the mountains and fragrant with sage and thyme,' he wrote to Marsh two days later.[63]

Brooke's body was taken ashore and buried just before his ship sailed for the Dardanelles. It lies there today in a quiet olive grove surrounded by grazing goats, a heavy marble tomb that looks as though it belongs in an English cathedral churchyard, strangely isolated in the Greek sunlight.

In *The Times* of 26 April 1915 Winston Churchill, his friend as well as his naval commander, formally inaugurated the Brooke cult, with his customary rhetorical mastery:

Rupert Brooke is dead. A telegram from the Admiral at Lemnos tells us that this life has closed at the moment when it seemed to have reached its springtime. A voice had become more audible, a note had been struck, more true, more thrilling, more able to do justice to the nobility of our youth in arms engaged in this present war, than any other – more able to express their thoughts of self-surrender, and with a power to carry comfort to those who watched them so intently from afar. The voice has been swiftly stilled. Only the echoes and the memory remain: but they will linger.

During the last few months of his life, months of preparation in gallant comradeship and open air, the poet-soldier told with all the simple force of genius the sorrow of youth about to die, and the sure triumphant consolations of a sincere and valiant spirit. He expected to die; he was willing to die for the dear England whose beauty and majesty he knew; and he advanced towards the brink in perfect serenity, with absolute conviction of the rightness of his country's cause, and a heart devoid of hate for fellow-men.[64]

Interestingly, Churchill added that the thoughts to which Brooke gave expression 'in the very few incomparable war sonnets which he has left behind' would be shared 'by many thousands of young men moving resolutely and blithely forward into this, the hardest, the cruellest, and the least rewarded of all the wars that men have fought'. It was not usual, at this relatively early stage of the War, to hear such an acknowledgement of the difficulty of the conflict.

A week later, in the *Cambridge Magazine*, Gilbert Murray wrote: 'I cannot help thinking that Rupert Brooke will probably live in fame as an almost mythical figure.'[65] A quieter note was struck by his mother a few months later in a letter to Maurice Browne: 'Very soon after war broke out, both my boys told me that they must go to fight for their country. I agreed at once, and much as I have suffered since, I have never regretted it ... Perhaps you don't know that seven weeks after Rupert's death my youngest son Alfred was killed in France and now I am quite alone ... One has to go on somehow, though I don't know how.'[66] In an essay, John Drinkwater compared Brooke to Sir Philip Sidney: 'It is truly as though the gods would have this man great; as though, having given him all bright and clear qualities of brain and heart, they were impatient of any slow moving to the authority for which he was marked, and must, rather in divine caprice than in nature, bring him to untimely and bewildering fulfilment ... Only once before in our history, I think, has a man passed to so large and just a renown with so unconsidered and slender a warrant.'[67] Like Sidney he will have a symbolic value even for those who do not know his poetry: 'Such a symbol, clear, almost spare, yet magnificently complete, is the radiant, perfectly poised story of Rupert Brooke.'

But what of the poetry? The first posthumous publication, in May 1915, a month after he died, was *1914 & Other Poems* which appeared with as frontispiece a 1913 picture of a dashingly handsome Brooke by Sherril Schell. By the end of the year this volume had run through eleven editions. It included the poems about the South Seas that he had been planning to publish, and though the strictly 'war poems' are few they contain lines that are among the most famous in English poetry. It was the combination of youth and beauty sacrificed to the nation's cause that made this collection so popular. In 'Peace' he writes:

> Now, God be thanked Who has matched us with His hour,
>   And caught our youth, and wakened us from sleeping ...

Youth has answered the call, found something to excite and lift it, cleanse and purify ('as swimmers into cleanness leaping'), rejecting stale Age:

> Glad from a world grown old and cold and weary ...
> And half-men, and their dirty songs and dreary
> And all the little emptiness of love!

There is an element of verbal posturing here because for Brooke love, as we have seen, was certainly not an 'emptiness' and it does force one to ask, How *sincere* is this poem? Is it just a rhetorical exercise, saying what he thinks people want to hear from a poet in wartime, or is it *meant*, profoundly felt?

Some of Brooke's fellow poets had their reservations. Isaac Rosenberg complained: 'I did not like Rupert Brooke's begloried sonnets.'[68] Rosenberg found 'second hand phrases . . . It should be approached in a colder way, more abstract, with less of the million feelings everybody feels; or all these should be concentrated in one distinguished emotion.' Rosenberg said his poems 'remind me too much of flag days' and his style generally offended him: 'It is gaudy and reminiscent.' A more temperate assessment by Gavin Ewart in his introduction to a reprint of *The Collected Poems* suggests: 'Brooke wrote a lot of sonnets. They are often well-intentioned rather than successful.'[69] But it was another of Brooke's contemporaries, the poet Charles Hamilton Sorley in a letter to his mother, who noted, in the most devastating dismissal of his work:

I think Brooke's earlier poems – especially notably 'The Fish' and 'Grantchester', which you can find in *Georgian Poetry* – are his best. That last sonnet-sequence of his, of which you sent me the review in the *Times Lit. Sup.*, and which has been so praised, I find (with the exception of the beginning 'These hearts were woven of human joys and cares, Washed marvellously with sorrow' which is not about himself) over-praised. He is far too obsessed with his own sacrifice, regarding the going to war of himself (and others) as a highly intense, remarkable and sacrificial exploit, whereas it is merely the conduct demanded of him (and others) by the turn of circumstances, where non-compliance with this demand would have made life intolerable. It was not that 'they' gave up anything of that list he gives in one sonnet: but that the essence of these things had been endangered by circumstances over which he had no control, and he must fight to recapture them. He has clothed his attitude in fine words: but he has taken the sentimental attitude.[70]

Another poem, 'The Dead', talks of the slaughtered soldiers who have 'poured out the red/Sweet wine of youth'. Brooke's poetry is far from the bitter realism of Sassoon and Owen and in his poems war is seen as cleansing, making heroic. His most famous poem, 'The Soldier', carved on the tomb in Skyros, is so well known as hardly to need quotation:

If I should die, think only this of me:
That there's some corner of a foreign field
That is for ever England . . .

In addition to this poetic conceit of the patch of foreign soil anglicised there is the notion that the buried heart now 'Gives somewhere back the thoughts by England given' to 'hearts at peace, under an English heaven'. Might this conceivably be a little smug? As if the survivors – or more likely non-combatants – can feel good as a result of others' deaths. The purified and purifying heart of the dead soldier thus rejuvenates a society seen in an earlier poem as old and expended. A contemporary critic, Edward Shanks, later observed percipiently that Brooke 'became the type of a war-poet'[71] but could not be compared with the later war poets of actual trench experience because his sonnets were only 'the expression of an ardent civilian preparing himself to be a soldier'. Such cavils, however, are beside the point. Brooke matched his poems with the hour and gave expression to the purest emotions of patriotism that the War in its first phase would provoke, and there is no doubt that they resonated universally.

They also triggered a poetry boom with scores of emulators rushing into print.

Conscription was still ten months away but during 1915 six more of our poets volunteered to fight. In January David Jones enlisted in the 15th (London Welsh) Battalion of the Royal Welch Fusiliers; in February Ivor Gurney was drafted into the 2nd/5th Gloucester Regiment ('B' Company); in July Edward Thomas joined the Artists' Rifles; in August Edmund Blunden was commissioned as 2nd lieutenant in the Royal Sussex Regiment; in October Isaac Rosenberg enlisted in the Bantam Battalion of the 12th Sussex Regiment (40th Division) and Wilfred Owen joined up in the Artists' Rifles.

In the same month, April 1915, that Brooke died a young officer in the Royal Dragoons, the Rt Hon. Julian Grenfell, wrote another famous poem of the War's first phase, 'Into Battle', during the second Battle of Ypres, in the course of which Germany first used poison gas on a large scale. Grenfell was just a year younger than Brooke and came from an aristocratic background, fascinatingly evoked in Nicholas Mosley's biography. He was untypical of the 'war poet' as generally conceived. He was not remotely anti-war and saw combat as an undiluted heroic adventure that was morally invigorating. The bitter satirical vein of Sassoon, the sardonic detachment of Rosenberg, the horrified recoil from slaughter of Owen, were all utterly foreign to him. He was a traditional English aristocrat who looks, in the only photograph we have of him, taken in 1915 in military uniform and wearing his DSO, handsome but austere, his dark, brooding eyes seeming to contemplate with dignified seriousness the gravity of his fate.

Julian Grenfell was born in 1888 in London, the second son of the first Baron Desborough and his wife the famous socialite Ettie, Lady Desborough. His parents were prominent in late

Victorian and pre-war society and were part of a group known as 'the Souls'. Educated at Eton and Balliol, Grenfell was a sporting man who boxed middleweight for Oxford, rowed at Henley and was passionate about hunting. At Eton he had started a paper called *The Outsider* and he frequently clashed with his mother and displayed a rebellious streak. There was something about the world of his parents that he loathed. Nicholas Mosley suggests: 'His fight for life was both with his mother and with the rest of the conventional world that seemed to have staked its faith on insubstantiality and death . . . Julian tried to fend off these feelings of sickness and of being out of place by violent physical exercise.'[72] He wrote in 1909 a long series of unpublished essays which sought to articulate his sense of what was wrong with the values of his parents and their set.

In 1910, after a short infatuation with Pamela Lytton, wife of the 3rd Earl of Lytton, he joined the Royal Dragoons and was sent to India at the end of the year and to South Africa in 1911, where he was seen as a dashing young cavalry officer sometimes in trouble for his womanising. In August 1914 the regiment was sent to France and Grenfell was joyful: 'Don't you think it has been a wonderful and almost incredible rally to the Empire . . . It reinforces one's failing belief in the Old Flag and the Mother Country and the Heavy Brigade and the Thin Red Line, and all the Imperial Idea, which gets rather shadowy in peace time, don't you think?'[73] In an echo of Brooke he described his first experience of sailing to France in October 1914 as 'all the best fun one ever dreamed of'.[74] Grenfell wrote about war like a young man writing about the hunt: bold, careless, light-hearted as if it were all a bit of high-spirited entertainment: 'One loves one's fellow man so much more when one is bent on killing him.'[75]

Grenfell's first engagement in action was at the first Battle of Ypres that began on 19 October 1914. He was in a cavalry division that fought south-west of Ypres, near the road to Menin. In a letter to his mother he showed some sense that life was administering a smack of realism to the heroic values he felt were his. After his first taste of fighting, and the shock of the men's 'most filthy language', he reflected: 'I longed to be able to say that I liked it, after all one has heard of being under fire for the first time. But it's bloody. I pretended to myself for a bit that I liked it; but it was no good; it only made one careless and unwatchful and self-absorbed. But when one acknowledged to oneself that it was bloody, one became all right again, and cool.'[76] The stiff upper lip, that had hardly quivered, swiftly reasserted itself.

In addition, as his biographer notes: 'Julian did not take part in any of the massed mechanical slaughters that were later characteristic of the war. In the conditions of 1914 and early 1915 he seemed to be able to see war as a matter of almost personal performance. He thought the Germans had to be beaten, but he did not dream of a better world. He seemed to feel that in war he could at last do what was expected of him without being false.'[77]

Towards the end of the Battle of Ypres, Grenfell offered to make a personal contribution to the problem of enemy snipers by setting off at night on his own, refusing an offer to take a section with him, in the direction of the enemy lines. Crawling slowly across the mud, he eventually arrived ten yards from the nearest German trench and heard voices. His description of this solitary feat reads like an entry in a hunt journal: 'So I crawled on again very slowly to the parapet of their trench. It was very exciting . . . I peered through their loophole, and saw nobody, in the trench. Then the German behind put his head up again. He was laughing and talking. I saw his teeth glisten against my foresight, and I pulled the trigger very steady. He just gave a grunt and crumpled up.'[78] After this exploit, Grenfell made two entries in his game book, in the space available after a record of '105 partridges' added back home in early October: 'November

16th: 1 Pomeranian'; 'November 17th: 2 Pomeranians'.[79] He failed to smoke out any more of the German soldiers, who were probably as frightened as he was, but for this small act of undoubted courage he was awarded the DSO.

On 29 April, a week after the first Ypres poison gas attack and six days after the death of Brooke, Grenfell wrote 'Into Battle'. As Nicholas Mosley puts it, the poem 'is almost unique amongst poems of the First World War in that it shows no outrage against war and yet its luminousness and serenity do not seem false',[80] though Grenfell himself later wondered if his lines were 'meretricious'. Although this poem is the polar opposite of Wilfred Owen's 'Dulce et Decorum Est', and is almost without parallel in the entire corpus of First World War poetry, the reader today will find it neither meretricious nor a pretext to sneer, because of its incontrovertible sincerity of feeling. In the poem, which is finely crafted, Grenfell not merely celebrates the warrior, without a shadow of hesitation or doubt, but he makes him seem a kind of elemental force, bound into nature's processes, his art of death a triumphant assertion of the force of life. It begins by celebrating the 'naked earth' warmed by the spring which shows that

life is colour and warmth and light,
And a striving evermore for these
And he is dead who will not fight;
And who dies fighting has increase.

The use of the word 'increase' with its Shakespearean echo of pregnancy directly links killing in war not with the 'futility' and 'senselessness' conventionally attributed to trench warfare but with the idea of creation and human fulfilment: 'The fighting man shall from the sun/Take warmth, and life from glowing earth.' Fighting is thus a creative act like the burgeoning of spring; it is, literally, natural. The trees, the birds, the stars, all urge the poet on into 'the joy of battle' which 'makes him blind' because it is a total self-surrender to 'the Destined Will'. The vague invocation of war's reality ('the brazen frenzy starts' or 'in the air death moans and sings') is secondary to the celebration of heroic, instinctual sacrifice. Death in battle is an affirmation of life. No English poet has subsequently written this way about war and it is highly unlikely that any poet will ever do so again. But Grenfell wrote it and he believed wholly in what he wrote.

The poem was published a month later in *The Times* of 28 May, accompanying news of Grenfell's death. On the 13th he had volunteered to be a messenger during a heavy burst of shelling and was wounded by a shell splinter in his head. He died in the military hospital in Boulogne on 26 May, after his parents had managed to cross the Channel and visit him in hospital, and his grave today is in one of the long lines in the military section on the edge of the municipal cemetery in Boulogne, where the stone reads, with no allusion to his poetry: 'Captain The Hon. J.H.F. Grenfell D.S.O. The Royal Dragoons'.

According to Robert Graves the three most important poets of those who died in the First World War were Isaac Rosenberg, Wilfred Owen, and Charles Hamilton Sorley. Sorley is less well known than the other two but he is an interesting figure from this first phase of the War because he is in some sense transitional. We see in Sorley the stirrings of a more critical, more unillusioned, view of the War.[81] The photographs show a rather boyish but confident-looking young man. He was lively, humorous, had experienced a happy and stable childhood, and had a spirited personality and independent mind. His biographer comments: 'He seems to have been in almost every situation happy and well-adjusted.'[82] He was also generous to others, asking his mother to stop sending him gifts but instead to dis-

patch Woodbines that he could give to his men, but then worrying that this act would make him look 'an egoist, sentimentalist
or poser'.[83] The Master of Marlborough recalled after his death
that Sorley was 'never dull or depressed. In fact a bubbling joy in
life was one of his greatest charms. He seemed to revel in all its
phases.'[84]

Sorley was born on 19 May 1895 in Aberdeen, the son of
William Ritchie Sorley, professor of moral philosophy at the university, and his wife Janetta Colquhoun Smith. They lived in 'a
fine Adam mansion standing high above the Old Town and
looking over the dream-like crown of King's College Chapel to
the rim of the North Sea'.[85] When Charles was five his father
was appointed Knightsbridge Professor of Moral Philosophy at
Cambridge University and elected a Fellow of King's College,
and the family left Aberdeen. Sorley was taught at home by his
mother until 1906, reading aloud from the Bible and *Pilgrim's
Progress*, and learning poetry by heart – ballads and passages of
Shakespeare, Walter Scott, Macaulay, and Blake. He would
write long passages of heroic verse in the style of Scott or
Macaulay. At the age of ten, he and his twin brother Kenneth
started to attend King's College Choir School. In spite of a not
particularly distinguished record there, he won an open scholarship to Marlborough College where his adolescent poems
started to appear in *The Marlburian* from 1912 onwards. In his
final year at school Sorley won several prizes and a scholarship to University College, Oxford, but it was decided that he
should first spend time with a German family in the state of
Mecklenburg and then three months studying philosophy and
political economy at the University of Jena. This German experience was clearly an important element in his ambivalence
towards the War.

In one of his letters home, written on 2 March 1913, the precocious schoolboy poet told his parents:

I have newly squandered 3s. 6d. on another new toy. It is called *Georgian Poetry* and is an anthology of the best poetry – short poetry of course – of the last two years. There is a little in it that is bad, and the vast majority is quite inconsequent. But there are two poets with strange names – Lascelles Abercrombie and Walter de la Mare – whom I am very glad indeed to have met: very striking both of them. Then there is a man Wilfrid Wilson Gibson whom I have come across before in the *English Review*, and he is the poet of the tramp and the vagabond, and he can write.[86]

On 13 December that year Sorley left Marlborough and in January 1914 he set off for Schwerin. He soon found himself writing a poem on the Kaiser's birthday for no better reason than boredom at watching a goose-stepping military parade in the Kaiser's honour. He gradually, however, became 'intoxicated by the beauties of the German language'[87] and, like everyone else, was well aware that war was a real prospect, even as early as the start of 1914, and that this was going to be problematic. He told his parents: 'I am getting more unpatriotic daily . . . I understood what a glorious country it is: and who would win, if war came. However, on that subject, the people here seem wonderfully pacific; they consider England is the aggressive party and affirm that Edward VII spent his life in attempting to bring about a German war.'[88] At the end of April he left the Beutin family, with whom he had been staying, to go to the University of Jena (which he found very medieval – 'a horrid little town and most unhealthily situated'[89]) for the summer semester to listen to lectures. Something of Sorley's independent-minded, lively, disrespectful tone can be seen in his comment on a visit to Weimar, where he 'spent most of a sunny afternoon inspecting Schiller's discarded pyjamas'.[90] He joined a student discussion club and made a lot of friends, played tennis, read the *Odyssey* in his cheap little bed-sit, and told a friend he was 'having a first-rate time' and 'discovering, one by one, the superiorities of the German nation to our own'.[91] In fact, he admired German poetry, especially Goethe, but thought they couldn't write prose. He wrote in characteristically bumptious style to the Master of Marlborough: 'I was never meant for a scholar: but I suppose the farce of making me one will go on for another four years.'[92]

Then a real adventure took place. On 28 July, Sorley left Jena in order to meet a friend called Arthur Hopkinson in Marburg for a walking tour in the Moselle region. On the very same day Austria-Hungary declared war on Serbia and both young men were promptly arrested at Trier. They spent the night of 2 August in prison in the town. Although they were released next day and sent home to England, making a joke out of the experience, they had probably been in real danger. Sorley later told a friend: 'I had a white cell, a bowl of soup, a pitcher of solidifying water, a hole in the wall through which I talked to the prisoner next door, a prison bed, a prison bible: so altogether they did the thing in style.'[93] He started a rumour in the prison that England had declared war on Russia, which made his captors relent. He then made his way back via Belgium, in blissful ignorance of the storm centre he was heading towards, and had extreme difficulty in getting out of Antwerp until he got a passage on a vessel chartered by the British consul. 'He reached home,' his mother recalled, 'on the evening of August 6th, still hatless and with little in his rucksack but a pair of sandals and a Jena beer-jug.'[94]

The next morning he applied to the University Board of Military Studies for a commission in the Army. There was no immediate response, so he was about to enlist as a private when he learned that he had been gazetted as 2nd lieutenant in the 7th Battalion of the Suffolk Regiment, known as the 'Old Dozen'. Soon he was training at Churn on the Berkshire Downs. 'It's a beastly nuisance this war,' he told his sister, 'especially as it's against such nice people as the Germans.'[95] To another friend he expressed exasperation: 'But isn't all this bloody? I am full of mute and burning rage and annoyance and sulkiness about it. I could wager that out of twelve million eventual combatants there aren't twelve who really want it. And "serving one's country" is so unpicturesque and unheroic when it comes to the point.'[96] But he resigned himself to life at the Moore Barracks, Shorncliffe, above Folkestone, with his unit in late September: 'With an identification disc stamped with a mythical number and "Church of England" round one's neck I've resigned all claims to my person, I no longer am my own property. I am not a living creature, but a temporary second lieutenant ... a kind of extemporized being called into life a month ago and fading at the end of the war.'[97] He was shrewd enough to see that the army was no place for a bolshie student poet, even one with a commission: 'We who are critics by nature are somewhat out of our element commanding.'[98]

Sorley settled down reluctantly to life as a soldier and expected the war to last three years and end in 'stalemate'. He had nothing to read all day and no time to do so, and 'when one thinks one does so on the sly; and as for writing poetry in the Officers' Mess – it's almost as bold a thing as that act of God's in writing those naughty words over the wall at Belshazzar's Feast'.[99] To friends he denounced 'this time of auto-trumpeting and Old-England-she's-the-same-as-ever-isms' and asserted 'we have temporarily renounced all our claim to the more articulate and individual parts of our individuality'. He saw Germany's fault as 'a lack of real insight and sympathy with those who differ from her. We are not fighting a bully, but a bigot.'[100] He was contemptuous of lazy British bourgeois opinion: 'Indeed, I think that after the war all brave men will renounce their country and confess that they are strangers and pilgrims on the earth ... What a worm one is under the cart-wheels – big

clumsy careless lumbering cart-wheels of public opinion. I
might have been giving my mind to fight against Sloth and
Stupidity: instead, I am giving my body (by a refinement of
cowardice) to fight against the most enterprising nation in the
world.'[101] Writing again to the Master of Marlborough he
insisted on Germany's good qualities: 'Curious, isn't it, that in
old days a nation fought another for land or money: now we are
fighting Germany for her spiritual qualities – thoroughness, and
fearlessness of effort, and effacement of the individual.'[102] And
the tedium of training camp dragged on: 'The monotony of this
existence is alarming, and on the increase ... The war is a
chasm in time. I do wish that all journalists etc., who say that
war is an ennobling purge etc., etc., could be muzzled. It simply
makes people unhappy and uncomfortable, if that is a good
thing. All illusions about the splendour of war will, I hope, be
gone after the war.'[103]

By the start of January 1915 Sorley was starting to sound like
a version of Siegfried Sassoon:

It is the most asphyxiating work ... War in England only
means putting all men of 'military age' into a state of routi-
nal coma, preparatory to getting them killed. You are being
given six months to become conventional: your peace thus
made with God, you will be sent out and killed. At least, if
you aren't killed, you'll come back so unfitted for any other
job that you'll have to stay in the Army. I should like so much
to kill whoever was primarily responsible for the war. The
alarming sameness with which day passes day until this
unnatural state of affairs is over is worse than any so-called
atrocities; for people enjoy grief, the only unbearable thing is
dullness.[104]

He started to look forward to the prospect of going out to
France (now rumoured to be March 1915) as a relief from the

boredom of camp, but his disillusion with war grew more vocal. He told his mother in March: 'If we had gone out earlier we would have gone out with a thrill in poetic-martial vein: now most of us have become by habit soldiers . . . After all, war in this century is inexcusable: and all parties engaged in it must take an equal share in the blame for its recurrence . . . I do wish also that people would not deceive themselves by talk of a just war. There is no such thing as a just war. What we are doing is casting out Satan by Satan.'[105] And then on 23 April Rupert Brooke died, and Sorley commented, 'I saw Rupert Brooke's death in *The Morning Post*. *The Morning Post*, which has always hitherto disapproved of him, is now loud in his praises because he has conformed to their stupid axiom in literary criticism that the only stuff of poetry is violent physical experience, by dying on active service.'[106]

Finally, at the end of May, Sorley crossed with his brigade to France as part of the 12th Division of the British Expeditionary Force. To his parents he made light of it: 'I have just been censoring letters: which hardly puts one in a mood for writing. Suffice it that we are in a little hamlet, or rather settlement of farms; the men on straw, the officers on old four-posters: within sound of guns. Nothing disturbs these people. I have never felt so restful . . . So far our company are separated from the rest. It is like a picnic, and the weather is of the best.'[107] And to a friend he reported:

> We arrived at dawn: white dawn across the plane trees and coming through the fields of rye. After two hours in an oily ship and ten in a grimy train, the 'war area' was a haven of relief . . . They make perfect cider in this valley: still, like them . . . It brings out a new part of one's self, the loiterer, neither scorning nor desiring delights, gliding listlessly through the minutes from meal-time to meal-time, like the stream through the rushes: or stagnant and smooth like their

cider, unfathomably gold: beautiful and calm without mental
fear. And in four-score hours we will pull up our braces and
fight.[108]

He had heard no more than the distant rumbling of the guns,
and news of the brigade's future movements was very hazy. He
was impressed by the apparent casualness that seemed to pre-
vail: 'France full of troops, marching up and down, but not
towards the firing line.'[109] Sorley was quietly writing poems,
however, and sending them home in batches, but he declined
his mother's suggestion that he publish a collection. And the
sense of futility continued to grow:

A large amount of organized disorderliness, killing the spirit.
A vagueness and a dullness everywhere: an unromantic
sitting still 100 yards from Brother Bosch. There's something rotten in the state of something. One feels it but
cannot be definite of what. Not even is there the premonition of something big impending: gathering and ready
to burst. None of that feeling of confidence, offensiveness,
'personal ascendancy', with which the reports so delight
our people at home. Mutual helplessness and lassitude,
as when two boxers who have battered each other crouch
dancing two paces from each other, waiting for the other to
hit. Improvised organization, with its red hat, has muddled out romance . . . This is not Hell as I hoped, but Limbo
Lake with green growths on the water, full of minnows . . .
We are busy, pleasantly busy: though riveted with small
and senseless orders. Everything is done on a small scale
here.[110]

The pettiness, the lack of action, the endless preparations,
the defensive precautions began to get to him and he was irri-
tated at the way in which the media back home reduced

everything to cliché: 'I hate the growing tendency to think that every man drops overboard his individuality between Folkestone and Boulogne, and becomes on landing either "Tommy" with a character like a nice big fighting pet bear and an incurable yearning and whining for mouth-organs and cheap cigarettes: or the Young Officer with a face like a hero and a silly habit of giggling in the face of death.'[111] He hated the 'colossal egoism' of the *Daily Mail* and 'its power of anticipating public opinion by twenty-four hours and giving it just the turn in the direction [it] wishes'.[112] But, behind the mocking pose, Sorley was capable of being moved: 'The existence is incredibly peaceful: till suddenly some officer whom one had known and not disliked – dies: one wonders; and forgets about him in a week.'[113] He found the friendships formed between soldiers to be extraordinarily close and felt he was learning 'the soldierly attitude of complete disconnection with our job during odd hours'.[114] And, slowly, things did start to happen. He became busier, with regular night patrols now and preparations for the approach of winter and the need to entrench against rains and frost. He described night time at the Front:

> Rustling of the grasses and grave tap-tapping of distant workers: the tension and silence of encounter, when one struggles in the dark for moral victory over the enemy patrol: the wail of the unexploded bomb and the animal cries of wounded men . . . One is hardened by now: purged of all false pity: perhaps more selfish than before. The spiritual and the animal get so much more sharply divided in hours of encounter, taking possession of the body by swift turns.[115]

In September, Sorley was promoted to captain, which meant he had to wait until October for leave. There were further signs of his growing maturation. To the Master of Marlborough, who

knew him as a rebellious student, he wrote: 'Perhaps afterwards, I and my likes will again become indiscriminate rebels.
For the present we find high relief in making ourselves soldiers . . . We no longer know what tomorrow may bring. As I
indicated, we no longer worry.'[116] At the same time he wrote to
another friend: 'To be able to prove oneself no coward to oneself, will be great, if it comes off: but suppose one finds oneself
fail[ing] in the test? I dread my own censorious self in the coming
conflict – I also have great physical dread of pain. Still, a good
edge is given to the sword here. And one learns to be a servant.
The soul is disciplined.'[117] And again to his father: 'We are now
embarked on a very different kind of life; whether one considers it preferable or otherwise to the previous depends on one's
mood. It is going to be a very slow business, but I hope a steady
one. There is absolutely no doubt that the Bosch is now on his
way home, though it is a long way and he will have many halts
by the wayside. That "the war may end any year now" is the
latest joke, which sums up the situation . . . O for a bath! Much
love to all.'[118]

Eight days later, on the night of 12–13 October, after the battalion moved south to take part in the Loos offensive, Charles
Sorley was shot in the head by a sniper's bullet while leading his
Company at the hair-pin trench near Hulluch to take over
trenches in preparation for the next day's attack. He died
instantly. He was twenty years old.

Professor Sorley, who gathered his son's letters for publication in 1919, offered a subtle assessment which did justice both
to Charles's dissident spirit and to his idealism:

The war moved him deeply, though it did not make him
either bitter or unjust. He never hesitated as to his own duty
in the matter, but he tried to understand the enemy's point
of view as well as our own. Some of his efforts in that direction may have been mistaken; but his views were always

honest and always his own. He looked on the world with clear eyes and the surface show did not deceive him. He saw that the spiritual values for which we fought could not be measured by material weapons or by material success. He saw too that the immediate effect of the war was to turn men's thoughts to material values and away from the things that are more excellent. And insight into these things underlies his occasional paradoxes.[119]

A posthumous collection of Sorley's work, *Marlborough and Other Poems*, was published in 1916 and went through six editions in that first year. Perhaps only half a dozen of these are directly 'war poems' but they show that his gift was considerable. One, 'To Germany', contains the lines: 'You are blind like us. Your hurt no man designed/ And no man claimed the conquest of your land.'[120] The poems are alert to the danger of false rhetoric and easy heroics. One of them, 'A Hundred Thousand Million Mites We Go', had an interesting genesis. When Sorley arrived at Paddington from his training camp at Churn in Berkshire on his way to join his regiment at Shorncliffe, he coincided with the special train that took the Marlborough boys back to school for the start of autumn term, and it provoked the poem. It expresses a sense of being caught up in something where the individual struggles to see the purpose and meaning like an insect caught in furious circles of pointless activity:

A hundred thousand million mites we sway
Writhing and tossing on the eternal plain,
Some black with death – but most are bright with Day!
Who sent us forth? Who brings us home again?

Sorley sent a draft of the poem to a friend, suggesting 'it should get a prize for being the first poem written since August

4th that isn't patriotic'.[121] Another poem on death suggests that, far from being a heroic moment, it is

> no triumph: no defeat:
> Only an empty pail, a slate rubbed clean,
> A merciful putting away of what has been.

Moreover: 'Victor and vanquished are a-one in death:/ Coward and brave: friend, foe.' Once again, Sorley is refusing to simplify the War into the rhetorical absolutes of opposing sides. His most famous poem, 'When You See Millions of the Mouthless Dead', is also about the finality of death, a refusal to give it meaning or sentimental justification. It was found in his kitbag after his death and seems to carry an implicit rebuke to poets like Brooke ('as other men have said') who varnished battlefield death. The poet warns against futile or rhetorical praise of the dead:

> Give them not praise. For, deaf, how should they know
> It is not curses heaped on each gashed head?
> Nor tears. Their blind eyes see not your tears flow.
> Nor honour. It is easy to be dead.

Rather than load the dead down with your synthetic emotion, he seems to say, admit that death now possesses your former comrades absolutely: 'Great death has made all his for evermore.' The poem, in its refusal of conventional panegyric, its insistence on facing the unadorned truth about mortality and about the War, points forward to the poems of 1916 and after, where a more explicitly anti-heroic mood increasingly emerged and became – and has remained in popular perception – the characteristic property of 'war poetry'.

3

The Somme and After: Siegfried Sassoon and the Poetry of Protest

In bitter safety I awake.[1]

The war, of course, did not end by Christmas 1914, nor, as the end of 1915 approached, with both armies settling into defensive positions, did a conclusion seem remotely in prospect. In December, two months after Wilfred Owen finally joined up in the Artists' Rifles, Sir Douglas Haig took over from Sir John French as the new Commander of the British Expeditionary Force, and on 2 February 1916 conscription was introduced. Five months later, the most notorious battle of the war, the Somme, commenced. The terrible casualties of this unprecedented engagement ensured that the relatively straightforward heroic style of the three poets of the last chapter, who were all dead by the autumn of 1915, would be, for serious poets, an increasingly untenable poetic model.

Siegfried Sassoon had joined up as soon as war broke out, enlisting in the Sussex Yeomanry, and in May 1915 he received a commission in the Royal Welch Fusiliers.[2] In November he finally arrived in France. Sassoon's memoirs – fluent, readable, and engaging – are, with Robert Graves's *Goodbye to All That* (1929), probably the most popular accounts by poets of service in the War. They are so well known that it is hardly necessary to précis them here, but one fact about them needs to be borne in mind. They were published a decade after the events they describe, the two poets surviving until 1967 (Sassoon) and 1985 (Graves). Sassoon's three volumes of memoir, *Memoirs of a Fox-hunting Man* (1928), *Memoirs of an Infantry Officer* (1930) and *Sherston's Progress* (1936), are lightly fictionalised, but when compared with the evidence of his letters and diaries they show that he did not embroider or fantasise.[3] George Sherston, his fictional alter ego, is a reliable witness.

This is clear from one of the more remarkable items in the Imperial War Museum's Sassoon collection of manuscripts (discussed in more detail later in this chapter).[4] Oddly under-utilised by recent scholars (possibly as a result of the exquisite refinement of torture involved in reading microfilm of pencilled scribblings in a notebook), this important document shows Sassoon's painstaking struggle to get the story right, his determination to reflect, without distortion, what actually happened. But, like Graves, he was looking backwards, a decade after the conflict, and he was not alone. It was as if many writers needed a decade to gather themselves after the War and reflect. The late 1920s and early 1930s saw a flood of such memoirs. Brooke, Sorley and Grenfell did not have the leisure for retrospection. Their poems – while we cannot be sure in every case exactly when and where they were written, and poems are often rewritten and revised at much later dates, frequently becoming different poems in the process, so that dating is always perilous – were contemporaneous and in some cases actually written in the field. They were more or less instant responses. Sassoon also wrote poems of this kind but his later prose versions of the War had the benefit of hindsight.

Thus, much of the literary 'anti-war' phenomenon was retrospective.

Literary critics have made much of this phenomenon. Influential works like Paul Fussell's *The Great War and Modern Memory* (1975), which was about 'some of the literary means by which [the conflict] has been remembered, conventionalized, and mythologized'[5] and about 'the literary dimensions of the trench experience itself', have focused on the ways in which literary models and preset responses modified not just how trench experience was described but even, in some cases, how it was lived. Military historians have sometimes been impatient with such approaches, seeing them as getting in the way of evidential inquiry into what actually happened, but they have proved suggestive and useful to analysts of war poetry and prose.

But not everyone, even at the time, was happy about the tenor of many of the late-1920s memoirs of the War. In *The Lie about the War* (1930), a short pamphlet published in T. S. Eliot's Criterion Miscellany series, Douglas Jerrold threw down a gauntlet to the memoirists. He marched into a London bookshop and asked for every current title of this kind, bearing off eleven volumes that purported to tell 'the truth about the War' – in order to demonstrate that they did no such thing. He inaugurated a lively critical tradition that persists today in books like Brian Bond's *The Unquiet Western Front* (2002).[6]

Jerrold analysed in the end sixteen books including *A Farewell to Arms*, *All Quiet on the Western Front*, *Death of a Hero*, *Goodbye to All That*, *Le Feu* (by the French writer Henri Barbusse, translated as *Under Fire*), *Rough Justice*, *The Enormous Room*, and *Storm of Steel* by Ernst Jünger. He quoted a recent opinion by the critic Desmond McCarthy: 'To the historian the year 1929–30 will chiefly be remembered as that in which men's emotions first began to turn against the idea of war . . . One of the symptoms of this change of attitude is the sudden and unexpected revival of interest in the actualities of war all over

Europe. Books which a year or so ago no publishers could hope to sell are now read eagerly by hundreds of thousands.'[7]

Confronting this explosion, Jerrold mocked the notion that the trend proved that people were 'unmoved by the deaths of nine million men in four years but waited till a novelist wrote a book about it before they sat up and took notice',[8] and claimed that the fashionable memoirists were presenting 'a picture of war which is fundamentally false even when it is superficially true, and which is statistically false even when it is incidentally true. If so, they are a danger to the cause of peace.' Moreover: 'There is no such thing as "the truth about war" . . . those who use this phrase about war are open to the charge that they believe that there is a truth about war which is different from the truth about peace. This is nonsense . . . To deny the dignity of tragic drama to the war in the interests of propaganda is not only unworthy but damnably silly and incredibly dangerous. My case is that this is what we are doing today, and that it is time to make an end of it.'

Surveying his pile of war memoirs, Jerrold found them, with the possible exception of Robert Graves's, to be 'lamentable' because they ignored the professional historians (like himself) and peddled 'a peculiar, unhistoric, and absurdly romantic vision of war which was popular, and that under the clever pretence of telling the truth about war, a farrago of highly sentimentalised and romantic story-telling was being foisted on to a new, simple and too eagerly humanitarian public'. Jerrold took particular exception to the anti-heroic flavour (which Sassoon, whom he doesn't mention, embodied so perfectly) of books which featured 'the callous, the brute, the fool and the coward' as equal partners with the hero. He claimed that, by contrast, books like Masefield's propagandist *Gallipoli* or Ian Hamilton's *Gallipoli Diary* or Charles Nevinson's *Gallipoli Campaign* were written 'not in printer's ink to flaunt an ill-considered personal emotion before a sensation-loving public for gain, propaganda or special pleading, but in letters of blood, impelled to break silence by the mere majesty of the events in which their lot was cast'.

Jerrold admitted that there had probably been 'too many' official and semi-official war histories. But the people reading the new genre of retrospective memoir ignored the actual existence in 1930 of '400,000 ex-service men on the verge of destitution' and were 'content to see holders of the Victoria cross starving in garrets'. He claimed that 'the people reading these books are mainly those who have chosen to forget or who are unable to remember'. His basic objection was that the war books ignored the fact that these were struggles of one army against another and that they concentrated too much on individual experience. They also harped consistently on the futility of war: 'The suffering, the horror and the desolation is presented always and brutally as without a meaning so far as the declared purposes of the struggle are conceived.' They refused to see the tragedy of war as inevitable, nor to allow its fatality. He urged that 'to accept the element of fatality would be to invest the war with a grandeur which these novelists are determined to deny it'. For Jerrold, 'the real tragedy of the war is being falsely reported as the death of so many men whose duty it was to live, whereas the real tragedy was that duty offered no alternative but death. And it was for this reason that death was accepted, not in fear, not in sullen indifference or in open or suppressed revolt, but deliberately and in the face of countless opportunities of evasion . . . A grotesque legend is being built up on a slender basis of hearsay.'

The fundamental problem was that they wrote of the War 'always and continuously from the standpoint of the individual, without pointing out, or even allowing the reader to guess, that the individual in modern national warfare is not a fighting unit'. By privileging personal experience they ignored the wider picture, to produce a 'damnably foolish cant about a futile war,

Rupert Brooke in characteristic 'Young Apollo' pose,
just before the outbreak of war

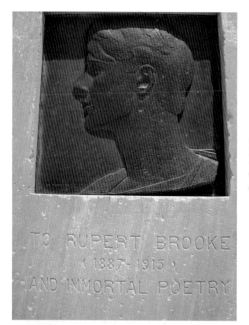

Detail from the memorial to Brooke 'and immortal poetry' on the Greek island of Skyros
(© Author)

Rupert Brooke's grave in an olive grove above Tris Boukes Bay on Skyros
(© Author)

The Rt Hon. Julian Grenfell, the aristocratic warrior-hero of the War's first phase
(© National Portrait Gallery)

Charles Hamilton Sorley, who died, aged twenty, in October 1915 at the Battle of Loos
(© National Portrait Gallery)

"Dottyville"

CRAIGLOCKHART WAR HOSPITAL,

SLATEFORD,

MIDLOTHIAN.

July. 26:

My dear Robbie.

There are 160 officers here, most of them half-dotty. No doubt I'll be able to get some splendid details for future use . .

Rivers – the chap who looks after me, is very nice – I am very glad to have the chance of talking to such a fine man.

Do you know anyone amusing in Edinburgh who I can go & see?

It was very jolly seeing Robert G. up here. We had great fun on his birthday – & ate enormously. R. has done some very good poems which he repeated to me. He was supposed to escort me up here; but missed the train & arrived 4 hours after I did!

Hope you aren't worried about my social position. Yrs ever. S.

Siegfried Sassoon's facetious letter from 'Dottyville' (Craiglockhart War Hospital), written shortly after his arrival there, to his friend Robbie Ross on 26 July 1917

(© Imperial War Museum)

Siegfried Sassoon, 1916, in the uniform of the Royal Welch Fusiliers
(© Getty Images)

Dr William Rivers, who treated Sassoon at Craiglockhart: 'Considering what he did for me I can hardly be blamed for seeing him in retrospect as a saint – a scientific saint'
(© Imperial War Museum)

Sassoon, the 'fox-hunting man', in more peaceful times
(© Imperial War Museum)

The Last Post

The bugler sent a call of high romance
"Lights out! Lights out!" to the deserted square.
On the thin brazen notes he threw a prayer
"God, if its this for me next time in France .....
Oh, spare ~~me~~ the phantom bugle as I lie
Dead in the gas & smoke & roar of guns,
Dead in a row with the other broken ones,
Lying so stiff & still under the sky,
Jolly young Fusiliers too good to die."

The music ceased & the red sunset flare
Was blood about his head as he stood there.

A dead Boche ~~in Mametz Wood~~.
~~Today I found in Mametz Wood~~
~~A certain cure for lust of blood~~
(2) Where, propped against a shattered trunk
In a great mess of things unclean
Sat a dead Boche: he scowled & stunk
With clothes & face a sodden green,
Big bellied, spectacled, crop-haired
Dribbling black blood from nose & beard.

(1) To you who'd read my songs of War
And only hear of blood & fame,
I'll ~~tell~~ ~~the Albany~~ (you've heard it said before)
~~"War's Hell!"~~ & if you don't the same,
Today I found in Mametz wood
A certain cure for lust of blood.

Early drafts of two poems by Robert Graves: 'The Last Post'
and ' A Dead Boche'

Robert Graves at work; the loyal friend who became an intermediary between Sassoon and the authorities at the time of Sassoon's protest against the War
(© Photoshot)

Robert Graves in later life. He revised many of his earlier poems and did not like to be thought of as a 'war poet'. He died in 1985
(© Corbis)

The infant Wilfred Owen in
military posture
(© Imperial War Museum)

Wilfred Owen, the tentative, aspiring
young Keatsian before the War
matured him and made him a poet
(© Imperial War Museum)

Wilfred Owen in 1916,
commissioned as second lieutenant
in the 5th Manchester Regiment,
just before his departure for France
(© National Portrait Gallery)

a war which broke up the structure of Europe, hurled three empires into the dust, brought into the very forefront of history three great new states, liberated the German people from a military despotism, established a new system of international relationships and, by a curious inversion, carried Western conceptions to Eastern nations'.

Jerrold denied that the War was either futile or avoidable or that the men who fought thought it to be so, either. He praised the stoicism and endurance of ordinary soldiers and observed with some justice that the modern literature of war 'is concerned only with the casualties to passengers. The majority, who never flinched, are forgotten.' He is hinting at a kind of posturing self-regard that showed little human sympathy now in peacetime for those who suffered. Such sympathy would be real, 'by which I mean a practical measure of revolt against the sufferings of other people *showing itself in a determination to make sacrifices in order to end or lessen such sufferings*; the post-war world has shown a callous and cynical indifference'. He was thinking of the Russian invasion of Poland: 'At no time in the history of Western European civilisation since the Thirty Years' War has there been a more complete and callous indifference to the devastation of vast tracts of country by irresponsible warfare.' He concluded that these books simply didn't understand what war was about, the tragic nature of human conflict, the fact that it could not be avoided:

The underlying *motif* of these books, the picture painted of the four years' conflict as an unbroken sequence of sanguinary, futile and purposeless horrors, debasing its participants, holds the seeds of a false doctrine which, once learnt, will be unlearnt only at a tragic cost. That doctrine is the inherent perfectibility of man. We are given by inference a picture of society as in a state of constant and automatic progress, senselessly checked in its course by the wicked incursion on to the political stage of soldiers and militarist politicians. Would to God that it were so . . . The object, conscious or unconscious, of all these books is to simplify and sentimentalise the problem of war and peace until the problem disappears in a silly gesture of complacent moral superiority, and the four years of war are shown idiotically as four years of disastrous, sanguinary and futile battles in which everything was lost and nothing gained, a struggle begun for no purpose and continued for no reason . . .

It is time we got back to the truth – unromantic, unchivalrous, unadventurous, unadorned by the marvellous, the epic or the obscene, simply WAR.[9]

It is a trenchant and important argument – which is why it has been dealt with at length here – and one that still gets made today, but it cannot compete with the received popular view of the Great War as an undifferentiated scene of pointless carnage.

Sassoon's *Memoirs of a Fox-hunting Man* concluded with the first descriptions of his war experience that would dominate his next volume. It was the spring of 1916, which came late that year in France, and he wrote: 'As for me, I had more or less made up my mind to die; the idea made things easier. In the circumstances there didn't seem to be anything else to be done.'[10] This rather languid, coolly patrician indifference to one's fate was very much Sassoon's personal literary trademark (though the private man was more prone to fears and anxieties). The next volume, *Memoirs of an Infantry Officer*, opens with the same scene, after Easter, at Morlancourt where Sassoon was just about to go to the Fourth Army School for a refresher course at Flixecourt, 'a clean little town exactly halfway between Amiens and Abbeville'. This was more like a holiday in the weeks leading up to the Somme, when 'the big Push' was constantly being talked about.

*

Siegfried Loraine Sassoon was born in 1886 at a country house called Weirleigh near Paddock Wood in Kent. He was the son of a prosperous financier, Alfred Sassoon, who left home when Siegfried was only seven. The Sassoons were descended from Sephardim in Spain, Portugal and North Africa, and by the eighteenth century the family had become successful traders in Baghdad. When the youthful Siegfried wrote a fan letter to the poet Charles Doughty, having read his epic *The Dawn of Britain* (1906), the senior poet replied that he had met some Sassoons in Poona. Siegfried was educated at Marlborough College during 1902–4 and at Clare College, Cambridge, but he left Cambridge without taking a degree in order to concentrate on the more agreeable pursuit of country sports, especially fox-hunting, on a private income.

The attractive ease and simplicity of his autobiographical writing belies, as has been said, a more complex man – a 'multiple personality'[11] – who sought solitude and tried most of his life to come to terms with his homosexuality. In 1911 he wrote to Edward Carpenter after reading *The Intermediate Sex*, a book which had been a revelation to him, in opening 'a new life to me, after a time of great perplexity and unhappiness . . . What ideas I had about homosexuality were absolutely unprejudiced and I was in such a groove that I couldn't allow myself to be what I wished to be, and the intense attraction felt for my own sex was almost a subconscious thing, and my antipathy for women a mystery to me. It was only by chance that (when I read your book) I found my brother (a year younger) was exactly the same.'[12] Sassoon once thought of writing a Proustian gay memoir, describing it in a letter to a friend: 'It is to be one of the stepping-stones across the raging (or lethargic) river of intolerance which divides creatures of my temperament from a free and unsecretive existence among their fellow men. A mere self-revelation, however spontaneous and clearly-expressed, can never achieve as much as – well, imagine another *Madame*

Bovary dealing with sexual inversion, a book that the world must recognize and learn to understand.'[13] In the imaginary library of adumbrated but unwritten literary texts Sassoon's queer memoir would have a privileged place. It was the law that prevented this, and he died in 1967, aged eighty-one, the very year that homosexual acts between consenting males over twenty-one were made legal.

Although Sassoon dabbled in verse during the fox-hunting years it was the War that made him a noticeable poet,[14] and after it he wrote little that was of poetic interest – though he would emerge as a prose writer of distinction. In late November 1915 he first made the acquaintance in France of Robert Graves, who features in his memoirs as 'David Cromlech'. They took tea in Béthune and Sassoon discovered that Graves, a young captain in 3rd Battalion, was 'very much disliked. An interesting creature, overstrung and self-conscious, a defier of convention.'[15] A few days later, Graves gave Sassoon his manuscript poems to read and an important friendship was sealed. None of the three poets in the preceding chapter knew each other, and none in subsequent chapters either, but Sassoon, Graves, and Wilfred Owen would all interact with each other in important ways. Initially, Sassoon had reservations about the poems of his new friend: 'some very bad, violent and repulsive. A few full of promise and real beauty. He oughtn't to publish yet.'[16] More vital, however, than poetry criticism was the first encounter with the realities of the Western Front at the end of 1915. On 3 December:

> We met an Infantry Brigade, Kitchener's army – Seventh Sussex, Eighteenth Middlesex and Eighth Royal Fusiliers. Men marching by, four after four, hideous, brutal faces, sullen, wretched. Some wore their steel basin-helmets, giving them a Chinese look. Strange to see, among those hundreds of faces I scanned, suddenly a vivid red-haired youth with green eyes

looking far away, sidelong – one clean face, among all the others brutalised. But their hearts are gold, I doubt not. The heavy transport-horses plodding through the sludge, straining at their weary loads; the stolid drivers munching, smoking, grinning, yelling coarse gibes; worried-looking officers on horses; young-looking subalterns in new rain-proofs. And the infantrymen, the foot-sloggers, loaded with packs, sweating under their water-proof capes, the men that do the dirty work and keep us safe . . . Everything out here goes past me like a waking dream. My inner life is far more real than the hideous realism of this land of the war-zone. I never thought to find such peace. If it were not for Mother and friends I would pray for a speedy death. I want a genuine taste of the horrors, and then – peace. I don't want to go back to the old inane life which always seemed like a prison. I want freedom, not comfort. I have seen beauty in life, in men and things; but I can never be a great poet, or a great lover. The last fifteen months have unsealed my eyes. I have lived well and truly since the war began, and have made my sacrifices; now I ask that the price be required of me. I must pay my debt. Hamo [Sassoon's brother, who died on 1 November from a wound sustained at Gallipoli] went: I must follow him. I will.[17]

These confused first thoughts show Sassoon's characteristic sharpness of observation, his sense of sympathy with, but social distance from, the ordinary soldiers, and the personal conflicts that he (like so many other sensitive young men on the Western Front at that time) was working out. Listening to the great guns booming thirty miles away, and Armageddon under way, he could still reflect: 'I have found peace here, anyhow, and the old inane life of 1913–14 seems lopped right off – never to return, thank heaven.'[18]

He told himself he was happy because he had escaped his former effete and purposeless existence and found peace unbelievable in this extraordinary existence which I thought I should loathe. The actual life is mechanical; and my dreams are mine, more lonely than ever. We're safe for another year of war, too, so next summer ought to do something for me. Anything but a 'cushy' wound! That would be an awful disaster. I must endure, or else die. And it's nice to look back on my childhood which lasted so long (until I was twenty-three, anyhow). What a confused idea I had of everything, except beauty; was that time *all* wasted? Lovely now seem the summer dawns in Weirleigh garden . . .'[19]

At the start of the second week of January 1916, Sassoon was once again making his senses alive to the landscape and exulting in his love of nature. His war memoirs are punctuated by passages in which he describes walking away on his own from camp or trench to commune with nature, observe the birds, the features of the landscape, sunsets and weather patterns. 'O this joy of today!' he exclaimed on 9 January in the valley of the Somme: 'My voice shall ring through the great wood, because I am glad for a while with beautiful earth, and we who live here are doomed to fall as best befits a man, a sacrifice to the spring; and this is true and we all know it – that many of us must die before Easter.'[20] But, again like many others, he experienced an odd conjunction of impending doom and exultation: 'How strange it is that I came to the war prepared to suffer torments and to see horrible sights; and I have found hours in heaven, and noble counties at my feet, and love inhabiting the hearts of men. Somewhere Hell awaits me, but it will be a brave place, where no devils are ramping.'[21]

Towards the end of January Sassoon was ordered to fill in for a transport officer who was on leave, and thus enjoyed a safe job when he had been seeking danger and hardship. It is worth pointing out that, in spite of his decorated bravery and his reputation as a courageous soldier and efficient killer, Sassoon

spent less than a month at the Front and was in a reserve battalion when the Somme offensive was launched. Nonetheless
he felt the strangeness of leave from the War when he went
back to England for ten days at the end of February, looking at
'the faces of my friends, smiling welcome, firelit rooms with
books and noble paintings on the walls, the beauty of London
streets by night with their mazes of red and orange lamps, passing and meeting, or burning steadily away into the vistas of
streets like dark waterways between the mystery of lofty buildings. Woods and fields in Sussex, in clear sunlight of early
March . . .'[22]

Not long after his return the brutal reality of war hit him
when his lover, 'Tommy' (Lieutenant David Thomas who is
the subject of 'A Subaltern', 'Last Meeting' and 'A Letter
Home'), was killed:

> they came afterwards and told that my little Tommy had
> been hit by a stray bullet and died last night. When last I saw
> him, two nights ago, he had his notebook in his hand, read-
> ing my last poem. And I said good night to him, in the
> moonlit trenches. Had I but known! – the old, human-weak
> cry. Now he comes back to me in memories, like an angel,
> with the light in his yellow hair, and I think of him at
> Cambridge last August when we lived together four weeks in
> Pembroke College in rooms where the previous occupant's
> name, Paradise, was written above the door.[23]

Sassoon went off after lunch into the woods to mourn:

> And I lay there under the smooth bole of a beech-tree, won-
> dering, and longing for the bodily presence that was so
> fair . . . Grief can be beautiful, when we find something
> worthy to be mourned. To-day I knew what it means to find
> the soul washed pure with tears, and the load of death was

lifted from my heart. So I wrote his name in chalk on the beech-tree stem, and left a rough garland of ivy there, and a yellow primrose for his yellow hair and kind grey eyes, my dear, my dear.

Robert Graves stood beside him at the burial: 'So Tommy left us, a gentle soldier, perfect and without stain.'[24]

Sassoon's mood was now defiant and careless:

To-night I'm going to try and spot one of their working-parties and chuck some bombs at them. Better to get a sling at them in the open – even if on one's belly – than to sit here and have a great thing drop on one's head. I found it most exhilarating – just like starting for a race. Great thing is to get as many sensations as possible. No good being out here unless one takes the full amount of risks, and I want to get a good name in the Battalion, for the sake of poetry and poets, whom I represent . . . No man's land fascinates me, with its jumble of wire-tangles and snaky seams in the earth winding along the landscape . . . I know I ought to be careful of myself, but something drives me on to look for trouble . . . I used to say I couldn't kill anyone in this war; but since they shot Tommy I would gladly stick a bayonet into a German by daylight. Someone told me a year ago that love, sorrow, and hate were things I had never known (things which every poet *should* know!). Now I've known love for Bobbie [Robert Hanmer at Salonika] and Tommy, and grief for Hamo and Tommy, and hate has come also, and the lust to kill. Rupert Brooke was miraculously right when he said 'Safe shall be my going,/ Secretly armed against all death's endeavour;/ Safe though all safety's lost.' He described the true soldier-spirit – saint and hero like Norman Donaldson and thousands of others who have been killed and died happier than they lived.[25]

In his *Memoirs of a Fox-hunting Man*, Sassoon described this eerie spring of 1916 in the Somme valley, when everyone listened out for rumours of the big push that they knew was coming, as a time of heightened sensation: 'Never before had I been so intensely aware of what it meant to be young and healthy in fine weather at the outset of summer.'[26] Yet the feeling of nature's beauty and seasonal regeneration wound itself in and out of thoughts of death: 'The sense of spring in England is very strong in me lately, and I dream of nice things and get rather weary of being out here. They say I am trying to get myself killed. Am I? I don't know . . . The existence one leads here is so much a thing of naked outlines and bare expanses, so empty of colour and fragrance, that one loves these things more than ever, and more than ever one hungers for them – the music and graciousness of life.'[27] And he remained haunted and saddened by the death of Tommy.

After eighteen days in the trenches, Sassoon was off to Army School at Flixecourt, where the music of ordinary life drowned out these thoughts of self-destruction. There was no more talk of being 'happier dead'. Instead he mocked the brawny Scots major who lectured him on bayonet warfare ('get your bayonet into his kidneys; it'll go in as easy as butter') and retreated when he could, as ever, to the solitude of nature: 'I told the trees what I had been hearing; but they hate steel, because axes and bayonets are the same to them . . . And a blackbird's song cries aloud that April cannot understand what war means.'[28]

In May at Fricourt on the Somme, Sassoon took part in a not particularly well judged raid, fully described in his memoirs. Of the twenty-eight men in his party eleven were wounded and one killed: 'This morning I woke up *feeling as if I'd been to a dance* – awful mouth and head . . . There was not terror there – only men with nerves taut and courage braced – then confusion and anger and – failure. I think there was more delight than dread in the prospect of the dangers, certainly I saw no sign of either.'[29] But his bravery in this raid earned him the Military Cross, an honour he was openly proud of, though the decoration, as we will see, would later suffer an ignominious fate. It was good for his reputation but he also had to confess: 'I can't read or enjoy poetry at all since I came back here.'[30]

Sitting in a dark dugout, a day before the Battle of the Somme, Sassoon reflected that he wanted to see the summer out, and get the experience of the big battle:

And, as for dying, I know it's nothing, and there's not much for me to lose except a few years of ease and futility. What I'm doing and enduring now is the last thing anyone could ask for; I'm being pushed along the rocky path, and the world seems all the sweeter for it . . . Death seems the only fact to be faced; the rest all twaddle and purposeless energy . . . I suppose I'm feeling what Robert Graves felt when he wrote 'Is this Limbo?'. Shut in; no chance of escape. No music; the quest for beauty doomed. But I *must* go on finding beauty *here* and now; not the sort of beauty I used to look for.[31]

After another short period of leave he was back in mid-June, and while sitting in a dugout reading Hardy's *Tess of the d'Urbervilles* the news came through about his MC. The next morning, after breakfast at 6 a.m., 1 July 1916, the Somme offensive began:

The morning is brilliantly fine, after a mist early. Since 6.30 there has been hell let loose. The air vibrates with the incessant din – the whole earth shakes and rocks and *throbs* – it is one continuous roar . . . Inferno – inferno – bang – smash! . . . A haze of smoke drifting across the landscape – brilliant sunshine . . . The sun flashes on bayonets, and the tiny figures advance steadily and disappear behind the mounds of trench-debris . . . The birds seem bewildered; I saw a lark start to go up, and then flutter along as if he thought better of it. Others were fluttering above the trench with querulous cries, weak on the wing. Just eaten my last orange. I am looking at a sunlit picture of Hell. And still the breeze shakes the yellow charlock, and the poppies glow below the Crawley ridge where a few Hun shells have fallen lately ... Weather hot and cloudless. A lark singing overhead ... I could see one man moving his left arm up and down as he lay on his side: his head was a crimson patch. The others lay still.[32]

Although he was able to report a lot of prisoners taken, Sassoon and others had no sense yet that it had been a wholesale slaughter. The attack had been seemingly well planned and in the preceding week a million and a half artillery shells had been fired at the enemy. 'The wire has never been so well cut nor artillery preparations so thorough,'[33] wrote General Haig, the night before, but he was over-optimistic. As the 120,000 men went over the top it turned out that the artillery bombardment had been much less effective than planned (many of the shells were duds), and so the hoped-for coordination of infantry and artillery collapsed in confusion and 21,000 men were dead or missing by the end of the day. Four months of attrition warfare later, the Allies had lost a total of 600,000 men and the Somme became a national byword for military disaster.

The next day Sassoon was lying in the sun in the long grass in front of his trench, still unaware of the extent of the slaughter. On the following day, 3 July, he wrote his poem 'At Carnoy', where 'I hear a sound of mouth-organs, ill-played,/ And murmur of voices, gruff, confused, and low'. Then: 'Tomorrow we must go/ To take some cursed Wood ... O world God made!'[34] In fact Mametz Wood was not taken, and on 4 July Sassoon saw some of the casualties: 'These dead are terrible and undignified carcases, stiff and contorted. There were thirty of our own laid in two ranks by the Mametz-Carnoy road, some side by side on their backs with bloody clotted fingers mingled as if they were hand-shaking in the companionship of death. And the stench undefinable. And rags and shreds of blood-stained cloth, bloody boots riddled and torn.'[35] But he somehow managed to conclude that it had been 'Great fun these last two days'.[36]

Sassoon, or 'Mad Jack' as he was known in his battalion, was recommended for a further decoration but it was disallowed seemingly because the whole attack had been a failure. Stuck in camp, reading Thomas Hardy, he tried to stop his mind from vegetating and wished he could see Graves, who was somewhere in the vicinity: 'This life begets a condition of mental stagnation unless one keeps trying to get outside it all. I try to see everything with different eyes to my companions, but their unreasoning mechanical outlook is difficult to avoid. Often their words go past me like dead leaves on the wind . . . Sometimes when I see my companions lying asleep or resting, rolled in their blankets, their faces turned to earth or hidden by the folds, for a moment I wonder whether they are alive or dead.'[37] Eventually he did make contact with Graves – 'whimsical and queer and human as ever'[38] – and the long talk and reflection put him in thoughtful mood after dinner in the tent:

I'm thinking of England, and summer evenings after cricket-matches, and sunset above the tall trees, and village-streets in the dusk, and the clatter of a brake driving home . . . So things went three years ago; and it's all dead and done with. I'll never be there again. If I'm lucky and get through alive, there's another sort of life waiting for me. Travels and adventures, and poetry; and anything but the old groove of cricket and hunting, and dreaming in Weirleigh garden. When war ends I'll be at the crossroads; and I know the path to choose.

I must go out into the night alone. No fat settling down; the Hanmer engagement idea was a ghastly blunder – it wouldn't work at all. That charming girl who writes to me so often would never be happy with me. It was my love for Bobbie [Hanmer, whose sister Dorothy Sassoon nearly got engaged to] that led me to that mistake.[39]

He had found that Robert Graves wanted to travel with him after the War: 'And whenever I am with him, I want to do wild things, and get right away from the conventional silliness of my old life . . . Blighty! What a world of idle nothingness the name stands for; and what a world of familiar delightfulness! O God, when shall I get out of this limbo? . . . I've still got my terrible way to tread before I'm free to sleep with Rupert Brooke and Sorley and all the nameless poets of the war . . . If I'm alive in July 1926 I'll be a decent poet at last.'[40]

On 21 July, however, Sassoon learned that Graves had been killed (a report that was later to prove false). It revived memories of Tommy, and his mood was, naturally, sombre. He soon went down with trench fever and by August was on a hospital ship, the *Aberdonian*, to London, feeling rotten at forsaking the battalion. He was taken from Southampton to Somerville College, Oxford, which was being used as a war hospital, to lie in a cream-white room listening to the bells of the university city at evening. On his way to Oxford he attempted a portrait of himself:

Lying in a hospital train on his way to London he looks out at the hot August landscape of Hampshire, the flat green and dun-coloured fields – the advertisements of Lung Tonic and Liver Pills – the cows – neat villas and sluggish waterways – all these came on him in an irresistible delight, at the pale-gold of the wheat-fields and the faded green of the hazy muffled woods on the low hills. People wave to the Red

Cross train – grateful stay-at-homes . . . he thinks 'All this I've been fighting for; and now I'm safe home again I begin to think it was worth while.'[41]

For the next three months Sassoon would convalesce at Weirleigh, do some hunting and riding, meet some old literary friends in London like Robert Ross and encounter for the first time at Garsington Lady Ottoline Morrell, who noted his 'lean face with green hazel eyes . . . He was not exactly *farouche* but he seemed shy and reserved, he was more *sauvage*; and, as I looked at his full face I said to myself, "He could be cruel."'[42] He would also try to 'work off some of the poetry bottled up in me . . . At the Front I had managed to keep my mind alive under difficulties, and had done some writing when we were away from the line. But it wasn't easy to be a poet and a platoon commander at the same time, and I was overflowing with stored-up impressions and emotional reactions to the extraordinary things I had observed and undergone.'[43] The poem 'Stretcher Case' was one of the first fruits of this period.

Sassoon was not really very ill and he was able to come and go as he liked. He paid a visit to his Uncle Hamo at Burford in the Cotswolds where, crossing the stone bridge over the Windrush, 'It was the first time I had fully realized what it meant to be well away from the war.'[44] He felt the contrast of Cotswold antique shops and old-fashioned tranquillity with what was happening in the trenches: 'I felt that no explanation of mine could ever reach my elders – that they weren't capable of wanting to know the truth . . . I resented their patriotic suppression of those aspects of war which never got into the newspapers . . . I began to feel that, although I didn't want to upset Uncle Hamo, I should like to give some of the comfortable civilians a few shocks, even if they were to accuse me of being wrong-headed and ungentlemanly. Needless to say, a good many of them did.'[45] Slowly, Sassoon was preparing himself for his very public condemnation of the War, beginning with one of the more powerful themes in his eventual indictment – that the older generation, the non-combatants, the comfortable gentlemen in the August Cotswold sunshine, did not properly appreciate the searing reality of what they were so easily condemning others to undergo.

Sassoon was back at Weirleigh at the end of August and now had some provisional sick leave that was due to start in October. This rural inaction left him bored and depressed, made worse by the fact that his mother was still affected by his brother's death at Gallipoli a year previously. Writing was the best relief and, settling to it, he started to reflect on how the War had slowly changed his attitude: 'The war had taught me one useful lesson – that on the whole it was very nice to be alive at all; and I had also acquired the habit of observing things with more receptiveness and accuracy than I had ever attempted to do in my undisciplined past.'[46] He worked in the smoking-room at Weirleigh, which brought back early 1915 when he had convalesced there after breaking an arm in training and had experienced 'a continuous poetic afflatus' that seemed at the time 'my last chance of being visited by the Muse'.

This rediscovery of writing seemed to Sassoon 'almost like a recovery of the vernal raptures of my juvenilia'.[47] He reflected how, in the early days of training, he hardly wrote anything except a Brooke-influenced poem, 'Absolution', which 'expressed the typical self-glorifying feelings of a young man about to go to the Front for the first time. The poem subsequently found favour with middle-aged reviewers, but the more I saw of war the less noble-minded I felt about it.' This process of becoming less 'noble-minded', or renouncing the heroic attitude, had begun, he considered, in the first months of 1916, 'with a few genuine trench poems, dictated by my resolve to record my surroundings' based on notes and 'aimed at impersonal description of front-line conditions, and could at least claim to be the first things of their kind'. The only satire as such was 'Good Friday Morning', which he considered 'one of the most effective of my war productions'.[48] Continuing this conspectus of his poetic career, Sassoon recalled how at the end of April 1916, when he was at the Fourth Army School at Flixecourt, he had indulged freely in what he called 'idyllic and melodious utterance . . . Alone with my *Concise Oxford Dictionary* when the long day's work was done, I became as much a poet as I have ever been in my life, though how I had the vitality to do it is now one of the mysteries associated with the superabundant energy of youth.'

For the subsequent three months, a period which included the Battle of the Somme, Sassoon 'lived very little with my private self'. His deep involvement in real fighting 'changed my emotional outlook on the war, but it had, of course, been impossible to do any independent thinking about it'. Now, in September 1916, he felt that this earlier poetry was 'tame and conventional compared with the material of recent experience which I was carrying about in my head, and the lively notions whereby I intended to convert some of that experience into a vehicle for candid and ironic comment'.[49] His witty friend Robbie Ross said of his early poems: 'They rather remind me of the delicious teas of thirty years ago.'[50]

Poems like 'The One-legged Man' and 'The Hero' gave Sassoon 'a strong sense of satisfaction that I was providing a thoroughly caddish antidote to the glorification of "the supreme sacrifice" and such like prevalent phrases. These performances [were] deliberately devised to disturb complacency.' In 'Died of Wounds' 'I had hit on a laconic anecdotal method of writing which astonished me by the way it indirectly expressed my passionate feeling about the agonizing episode described.' Pleased with this new sense of direction and purpose in his writing, he started to transcribe the drafts into an exquisite manuscript book given him by Lady Ottoline Morrell. He spent a week with her in September, when he was amused by 'Lady O's elevated notion of me as a romantic young poet'.[51] He loved the splendour and comfort of her Oxfordshire manor, which was also a salon and a refuge for, amongst others at this time, Aldous Huxley, who had been rejected for war service as a result of his poor eyesight, and who was working on the estate. He and Sassoon, however, seem not to have hit it off.[52]

It was at Garsington that Sassoon encountered for the first time arguments that the War was wrong and could be stopped. He had heard plenty of grumbling in the trenches, particularly in 1916 when it seemed as though the War was destined to drag on indefinitely, but here were people who actually thought there was a viable way of stopping it: 'It was the beginning of a process of disillusionment which afterwards developed into a fomentation of confused and inflamed ideas.'[53] But Sassoon still had a problem with the fully fledged conscientious objectors who sat holding forth in deckchairs on Ottoline's lawn in the summer of 1916 and who, in his view, 'seemed to be living in a mental world of their own'. He was very aware of the contrast between the idealist world of talk and intellectualising at Garsington and the real world of the trenches that he would soon be going back to. He resolved the tension by going hunting with the Fitzwilliam Hounds, relishing its 'unthinkingness' as an activity: 'Mounted on the hunt horses, I contrived to escape from the war atmosphere and to return to those sporting simplicities which I had provisionally rejected as a dead-end in the summer of 1914.'[54] He realised that the War had brought him 'a deepened consciousness of peace-time values and enjoyments and a new determination to get the best out of life wherever I happened to be.'[55] The master of the hunt, Wentworth Fitzwilliam, was a feudal character, and Sassoon's mother's simple, black-and-white patriotism further added to his sense that he was out of joint.

Good news came in September, with Heinemann offering to publish a collection of poems. Sassoon immediately went off to town to see the publisher, vaguely apprehensive that his literary mentor, Edmund Gosse, would like neither the note of realism nor the anti-heroic tone, but Robbie Ross was keen on his developing the satiric vein. Although Sassoon claimed that 'most of it was idyllic and graceful, and the war pieces were mainly descriptive', Gosse was indeed unhappy, describing some of the poems as 'savage, disconcerting silhouettes drawn roughly against a lurid background'.[56] The fact was that in 1916 'very few candid comments on the war had appeared in print, and . . . many people were genuinely shocked and startled by what I wrote'.

One of those appears to have been Sassoon himself, who surprised himself in the possession of 'a hitherto unpredictable talent for satiric epigram' and claimed that his famous 'Sassoonish' satires, as people came to call them, just happened: 'I merely chanced on the device of composing two or three harsh, peremptory, and colloquial stanzas with a knock-out blow in the last line.'[57] Robbie Ross, who hated war and militarism, was delighted and urged him on. One poem in particular, 'They', was written at Ross's rooms at 40 Half Moon Street, off Piccadilly, a sort of high-camp refuge for Sassoon in London, where, according to Ross's biographer, 'Robbie now discovered a new vocation, part literary midwife, part agony uncle to Sassoon and several other men in uniform.'[58] There was, however, 'no reason to think that any physical contact ever took place between the two'.

By the beginning of December, this civilised interlude over, Sassoon was back at 'The Huts, Litherland', the dull part of north Liverpool that is 'Clitherland' in his memoirs and the site of the barracks of the Royal Welch Fusiliers. It was thirteen months since he had first gone out to France in November 1915, 'resolved', as he put it, 'to put up as decent a performance as I could'.[59] In 'that year of adventure and mental expansion' he had 'made unexpected progress as a poet', helped by the fact that his military duties had been 'unexacting and perfunctory'. But he remained in 'a state of spiritual discomfort' as a poet in the trenches: 'Being in the army had always worked out as a sort of dual existence for me – a constant effort to combine efficiency in my duties with a detached and active brain . . . More than ever I wanted to be alone and write poetry – to read good literature and listen to good music . . . It was exasperating to be prevented from using my mind properly just when I was having a bit of success, for my war poems were getting themselves talked about.'[60]

At the end of December along came another month of home leave. Waiting to be sent back to the War was, he felt, in a way more uncomfortable than being actually out there and he was starting to lose his belief in the War itself. He felt he had expected too much of the Battle of the Somme, which had not in the end been the military 'Great Advance' promised. But it was at the Front that he would now need to find material for his war poems: 'My strength of mind thus consisted mainly in a ferocious and defiant resolve to tell the truth about the War in every possible way . . . My mental behaviour had become a typical case for the student of war psychology.'[61] Litherland, apart from its opportunities for golf at Formby and expensive luxury meals at the Adelphi Hotel in Liverpool, was a rather grim place. Indeed, 'The only merit of this hut-life is that there are no women about.'[62]

As the year drew to a close Sassoon was in reflective mood:

1916 has been a lucky year for me. This is a dreary drab flat place – fog and bleary sunsets and smoky munition-works at night . . . sirens hooting out on the Mersey mouth . . . The year is dying of atrophy as far as I am concerned . . . And the War is settling down on everyone – a hopeless, never-shifting burden. While newspapers and politicians yell and brandish their arms, and the dead rot in their French graves, and the maimed hobble about the streets.[63]

This was the turning point for Sassoon. What had begun as lively satire against the complacent people at home, combined with youthful impatience with his elders, was starting to turn into something more considered and deliberate. On Christmas Eve, 1916, he asked himself 'whether I shall be any better off through going to the War again next year. Of course I've *got* to go – I never doubted that; but if I'm there *another* eight months, and come back *safely wounded* (!) shall I have anything more to say about it all, or shall I be more bitter, and unbalanced and callous? . . . It will be good fun in its way.'[64] He was reading Charles Hamilton Sorley's posthumously published letters and Sorley's perspective would have touched him deeply. But he retained his sense of humour. A fellow officer, wounded in action in the Dardanelles, asked him in the huts one night why there were no women in his verse. 'I told him they are outside my philosophy.'[65] On Christmas Day he played a round of golf on his own at Formby and noted how the sideboard at the golf club groaned with food in spite of talk of wartime shortages to come in 1917.

Sassoon had now been away from action for four months and he felt that his sense of discipline was being eroded: 'My absurd decoration is the only thing that gives me any sense of responsibility at all. And the thought of death is horrible, where last year it was a noble and inevitable dream.'[66] Determined as he was to go back to the Front, he was occasionally seized by spasms of bitterness. On 10 January 1917 he wrote: 'Why should a little silver rosette on an M.C. ribbon make one want to go back to hell? . . . It is blood and brains that tell; blood in the mud, and brains smashed up by bullets. Where's all the poetry gone then?'[67] He was riding with the Cheshire Hunt at

the start of the new year and felt as though, in this rural aristocratic society, the War might never have happened:

> Pleasant enough; but what a decayed society, hanging
> blindly on to the shreds of its traditions . . . But comfort and
> respectable squiredom and the futile chatter of women,
> and their man-hunting glances, and the pomposity of
> port-wine-drinking buffers – what's all that but emptiness?
> These people don't reason. They echo one another and their
> dead relations, and what they read in papers and dull
> books. And they only *see* what they want to see – which is
> very little beyond the tips of their red noses. Debrett is on
> every table; and heaven a sexless peerage.[68]

Sassoon thought little more highly of his military superiors:
'I think nearly half the officers in our Army are conscripted
humbugs who are paid to propagate inefficiency. They aren't
even willing to be killed; I can at least say *that* for myself, for
I've tried often.' But he considered himself lucky to have
been freed to write some 'decent poems' and sort out a book
for publication and actually wanted to stay alive in order to
write: 'Now I've really got a grip of the idea of life and
describing it, I hope I shan't get myself killed in 1917. There's
such a lot to say. Love and beauty and death and bitterness
and anger.'[69] He watched the first draft of soldiers leaving
Litherland for France, sent off by the padre and the commanding officer in 'a pathetic scene of humbug and cant'.[70]
Robert Graves left next, the two poets having managed to
enjoy six weeks together, something to be grateful for in such
uncertain times. Sassoon's intimate friend Bobbie Hanmer
remained with him in the hut. He was not much of a conver-
sationalist, 'But he is a dear, though not *quite* so adorable as he
was in October 1915, when his radiance first broke in on me.
And I fell in love with his kind eyes and ingenuous looks. But

he would be a good person to die for, and suffer with, and I hope I'll get the chance.'[71]

In an echo of the spring of 1916 when the Somme loomed, now the 'spring offensive' began to be talked about and Sassoon went home in February for his last leave before departing for France. He lunched with Eddie Marsh and Robbie Ross at the Reform Club and took tea in Gower Street with Lady Ottoline who 'caused me to talk recklessly, with a sort of victimized bitterness'.[72] On 15 February 1917 he packed his kitbag with reading matter – Shakespeare's tragedies, Hardy's *Dynasts* and a selection of the poems, Conrad's *Nostromo* and *A Set of Six*, Lamb's *Essays*, and *The Canterbury Tales*. He left Waterloo Station 'feeling nervous and rattled'.[73]

Sassoon reached the infantry base at Rouen on 16 February but was taken to hospital two days later with German measles. At No. 25 Stationary Hospital, Rouen, 'a squalid little "compound"', he tried to sort out his turbulent feelings: 'My brain is so pitifully confused by the war and my own single part in it. All those people I have left in England have talked me nearly to death. The people I have seen out here so far have made me feel that there is no hope for the race of men. All that is wise and tender in them is hidden by the obsession of the war. They strut and shout and guzzle and try to forget their distress in dreary gabble about England (and the War!). It is all dull and hopeless and ugly and small.'[74] The bitterness here may have been exacerbated by his illness:

> Yet I should loathe the very idea of returning to England without having been scarred and tortured once more. I suppose all this 'emotional experience' (futile phrase) is of value. But it leads nowhere now (but to madness). There is little tenderness left in me: only bitter resentment . . . For the soldier is no longer a noble figure; he is merely a writhing insect among this ghastly folly of destruction . . . He does not cry for

wisdom . . . I *want* to find someone who has *some* faith in the war and its purposes. But they see nothing but their own tiny destinies.[75]

He was goaded by the 'stupid cynicism' of religion and hymns, but conceded: 'Such things come from a distempered brain: an infantry officer only sees the stupidest side of the War.' Nonetheless, Sassoon was now confiding to his diary something far stronger than ever before: not mockery or cynicism but a deep, passionate hatred of the War. Only nature could soothe him – as it always did. He walked out to contemplate some trees in the rain: 'And I am very lucky to be able to find happiness so quickly . . . And the war is of no importance as long as there are some trees left standing upright, with a clean wind to shake their branches.'[76]

On 11 March 1917 he joined the 2nd Battalion of the Royal Welch Fusiliers on the Somme Front, but by 25 March was noting that, after five weeks in France and two with the Fusiliers, he had not yet been within five miles of a German gun. On 7 April, at the village of Saulty, just off the Doullens–Arras Road, he reflected: 'I don't suppose anyone would believe me if I said I was absolutely happy and contented . . . But the fact remains that if I had a choice between England to-morrow and the battle, I would choose the battle without hesitation . . . my feeling of quiet elation and absolute confidence now is something even stronger than last summer's passionate longing for death and glory.'[77]

Nine days later Sassoon received a sniper's bullet through his shoulder. He was told he should go back to England but he wanted to stay because he felt 'warlike'.[78] On 20 April, however, he was sent back to the Fourth London Hospital at Denmark Hill in London. He was strained and tense and had nightmares about the battlefield dead. But still he saw no alternative to fighting on: 'Things must take their course; and I know I shall be sent out again to go through it all over again with added refinements of torture. I am no good anywhere else: all I can do is go there and set an example. Thank heaven I've got something to live up to. But surely they'll manage to kill me next time! Something in me keeps driving me on: I must go on till I am killed. Is it cussedness (because so many people want me to survive the war) – or is it the old spirit of martyrdom?'[79]

On 1 May Sassoon was out of hospital and lunching again at the Reform Club with Robbie Ross and others where he also met H. G. Wells and Arnold Bennett and J. C. Squire, pillars of the pre-war London literary establishment. He went to convalesce at Chapelwood Manor in Sussex, home of Lord and Lady Brassey, and felt that he had for a moment shaken off the Furies that were pursuing him. On 8 May *The Old Huntsman*, his first volume of poems, was published. He was a poet again, not a warrior. Virginia Woolf in the *Times Literary Supplement* wrote: 'What Mr Sassoon has felt to be the most sordid and horrible experiences in the world he makes us feel to be so in a measure which no other poet of the war has achieved.'[80] Lady Brassey was less impressed by his 'dangling about and writing poetry' and urged him to get a proper military posting in England: 'She is undoubtedly right, but I still think I'd better go back to the 1st Battalion as soon as possible, unless I can make some protest against the War.'[81]

At around this time Sassoon was having his portrait painted by Glyn Philpot, and during the fortnight of the sittings at the painter's Tite Street studio in Chelsea he began to formulate a course of action 'which not only asked for trouble but insisted on creating it for myself'.[82] There is something in that formulation that catches the flavour of deliberate attention-seeking and provocation, but also of self-punishment, which would define the eventual formal protest. He was still very much feeling his way and was assailed by doubts about his proposed statement of protest which had been divulged to no one except Lady Ottoline and her husband Philip, a Liberal MP, the latter actually advising against it. Sassoon went to see the critic and editor John Middleton Murry, who advised on tightening up the wording. Sitting in his club in St James's, he thought of the text as 'a moral equivalent of "going over the top" ... but what I disliked most was the prospect of being misunderstood and disapproved of by my fellow officers'.[83] In other words, Sassoon was not playing to the pacifist gallery, the Bloomsbury intellectuals who had been anti-war from the outset, but instead believed himself to be doing this thing for his fellow soldiers: 'It seemed that my companions of the Somme and Arras battles were around me ... It was for the fighting men that my appeal was made.' It was about this time that he wrote 'To Any Dead Officer', addressed to those men, with its savage last line: 'I wish they'd killed you in a decent show.' It was because Sassoon believed that this War was no longer a 'decent show' – not any war, that is, not *all* wars, but *this* War – that he would make his protest and remain adamant that it was 'a course of action that I have never regretted'.[84]

At his London club on 15 June 1917 he completed the final draft of his statement, drawn up with help from Bertrand Russell and John Middleton Murry; and, again with Russell's help, a sympathetic Labour MP, H. Lees-Smith, agreed to read it out in the House of Commons on 12 July, six days after Sassoon sent a copy to his commanding officer. In the event it was not read in the Commons until 30 July and published the next day in *The Times*.

At the time he wrote the statement, Sassoon was angry and emotional, though this does not come out in the text itself which is reasonably measured, if forthright. In his diary he let off steam, arguing that 'the Jingos' didn't truly know 'what useless suffering the war inflicts':

I only know, and declare from the depths of my agony, that these empty words (so often on the lips of the Jingos) mean the destruction of Youth ... And the Army is dumb. The Army goes on with its bitter tasks. The ruling classes do all the talking. And their words convince no one but the crowds *who are their dupes*.

The soldiers who return home seem to be stunned by the things they have endured ... Poor heroes! If only they would speak out; and throw their medals in the faces of their masters; and ask their women why it thrills them to know that they, the dauntless warriors, have shed the blood of Germans. Do not the women gloat secretly over the wounds of their lovers? Is there anything inwardly noble in savage sex instincts?

The rulers of England have always relied on the ignorance and patient credulity of the crowd ... Of the elderly male population I can hardly trust myself to speak. Their frame of mind is, in the majority of cases, intolerable. They glory in senseless invective against the enemy. They glory in the mock-heroism of their young men. They glory in the mechanical phrases of the Northcliffe Press ... In every class of society there are old men like ghouls, insatiable in their desire for slaughter, impenetrable in their ignorance.[85]

Sassoon's diaries at the time show that what was most exercising him was the idea that the War was somehow being continued indefinitely, that its aims had been lost or were undeclared, that there was simply no end in view, no articulated purpose. Had there been, it is unlikely that he would have made his protest. As he put it to his commanding officer when instructed to return to Litherland: 'I must inform you that it is my intention to refuse to perform any further military duties. I am doing this as a protest against the policy of the Government in prolonging the War by failing to state their conditions of peace.'[86] There is nothing here about the intrinsic evil of war as a pacifist would construe it.

The statement which was read out in the House and published the next day in *The Times* read as follows:

> I am making this statement as an act of wilful defiance of military authority, because I believe that the War is being deliberately prolonged by those who have the power to end it. I am a soldier, convinced that I am acting on behalf of soldiers. I believe that this War, upon which I entered as a war of defence and liberation, has now become a war of aggression and conquest. I believe that the purposes for which I and my fellow-soldiers entered upon this War should have been so clearly stated as to have made it impossible for them to be changed without our knowledge, and that, had this been done, the objects which actuated us would now be attainable by negotiation.
>
> I have seen and endured the sufferings of the troops, and I can no longer be a party to prolonging those sufferings for ends which I believe to be evil and unjust.
>
> I am not protesting against the military conduct of the War, but against the political errors and insincerities for which the fighting men are being sacrificed.
>
> On behalf of those who are suffering now, I make this protest against the deception which is being practised on them. Also I believe that it may help to destroy the callous complacence with which the majority of those at home regard the continuance of agonies which they do not share, and which they have not sufficient imagination to realise.[87]

The statement is judged by Sassoon's most recent biographer, Max Egremont, to be 'quite startlingly naive' and 'muddled'[88] – the adjectives we always expect to see applied in this country to principled statements of political dissent – but if there is some truth in this at the level of international realpolitik (Sassoon later conceded that a peace negotiated in 1917 might not have worked) there is also reasonable logical consistency to the argument, in my view. It is not an indictment of war itself or of 'incompetent generals' but a call for an end to drift in war policy, to the prolongation of human sacrifice when aims are not clear. It was a legitimate moral challenge that demanded a reply.

On 12 July Sassoon finally obeyed orders and went, late, to Litherland. He initially refused a medical board and was then persuaded by Robert Graves to attend another on 20 July at which he was ordered to go to the Craiglockhart War Hospital in Edinburgh. He would arrive on the 23rd, and remain there until boarded fit for general service on 26 November.

Craiglockhart was originally built, in Italianate style, as a hydropathic institute or 'hydro hotel' in 1877 by the Craiglockhart Hydropathic Company, and it remained so until the start of the War when it was requisitioned as a military hospital specialising in psychiatric damage and shell-shock. One of the most distinguished practitioners at Craiglockhart was Dr William Rivers, a captain in the Royal Army Medical Corps. Twenty-two years older than Sassoon, he took charge of his notorious new admission and a very strong relationship built up between the two men. Although Rivers never married there is no evidence to suggest that homosexuality was a common thread in their deep regard for each other. Rivers had already had an outstanding medical career in neurology at the National Hospital for the Paralysed and Epileptic in Queen Square, Bloomsbury, before specialising in psychology at Cambridge where he lectured and conducted psychological experiments, and he later worked at Jena and Heidelberg and did fieldwork in the Pacific. When war broke out he went to work with what would today be called post-traumatic stress disorders at Maghull

Military Hospital, Liverpool, and then in 1917 he arrived at Craiglockhart to work on the treatment of shell-shock. Rivers seems to have been a mild-mannered, donnish sort of man with a certain indifference to the military protocols imposed on Craiglockhart, but he was held in high regard by his peers.

Sassoon's friends were appalled and fearful for him. His old friend Bobbie Hanmer wrote from his war hospital bed in Reading: 'My dear old Sassons, What is this damned nonsense I hear from Robert Graves that you have refused to do any more soldiering? For Heaven's sake man don't be such a fool. Don't disgrace yourself and think of us before you do anything so mad.'[89] Lady Ottoline was naturally more sympathetic: '[Your statement] really couldn't have been better, I thought. Very condensed and said all that's necessary . . . You will have a hard time of it, and people are sure to say all sorts of foolish things. They always do – but nothing of that sort can really tarnish or dim the value and splendour of such a True Act . . . It is beastly being a woman and sitting still, irritating. Sometimes I feel I must go out and do something outrageous.'[90] Robbie Ross wrote from the Hotel Albion, Brighton, to say: 'I am quite appalled at what you have done . . . I am terrified lest you should be put under arrest.' Eddie Marsh, as Churchill's private secretary, could hardly be expected to say anything other than

Of course I'm sorry about it, as you expect . . . I do think you are intellectually wrong – on the facts. We agree that our motives for going to war were not aggressive or acquisitive to start with, and I cannot myself see that they have changed . . . it's too late to argue these points. One thing I do beg of you. Don't be more of a martyr than you can help! You have made your protest, and everyone who knows that you aren't the sort of fellow to do it for a stunt must profoundly admire your courage in doing it. But for God's sake stop there . . . if you find you have a choice between acceptance and further revolt, accept. And don't proselytise. Nothing that you can do will really affect the situation; we *have* to win the war (you must see that) and it's best that we should do it without more waste and friction than are necessary.

Arnold Bennett was the most stern:

I think you are very misguided and that your position cannot be argumentatively defended . . . you are not in a position to judge the situation . . . The overwhelming majority of your fellow citizens are against you . . . You are arrogating to yourself a right to which you are not entitled . . . And do not imagine that we chaps over age have not realised to a considerable extent what you soldiers have been through and are going through, and do not appreciate it . . . Your suspicion is correct. The Army will ultimately lay it down that you are 'daft'.

Bennett was prescient, for declaring Sassoon 'mad' was in effect what happened. Here 'confusion' and 'muddle' really do set in, for Sassoon's motives for so readily colluding with the solution found for him remain unclear. He certainly did not regret his protest and stood by it, yet he seems to have agreed, with remarkable alacrity, to a proposal, brokered by that subtle fixer Robert Graves, that he be sent to a hospital designed for the shell-shocked when it was clear that he was not ill, not mentally unbalanced, and wholly responsible for his thoughts and actions. Graves insisted in his account of the affair in *Goodbye to All That*, that Sassoon was 'very ill',[91] in which case the train journey to Edinburgh would prove startlingly therapeutic. Graves had originally written to his friend's commanding officer at Litherland (where Sassoon had compounded his anger by tossing his MC into the Mersey) and secured an agreement that he would be treated as a medical case rather than subjected to a court martial, which would have been the expected treatment. The crucial days are not covered by Sassoon's diaries and the account given in *Memoirs of an Infantry Officer* has him telling Graves, as they pounded the Formby foreshore, 'Can't you understand that this is the most difficult thing I've ever done in my life? I'm not going to be talked out of it just when I'm forcing them to make a martyr out of me.'[92] But talked out of it was exactly what he let himself be. In a few lines, Sassoon describes how, faced with the news that he was not to be court-martialled but would be locked up instead in a lunatic asylum for the rest of the War unless he agreed to a medical board, he gave in. 'So that was the end of my grand gesture,' he wrote. He always knew that 'the blighters would do me down somehow', but he seems to have relinquished his martyr's crown with remarkable ease, and felt that 'an enormous load had been lifted from my mind'.

The grand protest disappeared in a puff of smoke.

One detached observer, the poet Ivor Gurney, who did not know Sassoon, certainly got the message in a letter to a friend: 'There were questions in the House, and a general dust-up; but at last they solved it in a becoming official fashion, and declared him mad, and put him in a lunatic-asylum.'[93]

On 23 July 1917 Sassoon arrived at Edinburgh and made his way to the Craiglockhart War Hospital. The medical board had concluded that he was suffering from a nervous breakdown caused by 'the strain of active service, acting on a nervous temperament',[94] but that would not turn out to be the view of the specialist who treated him, and Sassoon himself seemed in very high spirits, like someone checking into a sporting holiday. On arrival he immediately wrote to Robbie Ross, facetiously heading his letter 'Dottyville', and asking gaily: 'Do you know anyone amusing in Edinburgh who I can go and see?'[95] He records no regret about the speed of his abandonment of the role of war protester nor his readiness to go along with what was a thinly disguised pretence that he was a serious medical case. Rivers certainly did not think that Dottyville had just taken delivery of a war victim. His typed medical notes, which are today in the Library of the Imperial War Museum, give his view of the state of the thirty-year-old 2nd Lieutenant Sassoon on his arrival:

The patient is a healthy-looking man of good physique. There are no physical signs of any disorder of the Nervous System. He discusses his recent actions and their motives in a perfectly intelligent and rational way, and there is no evidence of any excitement or depression. He recognises that his view of warfare is tinged by his feelings about the death of friends and of the men who were under his command in France. At the present time he lays special stress on the hopelessness of any decision in the War as it is now being conducted, but he left out any reference to this aspect of his opinions in the statement which he sent to his Commanding Officer and which was read in the House of Commons. His view differs from that of the ordinary pacifist in that he would no longer object to the continuance of the War if he saw any prospect of a rapid decision.[96]

There are two striking aspects to this candid and precise passage: first, it raises the question of whether the medical board in Liverpool had been 'leaned on' by someone in the War Office (Churchill, advised by Marsh?) to fabricate a nervous condition for the inconvenient celebrity protester; and secondly, it is noticeable that the doctor spends more time on analysing his patient's views of the war than his neural symptoms. Rivers, who is named without fictional disguise in the third volume of Sassoon's memoirs, *Sherston's Progress*, became a father figure to Sassoon, the latter describing him as 'the great and good man who gave me his friendship and guidance'.[97] The poet added: 'He liked me and he believed in me.' Rivers, entering into his patient's facetious sense of humour, concluded that he was suffering not from shell-shock but an 'anti-war complex'.

Sassoon also made, two weeks after his arrival, another momentous friendship at Craiglockhart – with a young, unknown soldier-poet called Wilfred Owen – which will be described fully in the next chapter. In the meantime, the putative invalid threw himself into writing poems, playing golf, and having long chats with Rivers and Owen. Sassoon always had a knack for landing on his feet and the Craiglockhart stay was a very productive period for his poetry. Nonetheless, he complained to Robbie Ross that having to share a room with a man he called 'the Theosophist' got in the way of his writing when he was 'full of poetry'. He added: 'I have great difficulty in doing any work as I am constantly disturbed by nurses etc & the man who sleeps in my room – an awful bore. It is pretty sickening when I feel like writing something & have to dry up & *try* to be polite (you can imagine with how much success!).' Sassoon hoped that Rivers would be able to get him a single room 'or get me away from these imbeciles'.[98]

In the pencilled notebook referred to earlier, which dated from 1929 to 1932 when he was at work on the second volume of autobiography, *Memoirs of an Infantry Officer* (1930), Sassoon explored his feelings about the Craiglockhart period and struggled to map out what he hoped would be a truthful rendering. In the notebook he confesses: 'While alone at Weirleigh in late June I worked myself into a state of belief in my protest – But when I had to discuss my view with "outsiders" my mental artifice began to crack and crumble, & my words sounded empty & unconvincing.'[99] It is fascinating to eavesdrop on Sassoon's preoccupation with getting it right and his sense that time brings shifting perspectives:

I must remember that <u>I knew very little at the time</u>. There must be no faked omniscience . . . I only saw the casualty lists in May & June 1917 & got bare details, in an occasional letter. The reality was not imaginable, even to one who knew the ground & the conditions – & the people engaged . . . My own war experience was only just adequate for my purposes (to contrast the conditions at the front with England). Anyone can find out photographic details of the war. What they can't find out is the secret drama inside a soldier's head. I must concentrate my efforts on that. [1–2 December 1928]

He is more explicit here than in the eventual memoir:

I expected Craiglockhart to be worse than it was. I wanted it to be 'good material for war poems' – harrowing sights etc. But the serious cases weren't visible, & most of the neuroses were below the surface. Those I played golf with, for instance, & the two I shared my room with in turn. Many were men who were obvious types that wouldn't be able to stay the distance. A few were wrong 'uns. Stammering was fairly frequent . . . There was a pervading note of war-weariness & disillusion – but there was also quite a lot of cheerfulness – thanks to the doctors – Acting plays – etc.

The more Sassoon thought about the men in the trenches 'the more I admired them – & regretted my own humiliated safety ("bitter safety"). The contrast was always being rubbed into me when I lay at night hearing the wind and the rain (& often half-despising my fellow patients).' Rivers asked him about his war experiences to find out if he had any very 'bad shows', but 'The truth was that I <u>hadn't</u>. My worst experience was the strain etc of the few days in April 1917. Not bad enough to cause a breakdown. If I had not been wounded I should have gone on quite all right. My "charmed life"!

Missing bad shows both times (April 17 and Sept 16).' In these pencilled notes Sassoon is much more frank about the trouble to his conscience, which doesn't really come out in his published accounts. Asking himself what his conscience said to him, he wrote:

It said – (after about six weeks? & when the weather began to get bad for the weather reminded me of the troops at the front) 'You are shortening the war nicely, for yourself, aren't you? Your separate peace is very convenient – for yourself!' It said. 'Does this count as being in prison for your principles?' (I was polishing my golf clubs with sand paper and oil!) It said. 'Do you notice that your protest has fizzled out, & that you are now living comfortably on it?' My pride (proper) put in a word too. It said, 'You may have been a man with a message two months ago, but you will soon be merely a man with a bee in his bonnet.'

And once he confessed to himself that the protest had ceased to be effective: 'you are here with false pretences'.

Every time Sassoon talked to Rivers

there seemed less to discuss and more that couldn't be discussed. I couldn't bluff Rivers! He waited his time and when I'd come to the point when I revealed – half-heartedly – my change of heart – he, for the 1st time ceased to look at my problem as confined to 'the present' & gently indicated the future. Had I considered the question of accepting another Medical Board? he asked. (Was I intending to try & get my discharge from the Army?) Once that bit of ice was broken the thaw set in. I looked ahead – beyond the war – & knew that to accept my Discharge would be ignoble defeat. (R. said 'the alternative is merely marking time. You will be kept here till the end of the war.')

Sassoon began to realise that he had to choose now

between discharge & – the front. It wasn't as simple as it
sounds – choosing between death and life! R. knew it – &
knew that he didn't want to send me back to be killed. But
he knew, & never doubted, which was the right way out. It
was touch and go – getting me through the Board which
passed me G.S. [general service]. And he got the assurance of
the W.O. that they'd send me back to the Front (I didn't trust
them as such).

In the notes Sassoon also confessed how he had 'pitted
myself against the Power of public opinion in 1917 and I want
to show how falteringly I did it (in my inward reality) and how
futile my achievement was'. Rivers was a vital catalyst in this
process of his moral self-knowing:

<u>Constructively</u> Rivers sums up my narrative of previous per-
plexities & development. He is, as it were, the bright clear
light which reveals my character (or mental condition
induced by war experience). Considering what he did for me
I can hardly be blamed for seeing him in retrospect as a sort
of saint – a scientific saint. <u>If R. had been a lesser man I
might have remained static – my clay hardening into obsti-
nacy – left to my own mental resources. I might have been
able to go on bluffing myself that my original attitude was
tenable till further notice. But when I went down to R's room
in the evening (3 times a week?) for an hour's talk, I was, as
it were, confronted by a mirror of honesty in which I saw
myself by the light of conscience. R's integrity was unevad-
able</u> [*sic*]. He was then an impartial umpire of my conflicting
problems & discussed things but <u>never</u> tried to influence,
persuade, convince etc. He was a sympathetic friend, so to
speak, and he managed to leave me detached and isolated –

respecting my position & patiently waiting for me to see my way to a reconsideration of it.

Sassoon never felt that Rivers was judging him but subtly: 'I became more and more aware that I was "skrimshanking" out of the war. The longer I stayed there the more ignominious my position became. My external life was not remarkable or impressive. – After the 1st few weeks my protest ceased to be significant – friends & relatives who wrote or visited me were glad I was "safely out of it".' He also felt that he must have been a demanding patient for the kindly Rivers: 'He was there to help me with advice, and I was Youth's Egotism personified. People always enjoy talking about themselves (I have outgrown the desire, thank goodness). R., of course, was interested in me as a psychological specimen (as well as liking me personally). If I had been less self centred & self important I shouldn't have been at C.L. at all! Once or twice I talked emotionally to R – usually, I think, when reminiscing about the behaviour of the troops, etc.'

From the first moment Sassoon saw Rivers he trusted him and loved him, '& realised that he was a haven of refuge for my troubled mind . . . R. was a sort of "Hound of Heaven" – often "I fled him" – but he was a visible incarnation of my conscience. Yes; Craiglockhart & everything there is only the backcloth for my duel with R. (which almost culminated when I "cut" the Medical Board – and caused him much pain & disappointment).'

The real truth was that Sassoon's grand gesture 'had resolved itself into an ignominious rest-cure – where I was continually reminded that I had a bee in my bonnet . . . The fact was that we were all mental and physical failures, as a result of war or inherent lack of guts. There were also the "lead swingers" & anyone might be one of them unless he showed psychologically shell shock symptoms. Only Rivers enabled me to preserve self-respect – he trusted me – until that moment when I "cut my board".'

Generally, Sassoon felt that 'The horde of war books is ever increasing, & most of them are inarticulately overloaded with details of infantry life from day to day.' He thought there was a danger of superimposition on past experiences but he was convinced that the truth of this episode was to be found in his decision to clear the ground for going back to the Front: 'The final fact of being passed – of deciding to go back – must be made an intense emotion. How that I went back without illusions – without hope – merely because "out there" was <u>the only place where I would find peace of mind.</u>' He knew that 'my mental conflict was severe. It was, at times, real anguish – <u>Renunciation of life.</u>' He also knew that without Rivers his morale might easily have disintegrated, 'for the atmosphere of Craigl was deadly', and there was also much pressure from outside to become, as he put it, 'a stop the war movement man'. Equally, he still hated the killing and told himself, when writing, to 'Show my aversion to going back to <u>fight.</u> I want to go back – but not to kill people. I want to save life – not take it.'

Sassoon remained at Craiglockhart for four months. His determination to go back to the War grew steadily. In the published works, in particular *Sherston's Progress*, he also recorded his thoughts about this move. In part he was exasperated with all those who had dismissed him as being wrong-headed or 'not quite normal' and he wanted to show them: 'In their opinion it was quite right that I should be safely out of it and "being looked after". How else could I get my own back on them but by returning to the trenches? Killed in action in order to confute the Under-Secretary for War, who had officially stated that I wasn't responsible for my actions.'[100] Rivers understood and helped to ensure that he was cleared for general service again, grasping that, as Sassoon put it, 'going back to the War as soon as possible was my only chance of peace'.[101] He expanded on this to Robbie Ross:

> I am at present faced with the prospect of remaining here for an indefinite period, and you can imagine how that affects me ... I have told Rivers that I will not withdraw anything that I have said or written, and that my views are the same, but that I will go back to France if the War Office will give me a guarantee that they really will send me there ... I hope that you and others will try to understand what I mean by it. After all I made my protest on behalf of my fellow-fighters, and (if it is a question of being treated as an imbecile for the rest of the war) the fittest thing for me is to go back and share their ills. By passing me for General Service (which Rivers says is 'the only thing they can do') they admit that I never had any shell-shock, as it is quite out of the question for a man who has been three months in a nerve-hospital to be sent back at once if he really had anything wrong.[102]

He told Graves, who had much more caste loyalty than his friend Ross, that his position was unbearable and that he felt isolated and depressed, and lost patience with Graves' acquiescence: 'O Robert, what ever will happen to end the war? It's all very well for you to talk about "good form" and acting like a "gentleman". To me that's a very estimable form of suicidal stupidity and credulity ... If you had real courage you wouldn't acquiesce as you do.'[103] He told the War Office that he would only go back to the war if he was allowed to join his old battalion in France. Above all he wanted to be active again, and on 26 November he was passed for general service: 'The Board asked if I had changed my views on the war, and I said I hadn't, which seemed to cause surprise.'[104] He returned to Litherland and immediately felt much better: 'I intend to lead a life of light-hearted stupidity. I have done all I can to protest against the war and the way it is prolonged. At least I will try and be peaceful-minded for a few months – after the strain and unhappiness of the last seven months. It is the only way by which I can hope to face the horrors of the front without breaking down completely. I must try to think as little as possible. And write happy poems. (Can I?)'[105]

At the start of January 1918 Sassoon was sent to new barracks in Limerick and was very glad to get away from Litherland. He picked up Barbusse's war novel *Le Feu* (1916) which he had been reading in Craiglockhart, went hunting, and heard rumours that he might be going to Egypt. In February he rejoined his Company and set off for Alexandria via Sicily but the experience turned out to be mostly a pointless hanging-about base camp: 'This place is the absolute visible expression of time wasted at the war . . . Just a crowd of people killing time. Time wasted in waste places. I wish I could see some meaning in it all. But it is soul-less . . . People go "up the line" almost gladly – for it means there's some purpose in life.'[106] He railed against the 'coarse stupidity' of the men and officers: 'Minds like the front page of the *Daily Mirror* . . . Suffocating boredom of the forced intimacy of living with them. They see nothing clearly. Minds clogged with mental deadness.'[107] At the end of April the Company finally started its return journey to France and Sassoon, contemplating that Front again, was confused about what it meant to him: 'It is all like a pilgrimage – leading me deathward. It seems an irresistible procession of events – toward completion and fulfilment. Everything seems to fit in. I am working up to another climax – steadily. The nearer I get to the war the more I desire to share its terrors again – that I may learn yet more the meaning of it – and the effect. But I can't believe that I'm going there to kill people – or to help in the destruction of human life. It is inconceivable.'[108]

Back in France he thought the Company was the best he had

struck in the War and, not far from Arras, he reflected: 'Getting nearer the line is working me up to a climax. Same old feeling of confidence and freedom from worry.'[109] After a period of training he was glad to do some more reading:

> One cannot be a good soldier and a good poet at the same time . . . Life will be easier and simple when we get into the line again . . . Everything up there is 'soul-deadening'; there is no time for emotion, no place for beauty. Only grimness and cruelty and remorse . . . But under all that mask of animal satisfaction the mind rebels and struggles to dominate the situation as it should do. For all these details of soldiering are not exercises for the mind; they are mechanical and utterly stupid, and (to me) unnatural . . . I am merely recording what thousands of sensitive gifted people are enduring in the name of 'patriotism'. And O how I long for music. *That* is what I need *most of all*.[110]

But, once again, he was not to see service at the Front. In July 1918 he was wounded, shot in the head by one of his own sergeants. This happened the day after there had been a direct hit on his dugout, on 11 July. Against advice, Sassoon set off on the 12th to crawl within fifty yards of a German machine-gun post, which fired on him. As he returned in the small hours of 13 July he stood up to look back at the enemy lines and one of his own men mistook him for a German and fired. He was taken to a casualty clearing station, then to a hospital at St Omer, then to the British Red Cross Hospital in Boulogne from where he announced that 'an angry, tortured feeling has come over me. I'll stay in France just to spite those blighters who yell about "our alien enemies" in Trafalgar Square. But, after all, what do *they* care about me?'[111] It wrung Sassoon's heart to be separated from his Company again: 'There at least I had something real, and I had lived myself into a feeling of responsibility for them –

inefficient and excitable though I was when in close contact with Germans. All that was decent in me disliked leaving them to endure what I was escaping from. And somehow the idea of death had beckoned to me – ghastly though it had been when I believed that I had been killed.'[112] Not going back home, he believed, 'is the only way I can keep my soul clean, and vindicate my pride in the men who love and trust me ... I am weakening in my proud, angry resolve; all my tenderness is fading into selfish longing for safety. I close my eyes, and all I can see is the door into the garden at home, and Mother coming in with a basket of roses. And my terrier ... and the piano ...'[113]

On 18 July Sassoon arrived at the American Red Cross Hospital for Officers at Lancaster Gate in London. He would never see service again. His new book of poems, *Counter-Attack*, published on 27 June, was his only consolation. He had an idea of being sent out by the Ministry of Information as a writer, in the manner of a war artist, but this was rather unrealistic, Marsh believed, when sounded out. He rejected an offer to join Beaverbrook's staff but was developing 'a more controlled and objective attitude towards the War. To remind people of its realities was still my main purpose.'[114] On 18 August he met Wilfred Owen in London at Osbert Sitwell's but he did not know that it would be for the last time: 'I have never been able to accept that disappearance philosophically. A blank miserable sense of deprivation has dulled my mind whenever I have thought of him ... the chasm in my private experience remains.'[115]

Sassoon thus survived the War. On the night of the Armistice he was back in London: 'I got to London about 6.30 and found masses of people in streets and congested Tubes, all waving flags and making fools of themselves – an outburst of mob patriotism. It was a wretched wet night, and very mild. It is a loathsome ending to the loathsome tragedy of the last four years.'[116]

After the War he continued to write poetry but it is as a 'war poet' that he is remembered. Introducing the definitive edition of *The War Poems of Siegfried Sassoon*, Rupert Hart-Davis wrote: 'In later years, when Siegfried Sassoon had written much else in prose and verse, he was annoyed at always being referred to simply as a war poet, but it was the Great War that turned him into a poet of international fame, and I feel sure that his ghost will forgive me for thus bringing together these magnificently scarifying poems.'[117] The first, 'Absolution', which contained the line 'And, fighting for our freedom, we are free', Sassoon thought typical of the way people felt when they first joined up in 1914 and 1915. 'No one feels it when they "go out again". They only feel, then, a queer craving for "good old times at Givenchy" etc.'[118] It was the poem 'The Redeemer' that he was to describe as 'My first front-line poem'. It was written in November 1915, inspired by working parties at the Battle of Festubert earlier in the year when the British Army in the Artois region attacked German forces, heading them off in order to assist the French offensive near Arras: 'We were soaked, chilled and wretched, every one.' Very early, he struck the note of unillusioned realism and in the poem he shows a Lancaster soldier illuminated by a flare: 'I say that he was Christ; stiff in the glare.'

> But to the end, unjudging, he'll endure
> Horror and pain, not uncontent to die
> That Lancaster on Lune may stand secure.
> He faced me, reeling in his weariness,
> Shouldering his load of planks, so hard to bear.

But it was 'In the Pink' that he described as 'The first of my "outspoken" war poems. I wrote it one cold morning at Morlancourt, sitting by the fire in the Quartermaster's billet, while our Machine-Gun Officer shivered in his blankets on the floor. He was suffering from alcoholic poisoning, and cold feet, and shortly afterwards departed from England, never to return. Needless to say, the verses do not refer to him, but to some typical Welshman who probably got killed on the Somme in July, after months of a dog's life and no leave. The *Westminster Review* refused the poem, as they thought it might prejudice recruiting!!'[119] The poem is about a Welsh soldier who writes to his sweetheart that he is 'in the pink', but he can't sleep that night, remembering 'Sundays at the farm' with Gwen:

> And then he thought: tomorrow night we trudge
> Up to the trenches, and my boots are rotten.
> Five miles of stodgy clay and freezing sludge,
> And everything but wretchedness forgotten.
> To-night he's in the pink; but soon he'll die.
> And still the war goes on – *he* don't know why.

There is an assumption here that the ordinary soldier in February 1916 does not know what the war is for. Some of these early trench poems have a plainness of diction and a flavour of reportage that make their content more impressive than their form. Compared with his friend and protégé, Wilfred Owen, Sassoon's language is less rich and sensuous and evocative. But the feeling is often very powerful, as in 'The Last Meeting' which is for his dead lover, David Thomas: 'him that I have lost'. He goes in search of Thomas's ghost thinking that he might 'loom above me like a tree,/ With lifted arms and body tall and strong', but the abandoned house he comes across does not contain him:

> Quite empty was that house; it could not hold
> His human ghost, remembered in the love
> That strove in vain to be companioned still.

But in the woods he finds him:

> He was beside me now, as swift as light.
> I knew him crushed to earth in scentless flowers,
> And lifted in the rapture of dark pines.

The poet will henceforth identify him with the beauty of nature (it is springtime in France):

> So he will never come but in delight,
> And, as it was in life, his name shall be
> Wonder awaking in a summer dawn,
> And youth, that dying, touched my lips to song.

In the poem 'A Night Attack', written in July 1916, the poet recalls:

> The rank stench of those bodies haunts me still,
> And I remember things I'd best forget.
> For now we've marched to a green, trenchless land
> Twelve miles from battering guns . . .

Sassoon can still 'smell the battle' and observes:

> If any friend be there whom I have loved,
> God speed him safe to England with a gash.

He then hears a soldier talking about 'the bloody Bosche' and remembers having seen someone

> Dead in a squalid, miserable ditch,
> Heedless of toiling feet that trod him down.
> He was a Prussian with a decent face,
> Young, fresh and pleasant, so I dare to say.

No doubt he loathed the war and longed for peace,
And cursed our souls because we'd killed his friends.

These poems exhibit a kind of documentary realism, like a
modern war photograph, that shows the dead Prussian without
further commentary. Some poems, of course, were more angry
and opinionated – like 'Christ and the Soldier' about a roadside
Calvary in France which, for most soldiers, was merely a
reminder of the inability of religion to cope with the carnage
and catastrophe they experienced:

The dilemma of an ignorant private is demonstrated. But
I was a very incomplete and quite unpractising Christian,
and understood little more than he of the meaning of Our
Lord's teaching. Like Wilfred Owen, I was anti-clerical,
and the Churches seemed to offer no solution to the
demented doings on the Western Front . . . As far as I can
remember, no one at the Front ever talked to me about
religion at all. And the padrés never came near us – except
to bury someone . . . This poem cannot be read as showing
any clue to my own mental position, which was altogether
confused, and became increasingly disillusioned and
rebellious.[120]

In Denmark Hill Hospital on 23 April 1917 (two years to the
day after the death of Brooke) he wrote a poem 'To the
Warmongers':

For you our battles shine
With triumph half-divine . . .
But a curse is on my head,
That shall not be unsaid,
And the wounds in my heart are red,
For I have watched them die.

Most of these poems were written on periods of leave or convalescence and the Craiglockhart months were particularly productive, resulting in no fewer than eighteen poems, some published in the hospital paper, *The Hydra*. One of these, 'Sick Leave', captures in a few lines the whole significance of the Craiglockhart experience. When the poet is asleep 'dreaming and lulled and warm' they come, 'the noiseless dead', to ask why he is not with them. 'In bitter safety I awake.'

> I think of the Battalion in the mud.
> 'When are you going out to them again?
> Are they not still your brothers through our blood?'

This is why Sassoon went back to the Front after his protest. He could not tolerate the thought of the 'bitter safety' he enjoyed in Blighty. Another poem, 'Banishment', again articulates his personal dilemma in relation to the men he had left behind in the trenches. 'I am banished from the patient men who fight,' he wrote, adding, 'Their wrongs were mine'. And then he says he let out a 'mutinous' shout to 'those who sent them out into the night', but it was in vain:

> Love drove me to rebel.
> Love drives me back to grope with them through hell;
> And in their tortured eyes I stand forgiven.

That last line may be wish-fulfilment, but it was the outcome he hoped for.

After the War Sassoon was drawn to Labour politics and became the first literary editor of the socialist *Daily Herald* when it was relaunched. In 1928 his popular and highly readable memoirs started to be published, based on the copious diaries and notebooks he had kept all his life. Although he married in 1933 – one Hester Gatty – and settled for the rest of his life at

Heytesbury House near Warminster in Wiltshire, his private life was troubled, largely as a result of his homosexuality, and the marriage ended in 1944.

He had one son, George, and many relationships, the most significant of which was with the extraordinary aristocratic aesthete Stephen Tennant, described by his biographer as 'part Peter Pan, part Dorian Gray – a glittering androgynous figure invested with an almost alien sexuality'.[121] The pair met in 1927 and Peter Quennell described it as 'a tremendous *coup de foudre*. Sassoon was like the worthy vicar of a parish coming to town and meeting this great society beauty.'[122] After it was rumoured that while they were staying in Bavaria together Sassoon had been sent back to the hotel by his lover to collect his pearls, Edith Sitwell dubbed them 'the Old Earl and Little Lord Fauntleroy'.[123] But Tennant – who lived on until 1987 – eventually tired of the Old Earl and, in May 1933, Sassoon wrote despairingly: 'O Steenie, I have given you the last four years of my life.'[124]

In 1957 Sassoon was received into the Catholic Church and when he died ten years later he was buried in Mells churchyard near to his friend Monsignor Ronald Knox.

4

The Poetry and the Pity: Wilfred Owen and Robert Graves

I hate washy pacifists as temperamentally as I hate whiskied prussianists.[1]

WILFRED OWEN

Siegfried Sassoon made his entrance in the last chapter in France in November 1915, when the War was increasingly looking as though it was going to last far longer than anyone had feared. He had joined up more than a year earlier, in August 1914, but it was not until 21 October the next year that a young teacher of English in France called Wilfred Owen – who had toyed with the idea of joining the French Army – eventually signed up with the Artists' Rifles. Owen's observations on the poetry of war have been discussed in the Prologue, but it should be stressed that these were the product of rapidly acquired experience on the battlefield. The young poet who joined up in the autumn of 1915 still had much to learn about poetry and about war.

Wilfred Owen was born on 18 March 1893[2] at Plas Wilmot, near Oswestry in Shropshire, the first child of a local railway clerk, Tom Owen, and his wife Susan, who was the daughter of Edward Shaw, an Oswestry ironmonger and municipal worthy – a provincial lower-middle-class background received rather sniffily by the patrician Siegfried Sassoon at his first meeting with Owen in the summer of 1917. In 1898 Tom Owen was transferred to Birkenhead, which meant that between 1899 and 1907 Wilfred was educated at the Birkenhead Institute. In that latter year his father was appointed assistant superintendent of the Joint Railways and Wilfred now moved to Shrewsbury Technical School. He had already started writing poetry by this time but a much more passionate interest was religion, spurred on by his devout mother. With his two cousins he started an Astronomical, Geological and Botanical Society of three and also became interested in local archaeology, incited by the presence nearby of the Roman city of Uriconium at Wroxeter.

Owen's childhood was dominated by the changes of residence which his father's shifting employment dictated, but the Birkenhead years seem to have been relatively calm and secure. His parents were Evangelical Christians, and home life was pious and high-minded with Wilfred studying the Bible at home with mother and attending Sunday School. Both he and his younger brother Harold were reared protectively by their rather snobbish mother, who kept them away from other children in the street. Owen's biographer suggests: 'The adult Wilfred cannot be understood as man or poet unless his youthful experience of Evangelical religion is remembered. It was a religion based on the Word, on words, on language.'[3] His close, if not stiflingly protective, relationship with his mother probably created a barrier between Wilfred and the rest of the family and he became burdened with her pious expectations of him. This also created tensions with his father, who was seemingly shut out of the intense partnership.

When Owen left school he hoped to go to the University of London but his results were not good enough to secure the necessary scholarship, so he took an unpaid position as lay assistant to the vicar of Dunsden near Reading. In exchange for parish duties Owen received free board and lodging and some tuition to help prepare him for a renewed attempt at the university entrance, but in the end the latter arrangement did not work out. He received more literary encouragement from the head of the English Department at the University of Reading where he attended botany classes.

Meanwhile, Wilfred's enthusiasm for Evangelical religion was beginning to wane and he eventually left Dunsden in a state of nervous collapse, made worse by congestion of the lungs. In June 1912 he declared: 'All Theological lore is growing distasteful to me. All my recent excursions into such fields prove it to be a shifting, hypothetical, doubt-fostering, dusty and unprofitable study.'[4] By the start of January 1913 he had grown more determined to put this phase of his life behind him: 'Escape from this hotbed of religion I now long for.'[5] Faced with 'overbearing elders', by contrast he was able to 'find great comfort in scribbling'. Writing poetry had now become a central experience for Owen. After a second failed attempt in July that year at the scholarship examination for University College, Reading, he decided to go and teach English at the Berlitz School in Bordeaux. Less than a year later, while he was tutoring a young girl at her parents' house in the Pyrenees, war was declared. In France he had met the 'decadent' poet Laurent Tailhade who introduced him to writers like Flaubert and Verlaine and whose own pacifist beliefs – which Tailhade somehow contrived to combine with a passion for duelling – may have influenced Owen against war. But, like Tailhade, he eventually decided to enlist.

Criticism of Wilfred Owen the poet always begins with a reference to his early fondness for Keats, and a derivative lushness is certainly present in his first attempts at verse. As early as 1910 he bought Sidney Colvin's *Life of Keats* and declared: 'I sometimes feel in reading such books that I would give ten years of life to have been born a hundred years earlier.'[6] When he saw Keats's house in London in April 1911 he 'gaped at it . . . to my heart's content', and considered the garden in which 'Ode to a Nightingale' was written to be 'one of London's most holy spots'.

When war was declared, Owen was in the town of Bagnères in the Pyrenees and had to declare himself and get a permit to stay under penalty of arrest and sentence as a spy. He told his parents, less than a week later: 'I feel shamefully "out of it" up here, passing my time reading the Newspapers in an armchair in a shady garden . . . After all my years of playing soldiers, and then of reading History, I have almost a mania to be in the East, to see fighting, and to serve. For I like to think this is the last War of the World! I have only a faint idea of what is going on, and what is felt, in England.'[7]

As the news of war became more grave, including the invasion of Belgium and the consequent French and English losses, Owen admitted: 'We are very unquiet.'[8] In a comment reminiscent of Charles Hamilton Sorley, he expressed his mixed feelings about the national polarisations that war made inevitable and the cultural losses that are incurred when one European nation is required officially to hate another. His words at this time also embody an ambivalence about commitment, as well as an occasional insouciance or even flippancy:

The war affects me less than it ought. But I can do no service to anybody by agitating for news or making dole over the slaughter . . . I feel my own life all the more precious and more dear in the presence of this deflowering of Europe. While it is true that the guns will effect a little useful weeding, I am furious with chagrin to think that the Minds which were to have excelled the civilization of ten thousand years, are being annihilated – and bodies, the product of aeons of Natural Selection, melted down to pay for political statues. I regret the mortality of the English regulars less than that of the French, Belgian, or even Russian or German armies: because the former are all Tommy Atkins, poor fellows, while the continental armies are inclusive of the finest brains and temperaments of the land.[9]

Now in Bordeaux, Owen confessed to his parents that he was having a very agreeable time – many Parisians had arrived there to escape the conflict – but he was a little lonely. He resembled Sassoon in that 'All women, without exception, *annoy* me',[10] but equally: 'I begin to suffer a hunger for Intimity. At bottom, it is that I ought to be in love and am not.'[11] Although he claimed to have no friends in England, Owen was beginning to realise that he must return and enlist: 'It is a sad sign if I do: for it means that I shall consider the continuation of my life of no use to England. And if once my fears are roused for the perpetuity and supremacy of my mother-tongue, in the world – I would not hesitate, as I hesitate now – to enlist.'[12] He could hardly be said to have been infected by the war-spirit and it was an aesthetic impulse – to preserve the language – rather than any pity for the victims that started to drive him on:

The *Daily Mail* speaks very movingly about the 'duties shirked' by English young men. I suffer a good deal of shame. But while those ten thousand lusty louts go on playing football I shall go on playing with my little axiom: – that my life is worth more than my death to Englishmen. Do you know what would hold me together on a battlefield?: the sense that I was perpetuating the language in which Keats and the rest of them wrote! I do not know in what else England is greatly superior, or dearer to me, than another land and people.[13]

It was the German shelling of Scarborough, Whitby and Hartlepool that finally unseated him from his fence: 'When I read that a shell fell into a group of sixteen schoolboys and killed fifteen, I raved. Talk about rumours of wars and earthquakes in divers places; all that's historic now. The beginning of the End must be ended, and the beginning of the middle of the end is now.'[14] Owen was short of money and was not equipped to teach in England without a degree, so if he returned he would have to enlist anyway, just to survive. He discussed this with his parents, telling them,

> I have not abandoned all idea of enlisting, but it need be discussed before I get home. My present life does not, as Father points out, lead to anywhere in particular; but, situated where I was, say in 1911, I don't think I could have done wiselier than I did. I have not struck out in any direction yet. I have made soundings in deep waters, and I have looked out from many observation-towers: and I found the deep waters terrible and nearly lost my breath there ... I seem without a footing on life; but I have one. It is as bold as any, and I have kept it for years. For years now. I was a boy when I first realised that the fullest life liveable was a Poet's. And my later experiences ratify it.[15]

The awkward youthful self-consciousness in these letters, together with the capitalisation of certain words, suggests occasionally a rather strained pastiche of the letters of Keats. For Owen poetry demanded dedication and concentrated attention with which the life of a soldier would clearly conflict: 'A poem does not grow by jerks. If it is to be worth a place in Human Time, it must be worth more than the fag-ends of the Poet's time.'[16]

In the end, however, he realised that he had no choice. On a brief trip to London he read an advertisement which said that 'any gentleman . . . returning to England from abroad will be given a Commission – in the "Artists' Rifles". Such officers will be sent to the front in 3 months. Thus we shall watch the Dardanelles with a little more interest than before . . . I don't want the bore of training, I don't want to wear khaki; nor yet to save my honour before inquisitive grand-children fifty years hence. But I now do most intensely want to fight.'[17]

Owen asked his mother for the address of the Artists' Rifles and said that he might even consider joining the Italian Army if he were refused an English commission. In spite of telling his old friend Leslie Gunston that 'Keats remained absolutely indifferent to Waterloo and all that commotion',[18] he came back to England in September 1915 and enlisted on 21 October. His first task was to present himself to the Artists' Rifles regimental HQ off Euston Road for a medical examination. One of the advantages of this regiment was that its initial training was in London and he took lodgings in Tavistock Square, Bloomsbury: 'Tavistock Square is a replica of every other Bloomsbury square; wadded with fog; skeletons of dismal trees behind the palings; but the usual west-end pervasion of ghostly aristocracy.'[19] That same day he took the oath ('This time it is done: I am in the British Army!'[20]) and was immediately inoculated against typhoid. He then set off the same night for a poetry reading around the corner at the Poetry Bookshop, at 35 Devonshire Street. He met Harold Monro at another reading there on 27 October but it was drill and parade ground that would now take over his life ('the discipline is frightfully minute'[21]). He did physical training instruction at nearby Cartwright Gardens and learned with difficulty to acknowledge the authority of the drill sergeants:

I never felt devotion, and not much respect, for any authority or individual in this world since I left the 3rd form of the Institute; but I am beginning again under these fellows . . . I spend a good part of my leisure polishing my buttons and badges. It is a frightful bore ... I have bought my swagger cane, and now feel perfectly normal in Khaki ... When I clamp-clump-clamp-clumped into the Poetry Bookshop on Thursday, the poetic ladies were not a little surprised ... I could not speak to Monro, but he smiled sadly at my khaki.[22]

Owen was disappointed in November not to get a room over the Poetry Bookshop, which some writers had succeeded in doing, but he managed to rent one over the coffee shop opposite for 5s 6d a week with candle-light and no bath. Preparing to depart for serious military training in Essex, he complained: 'There seem *no* Artists whatever among us!'[23]

On 15 November Owen started a seven-and-a-half-month training period, mostly at Hare Hall Camp in Gidea Park, Essex. Refused a commission with the Lancashire Fusiliers in early January 1916, he pressed on with intensive musketry drill and other courses. One of these lasted ten days and was in London, so from 27 February to 5 March he did stay at the Poetry Bookshop in one of the upper bed-sits that Monro let out. Late at night on 4 March, Monro came up to his room with Owen's manuscripts in his hand: 'So we sit down, and I have the time of my life. For he was "very struck" with these sonnets. He went over the things in detail and he told me what was fresh and clever, and what was second-hand and banal; and what Keatsian, and what "modern". He summed up their value as far above that of the Little Books of Georgian Verse.'[24]

Unfortunately this literary episode was all too brief and by the middle of March it was back to Essex and 'the same old, insupportable drill. This last week has been enough to send crazy any thinking being – eternal inspections, parades, inspections, punishment parades, & more inspections.'[25] Relief eventually came in the shape of a commission on 4 June into the 5th Battalion, the Manchester Regiment. He was initially in camp in Guildford: 'I am an exile here . . . It is due to the complete newness of the country, the people, my dress, my duties, the dialect, the air, food, everything. I am marooned on a Crag of Superiority in an ocean of Soldiers.'[26]

Owen finally crossed to France on 29 December 1916 to join the 2nd Manchesters on the Somme. In the second week of January 1917 he led his frozen platoon into the trenches for the first time. 'There is a fine heroic feeling about being in France,' he had already reported to his mother, 'and I am in perfect spirits. A tinge of excitement is about me, but excitement is always necessary to my happiness . . . On all the officers' faces there is a harassed look that I have never seen before, and which in England, never will be seen – out of jails . . . I am perfectly well and strong, but unthinkably dirty and squalid.'[27]

It was now that he found he must start to come to terms with the sounds and sights of the Western Front at one of the worst parts of the line: 'As I was making my damp bed, I heard the Guns for the first time. It was a sound not without a certain sublimity . . . At night it is like a stupendous thunderstorm, for the flashes are quite as bright as lightning.'[28] Yet he held on to his shreds of youthful nonconformity: 'The Victoria Cross! I covet it not. Is it not Victorian?'[29] He reported home that he was wearing 'a steel helmet, buff jerkin of leather, rubber-waders up to the hips, & gauntlets. But for the rifle, we are exactly like Cromwellian Troopers', yet he had 'no anxiety. I cannot do a better thing or be in a righter place.'[30]

That initial enthusiasm was immediately tested in mid-January by five days of hell at an advanced post, a dugout in the middle of No Man's Land mud ('an octopus of sucking clay') and high explosives: 'Those fifty hours were the agony of my happy life . . . I nearly broke down and let myself down in the water that was now slowly rising over my knees', and 'I am never going back to this awful post.'[31] He was glad to withdraw, after this episode, to a ruined village: 'We are wretched beyond my previous imagination – but safe ... I have not seen any dead. I have done worse. In the dank air I have *perceived* it, and in the darkness, *felt*.'[32]

February 1916 in the trenches was bitterly cold (a date in one of Owen's notebooks suggests that his poem 'Exposure' could have been at least conceived at that time, though it was drafted much later). Nevertheless, 'I was kept warm by the ardour of Life within me.'[33] He could bear the cold but not

> the universal pervasion of *Ugliness*. Hideous landscapes, vile noises, foul language and nothing but foul, even from one's own mouth (for all are devil ridden), everything unnatural, broken, blasted; the distortion of the dead, whose unburiable bodies sit outside the dugouts all day, all night, the most execrable sights on earth. In poetry we call them the most glorious. But to sit with them all day, all night ... and a week later to come back and find them still sitting there, in motionless groups, THAT is what saps the 'soldierly spirit'.[34]

Here is the genesis of the distinctive Wilfred Owen poetic presentation of the war experience: the contrast between the reality and the conventional fine words. He was resolved to make poetry out of the former, not the latter.

While he was working at the advanced horse transport depot during February and March, life got a little better and Owen was able to write a little. The poet David Jones later expressed his astonishment that he could write in these conditions. Isaac Rosenberg was another who scribbled on any mud-spattered odd sheets that he could lay his hands on.[35] Looking back in 1973, Jones wrote: 'What astonished me about Owen whose poems I have been familiar with only in recent years is how on earth he was able to write them while actually in the trenches, it was an astonishing achievement – I can't imagine how it was done – a unique and marvellous detachment.'[36] Other poets wrote, more typically, while on leave or in hospital or convalescing.

In March, however, Owen fell into a shell-hole and was concussed and later sent to 13th Casualty Clearing Station, a field hospital where he lamented the lack of reading matter and began to dream of a post-war career as a pig farmer. Morale, he found, was harder to sustain away from the front line: 'My long rest has shaken my nerve. But after all *I hate old age*, and there is only one way to avoid it,' he wrote to his mother. Without her letters, he said, he should give in. He needed an object for carrying on: 'And that object is not my Motherland, which is a good land, nor my Mother tongue, which is a dear language, but for my Mother, of whom I am not worthy to be called *The Son*xxx.'[37]

Owen returned to the Front just too late to be in at the start of a major operation, or 'stunt', against the outposts of the Hindenburg Line. The Hindenburg Line was a complex defensive system of trenches, barbed wire and concealed pillboxes, and the offensive launched on 1 April resulted in two brigades taking an area known as Savy Wood and a village where Owen had now been sent. This was one of the notable successes of the war, as Germans were forced to flee and prisoners were taken and a great deal of ammunition and guns captured, possibly the most striking achievement of its kind since 1914.

During this action Owen had some extraordinary escapes from shells and bullets, and for days could not wash his face nor take off his boots nor get any real sleep: 'For twelve days we lay in holes, where at any moment a shell might put us out. I think the worst incident was one wet night when we lay up against a railway embankment. A big shell lit on the top of the bank, just 2 yards from my head. Before I awoke, I was blown in the air right away from the bank! I passed most of the following day in a railway Cutting, in a hole just big enough to lie in, and covered with corrugated iron.'[38] (It was this incident that caused his shell-shock and eventual invaliding home.) At first the doctor forbade him to take part in any further action:

> he is nervous about my nerves, and sent me down yester-day – labelled Neurasthenia. I still of course suffer from the headaches traceable to my concussion ... Do not for a moment suppose I have had a 'breakdown'. I am simply *avoiding* one ... If I haven't got a Blighty [the soldiers' term for a wound that would mercifully get one sent home] in this war, I will take good care not to get a *Blight*, as many have done, even from this Regiment. I should certainly have got a bullet wound, if I had not used the utmost caution in wrig-gling along the ground on one occasion.[39]

With time to reflect on things, Owen tried to work out what was the right response of a Christian to warfare:

> Already I have comprehended a light which will never filter into the dogma of any national church: namely that one of Christ's essential commands was: Passivity at any price! Suffer dishonour and disgrace; but never resort to arms. Be bullied, be outraged, be killed; but do not kill ... Christ is literally in no man's land. There men often hear His voice: Greater love hath no man than this, that a man lay down his life – for a friend ... Thus you see how pure Christianity will not fit in with pure patriotism ... This practice of *selective ignorance* is, as I have pointed out, one cause of the War. Christians have deliberately *cut* some of the main teachings of their code.[40]

Late in May, Owen was moved to 41st Stationary Hospital at Gailly, a village on the Somme canal, in a feverish condition and felt a prisoner. He was convinced that if he could just get away from the Front for a week to a town he would be cured, but he was put on a list for evacuation and then crossed off it again. He drafted a mock questionnaire about his condition which included: 'Health: quite restored ... Mood: highest variety of jinks ... Aim in War: Extinction of Militarism *beginning* with Prussian.'[41] On 12 June he was moved again to the General Hospital at Étretat, where he was lodged in a marquee on the front lawn. Finally, the decision was taken to send him home for treatment, to the Welsh Hospital at Netley, Southampton Water, where boredom awaited him, alleviated only by the presence of the Welsh whom he was glad to be among. The voyage across the Channel had been on a luxurious West Indian liner with a cabin to himself and excellent food.

On 26 June 1917, Owen was transferred to Craiglockhart War Hospital. He went via London where he made for Burlington House to see the Royal Academy Summer Exhibition and had tea at the exclusive Shamrock Tea Rooms, met a few familiar faces, and got himself measured for some new trousers at Pope & Bradley's the tailor. On arrival at Edinburgh's Waverley Station he tucked into an enormous breakfast before setting off for Craiglockhart. 'There is nothing very attractive about the place, it is a decayed Hydro, far too full of officers, some of whom I know,' he reported.[42] He was uncomfortable and vaguely guilty at being there. He wrote to his aunt: 'I feel a sort of reserve and suspense about everything I do ... I have endured unnameable tortures in France; but I know that I have not suffered by this war as you have and are suffering.'[43] He was put under the care of a Dr Brock and became editor of *The Hydra*, which would publish some remarkable things by several war poets in the summer of 1917. He lectured the natural history club on the topic of 'Do Plants Think?', considered taking German lessons at a Berlitz school, and went swimming:

At present I am a sick man in hospital, by night; a poet, for a quarter of an hour before breakfast; I am whatever and whoever I see while going down to Edinburgh on the tram:

greengrocer, policeman, shopping lady, errand boy, paper-boy, blind man, crippled Tommy, bank-clerk, carter, all of these in half an hour; next a German student in earnest; then I either peer over bookstalls in back-streets, or do a bit of a dash down Princes Street, – according as I have taken weak tea or strong coffee for breakfast.[44]

He also did some acting and wrote a (lost) play, which his surviving notes say intended 'To expose war to the criticism of reason'.[45] Reading a biography of Tennyson, Owen concluded that the Victorian poet was 'a great child' and 'So should I have been, but for Beaumont Hamel.* Not before January 1917 did I write the *only lines* of mine that carry the stamp of maturity: these:

But the old happiness is unreturning.
Boys have no grief so grievous as youth's yearning;
Boys have no sadness sadder than our hope.'[46]

In the middle of August, Owen was reading the poems of one of the other patients, Siegfried Sassoon, who had not long been a resident, and to whom he had not yet dared to introduce himself:

I have just been reading Siegfried Sassoon, and am feeling at a very high pitch of emotion. Nothing like his trench life sketches has ever been written or ever will be written. Shakespeare reads vapid after these. Not of course because Sassoon is a greater artist, but because of the subjects, I mean. I think if I had the choice of making friends with

---

* Owen's first taste of action was when he joined the 2nd Manchesters at Beaumont Hamel on the Somme on 22 January 1917 and experienced fierce fighting in bitter cold.

Tennyson or with Sassoon I should go to Sassoon. That is why I have not yet dared to go up to him and parley in a casual way. He is here you know because he wrote a letter to the Higher Command which was too plain-spoken.[47]

Owen had already come a long way from his days as a dreamy adolescent sub-Keatsian poet. He was now ready to write a poetry tempered and validated by what he had known, braced by extreme experience.

Somewhere around 17 August, he screwed up his courage and resolved to call on the great man. He gave no report of that first meeting but it must have been a success because he went back for a second time on the 21st: 'The sun blazed into his room making his purple dressing suit of a brilliance – almost matching my sonnet! He is very tall and stately, with a fine firm chisel'd (how's that?) head, ordinary short brown hair. The general expression of his face is one of boredom.'[48] Sassoon, when Owen found him, was struggling to read a letter from H. G. Wells, who planned to visit him. After leaving him, Owen wrote the poem 'The Dead-Beat', an effective pastiche of Sassoon's bitter satirical style about a soldier who collapses – causing the doctor to say at the end: 'That scum you sent last night soon died.' Sassoon was shown some of Owen's pre-war verse, but 'Some of my old sonnets didn't please him at all . . . So the last thing he said was "Sweat your guts out writing poetry" . . . He also warned me against early publishing: but recommended Martin Secker for a small volume of 10 or 20 poems. He himself is 30! Looks under 25! . . . Sassoon admires Thos. Hardy more than anybody living. I don't think much of what I've read . . . A better mode of life than this present I could not practically manage.'[49]

In fact Owen was so impressed by Sassoon that he tried to interest his father in his work: 'I think this work of Sassoon's will show you to the best possible advantage the tendencies of

Modern Poetry ... There is nothing better this century can offer you.'[50] On Sassoon's side the adulation was a little more muted at first. He describes the meeting above, which took place a couple of weeks after Sassoon's arrival at Craiglockhart, in *Siegfried's Journey* (1945). He was in his room, cleaning his golf clubs, when a young officer knocked on his door with copies of the older poet's latest volume, *The Old Huntsman*, to be signed. Owen appeared at the door, 'short, dark-haired, and shyly hesitant', and the languid Sassoon, whose manner even he himself knew could be offputting (and it must have been especially so to a nervous tiro), received him patronisingly and not a little snobbishly: 'interesting little chap ... perceptibly provincial ... Owing to my habit of avoiding people's faces while talking, I had not observed him closely.'[51]

The meeting was momentous for Owen, as he later told Sassoon, but the latter was slow to recognise his gifts. He criticised Owen's 'over-luscious writing' and the 'embarrassing sweetness in the sentiment of some of his work'.[52] Nonetheless he considered 'Strange Meeting' to be a 'masterpiece ... the finest elegy written by a soldier of that period'. But it was 'Anthem for Doomed Youth' that was the 'revelation'. Sassoon claimed that his only influence on Owen was that 'I stimulated him towards writing with compassionate and challenging realism.' He did, however, record that their relationship quickly blossomed, and he talked of 'the luminous animation of our intimacy'.[53] He came to value Owen's 'unassumingness' and thought that 'in a young man of twenty-four his selflessness was extraordinary ... highly strung and emotional though he was – his whole personality was far more compact and coherent than mine'. In addition, there was the 'velvety quality of his voice'.[54]

By October Sassoon had his own room and Owen visited him every evening until he left at the beginning of November, and this was a great comfort to Sassoon: 'For I was enduring the difficult and distressing experience of making up my mind to withdraw from my "stop the war" attitude and get myself passed for service abroad.'[55] The two poets, as Sassoon put it, 'vowed our confederacy to unmask the ugly face of Mars'.[56] Sassoon also introduced Owen to some influential people in literary London such as Robbie Ross, and he wrote to Robert Graves on 19 October saying, 'His work is very unequal, and you can help him a great deal.'[57]

On Owen's side, the relationship meant much more, as he wrote to a friend: 'A word from Sassoon, though he is not a cheery dog himself, makes me cut capers of pleasure.' He added that except in Sassoon's poems 'you will find nothing so perfectly truthfully descriptive of war'.[58] One night Sassoon called him in to his rooms. He had some more criticism of his poems, and read to his friend what he had written the previous night. Owen called this 'a piece which is the most exquisitely painful war poem of any language or time.* I don't tell him so, or that I am not worthy to light his pipe. I simply sit tight and tell him where I think he goes wrong.'[59] He told his mother that he liked Sassoon

as a man, as a friend, as a poet. The *man* is tall and noble-looking ... He is thirty-one. Let it be thoroughly understood that I nourish no admiration for his nose or any other feature whatever. The *Friend* is intensely sympathetic, with me about every vital question on the planet or off it. He keeps all effusiveness strictly within his pages. In this he is eminently *English* ... We have followed parallel trenches all our lives, and have more friends in common, authors I mean, than most people can boast of in a lifetime.[60]

---

* Unfortunately, it is not possible to identify exactly which poem Sassoon read to Owen on this occasion.

Aside from these encounters, Owen was getting to meet the higher Edinburgh society and doing some teaching at a local school, Tynecastle. He read an article by H. G. Wells in the *Daily Mail* which argued for a 'United States of the World' to prevent future wars and eagerly endorsed it, but added: 'As for myself, I hate washy pacifists as temperamentally as I hate whiskied prussianists. Therefore I feel that I must first get some reputation of gallantry before I could successfully and usefully declare my principles.'[61]

In mid-October 1917, Owen met another poet friend of Sassoon, Robert Graves, who had arrived at Craiglockhart to see his friend. Unfortunately, a sacrosanct round of golf had forced Graves to wait for an audience with Sassoon. 'He is a big, rather plain fellow, the last man on earth apparently capable of the extraordinary, delicate fancies of his books,' thought Owen of Graves.[62] When Sassoon finally emerged he decided to show Owen's poem 'Disabled' to Graves: '& it seems Graves was mightily impressed, and considers me a kind of *Find*!! No thanks, Captain Graves! I'll find myself in due time.'[63] Owen's confidence was clearly growing, helped by Sassoon's increased confidence in him: 'I think it a rather precious exhibition of esteem that S.S. lends me the MSS. of his next book,' he reported.[64] Graves later wrote to him: 'Don't make any mistake, Owen, you are a ___ fine poet already & are going to be more so . . . Puff out your chest a little, and be big for you've more right than most of us . . . You must help S.S. & R.N. [Robert Nichols] & R.G. to revolutionize English Poetry.'[65]

Owen sent to his sister on 16 October the draft of what would become his most famous poem, 'Dulce et Decorum Est', observing, 'Here is a gas poem, done yesterday.'[66] He wrote a further six poems over the course of that week, 'and when I read them to S.S. over a private tea in his room this afternoon, he came round from his first advice of deferred publishing, and said I must hurry up & get what is ready typed. He & his friends will get Heinemann to produce for me. Now it is my judgement alone that I must screw up to printing pitch.'[67]

After Owen left Craiglockhart he wrote to Sassoon from Shrewsbury, where he was visiting his family before returning to the Front, in very physically warm terms:

Know that since mid-September, when you still regarded me as a tiresome little knocker on your door, I held you as Keats+Elijah+my Colonel+my father-confessor+Amernophis IV in profile.

What's that mathematically?

In effect it is this: that I love you, dispassionately, so much, so *very* much, dear Fellow, that the blasting little smile you wear on reading this can't hurt me in the least.

If you consider what the above Names have severally done for me, you will know what you are doing. And you have *fixed* my Life – however short. You did not light me: I was always a mad comet; but I shall swing out soon, a dark star in the orbit where you will blaze. It is some consolation to know that Jupiter himself sometimes swims out of Ken! . . . What I miss in Edinburgh (not Craiglockhart) is the *conviviality* of the Four Boys . . . we loved one another as no men love for long.[68]

In London, before his leave ended, Owen met more literary people, including Arnold Bennett at the Reform Club where he discovered that 'I and my work are a success. I had already sent something to the *Nation* which hasn't appeared yet ['Miners'], but it seems the Editor has started talking of me, and Wells told me he had heard of me through that Editor! H.G.W. said some rare things for my edification, & told me a lot of secrets.'[69] He looked in too at the Poetry Bookshop, and then on 24 November he joined the 5th (Reserve) Battalion, the Manchester Regiment, at Scarborough's Northern Cavalry Barracks.

He was put on light duties as a sort of major domo of the barracks and was touched by the way the men of all ranks showed him unexpected consideration and respect on his return from sick leave. He was still pleased, more widely, at the growing evidence that he was being accepted as a poet and winning the sought-after respect of the dominantly fashionable group, the Georgians: 'They believe in me, these Georgians, and I suffer a temptation to be *satisfied* that they read me; and to remain a poet's poet! . . . I have had some good inspirations in Scarboro', but my need is to revise now, rather than keep piling up "first drafts".'[70] He told his mother that he was 'not dissatisfied' with where his writing career had reached, repeating: 'I go out of this year a Poet, my dear Mother, as which I did not enter it.'[71] Once again there is the faintest echo of Keats's letters in these asseverations.

But that was poetry. The imminent return to the Front was something else. He thought of the previous year 'in a windy tent in the middle of a vast, dreadful encampment' and the 'strange look' on all the faces: 'It was not despair, or terror, it was more terrible than terror, for it was a blindfold look, and without expression, like a dead rabbit's. It will never be painted, and no actor will ever seize it. *And to describe it, I think I must go back and be with them* [my italics].'[72] Like Sassoon, Owen felt that – whatever view he might have of the War and its rights and wrongs – his place was out there alongside his men. In an after-echo of this sentiment, understandably very strong in fighting men, the *Observer* newspaper in July 2009 printed a selection of emails from British soldiers serving at the front line in Helmand province in Afghanistan. One anonymous soldier wrote to his family: 'I really cannot understand why we are here . . . If anything happens to me, don't let them tell people I believed in the mission, because I don't. I am here because I'm a paratrooper. I wanted to test myself in combat and that's the truth.'[73]

After the effective laying-on of hands by the Georgians, Owen became more confident as a poet and at the same time realised how much he was sacrificing to his art by being at war and how he needed concentration in order to write: 'For it is an art, & will need the closest industry. Consider that I spend – what? – three hours a week at it, which means one fruitful half-hour, when I ought to be doing SIX hours a day by all precedents.'[74] He also knew that the art of poetry was one that developed: 'Did Poetry ever stand still? You can hark back if you like, and be deliberately archaic, but don't make yourself a lagoon, salved from the ebbing tide of the Victorian Age ... We Georgians are all so old.'[75] He began to speculate about whether to issue his first collection in spring 1919 and celebrated his first acceptance – by the *Nation*, of the poem 'Miners' – together with the handsome cheque paid for what he claimed was only thirty minutes' work.

At Robert Graves's wedding reception in January 1918 Owen met Max Beerbohm, Sassoon's publisher William Heinemann, and Eddie Marsh. 'I was introduced as "Mr. Owen, Poet" or even "Owen, the poet".'[76] He further claimed, surprisingly perhaps to modern critical eyes, 'I suppose I am doing in poetry what the advanced composers are doing in music. I am not satisfied with either.'[77] When not polishing his self-image as the emerging poet Owen was killing time in Scarborough, going to boxing matches and poking around antique shops, until he was instructed to go to Northern Command Depot at Ripon on 12 March: 'An awful Camp – huts – dirty blankets – in fact WAR once more. Farewell Books, Sonnets, Letters, friends, fires, oysters, antique-shops. Training again!'[78] He was upset by the news of casualties from the second Battle of the Somme and concluded that there was now no prospect of his being demobilised. On the contrary he was trying to get himself fully fit: 'I consider myself completely restituted now from Shell Shock.'[79] He was growing increasingly alarmed at the state of the War:

'The enormity of the present Battle numbs me. Because I perfectly foresaw these days, it was that I said it would have been better to make peace in 1916. Or even last Autumn. It certainly is "impossible" now . . . All the joy of this good weather is for me haunted by the vision of the lands about St. Quentin crawling with wounded . . . Our Staff is execrable . . . I must buck up and get fit!'[80]

On a trip to London from Ripon to see the War Office about a job training cadets, Owen visited publishers and drew the conclusion: 'Judging from my own diffidence, *and* the state of the paper supply a book is not likely to appear before next Spring. I am rather proud – to have got so far on *one* published poem. Almost an unparalleled case, what!'[81] He was learning fast about the literary world but also about his own private sense of literary value. The editor of the *Burlington Magazine* told him it would not be politic to send his poem 'Mental Cases' to the *English Review*. Five years earlier, he knew this would have turned his head, being taken so seriously by editors and drawn into their machinations, 'but nowadays my head turns only in shame away from these first flickers of the limelight. For I am old already for a poet, and so little is yet achieved. And I want no limelight, and celebrity is the last infirmity I desire. *Fame is the recognition of one's peers*. I have already more than their recognition: I have the silent and immortal friendship of Graves and Sassoon and others. Behold are they not already as many Keatses?'[82]

Still he waited in Yorkshire. A ship was torpedoed off Scarborough and only ten lives saved, which prompted a spasm of soldier's anger (identical to the rage of Rupert Brooke) at those at home who did not appreciate the true meaning of the war experience: 'I wish the Bosche would have the pluck to come right in & make a clean sweep of the Pleasure Boats, and the promenaders on the Spa, and all the stinking Leeds & Bradford War-profiteers now reading *John Bull* on Scarborough Sands.'[83]

At the end of August 1918 Owen finally set off for France, to report at base camp at Étaples on the 31st to the 2nd Battalion, the Manchester Regiment, but not before he had enjoyed a brief sensual idyll: 'My last hours in England were brightened by a bathe in the fair green Channel [at Folkestone], in company of the best piece of Nation left in England – a Harrow boy, of superb intellect & refinement, intellect because he detests war more than Germans, and refinement because of the way he spoke of my going away; and the way he spoke of the Sun; and of the Sea, and the Air; and everything. In fact the way he spoke.'[84] He repeated this story archly to Sassoon: 'Moreover there issued from the sea distraction, in the shape, Shape I say, but lay no stress on that, of a Harrow boy.'[85]

After the horrors of the previous year, Owen felt that his return to France this time was going to be 'an amusing little holiday ... nowhere in the universe, and at no time, can I experience anything again like – and – in 1917'.[86] On arrival at Amiens, to serve with the 2nd Manchesters, he was appointed bombing officer to the battalion – though he had to confess 'I know nothing specially about bombs.'[87] He wrote to Sassoon reminding him, 'You said it would be a good thing for my poetry if I went back. That is my consolation for feeling a fool. This is what shells scream at me every time: Haven't you got the wits to keep out of this?'[88]

From 29 September to 3 October Owen was involved in the successful assault on the Beaurevoir–Fonsomme line, and would be awarded the MC for his performance:

I can find no word to qualify my experiences except the word SHEER. (Curiously enough I find the papers talk about sheer fighting!) It passed the limits of my abhorrence. I lost all my earthly faculties, and fought like an angel ... I captured a German Machine Gun and scores of prisoners ...

I only shot one man with my revolver. I have been recommended for the Military Cross; and have recommended
every single N.C.O. who was with me! My nerves are in perfect order. I came out in order to help these boys – directly by
leading them as well as an officer can; indirectly, by watching
their sufferings that I may speak of them as well as a pleader
can. I have done the first . . . The War is nearing an end.[89]

The War may indeed have been nearing its end but there
was no let-up for Owen:

All one day (after the battle) we could not move from a small
trench, though hour by hour the wounded were groaning just
outside. Three stretcher-bearers who got up were hit, one
after one. I had to order no one to show himself after that, but
remembering my own duty, and remembering also my fore-
fathers the agile Welshmen of the Mountains I scrambled out
myself & felt an exhilaration in baffling the Machine Guns
by quick bounds from cover to cover. After the shells we had
been through, and the gas, bullets were like the gentle rain
from heaven.[90]

After the battle, as the boy by his side, shot through the head,
lay on top of him, his blood soaking the poet's shoulder, Owen
admitted: 'My senses are charred. I shall feel again as soon as I
dare, but now I must not. I don't take the cigarette out of my
mouth when I write Deceased over their letters. But one day I
will write Deceased over many books. I'm glad I've been recommended for M.C., & hope I get it, for the confidence it may
give me at home.'[91]

But he still felt that his time on the Somme in 1917 had been
far worse in terms of cold, privation and fatigue, and that nothing now daunted him. He was amused, when censoring a letter,
to read a reference to '"that little officer called Owen who was

at Scarborough" – "he is a *toff* I can tell you. No na-poo. Compree?" Interpreted: "a fine fellow, no nonsense about him".'[92]

On the night of the official news of the German 'acceptance' of peace terms everyone celebrated and Owen even discovered he could sing – though he was deeply saddened to learn the news from home that Robbie Ross had died. Reading in *The Times* of the break-up of the Austro-Hungarian Dual Monarchy really did make him think that at last the guns were to be silenced. But life in the trenches went on. He was amused at the jealousy his fluency in French aroused amongst the men when he chatted to two French girls, telling Sassoon, 'The dramatic irony was too killing, considering certain other things, not possible to tell in a letter.'[93] He claimed that in the villages exposed by the German retreat there was no evidence of German atrocities and that the girls were treated with respect, all the serious damage having been caused by British guns. Learning that five healthy girls had died of fright in one night of shelling he was unusually vocal in his anger: 'The people in England and France who thwarted a peaceable retirement of the enemy from these areas are therefore now sacrificing aged French peasants and charming French children to our guns. Shells made by women in Birmingham are at this moment burying little children alive not very far from here.'[94]

On 31 October, Owen wrote what was to be his last letter home, to his mother: 'It is a great life. I am more oblivious than alas! yourself, dear Mother, of the ghastly glimmering of the guns outside, & the hollow crashing of the shells. There is no danger down here, or if any, it will be well over before you read these lines. I hope you are as warm as I am; as serene in your room as I am here; and that you think of me never in bed as resignedly as I think of you always in bed. Of this I am certain, you could not be visited by a band of friends half so fine as surround me here.'[95]

A few days later, on 4 November, the Battalion prepared for an attack across the Oise–Sambre Canal at Ors where the enemy was ranged on the eastern side of the canal and where casualties were likely to be high. At dawn the two leading Manchester companies, of which Owen's was one, launched their attack, which would depend on surprise and superior fire and entail an attempt to span the canal by launching rafts to make a bridge under heavy fire and secure the opposite bank. Many were lost in this operation and, while leading his men, seemingly afloat on a raft, Owen was hit by a sniper's bullet and killed instantly.

Seven days later the Armistice was signed and, on that day, 11 November, the bells were ringing in Shrewsbury when his parents received the telegram with news of his death.

It was not until 1921 that Owen's poems were first published, with an introduction by Siegfried Sassoon in which he claimed that they were

> backed by the authority of Owen's experience as an infantry soldier, and sustained by nobility and originality of style . . . His conclusions about War are so entirely in accordance with my own that I cannot attempt to judge his work with any critical detachment. I can only affirm that he was a man of absolute integrity of mind. He never wrote his poems (as so many war-poets did) to make the effect of a personal gesture. He pitied others; he did not pity himself. In the last year of his life he attained a clear vision of what he needed to say, and these poems survive him as his true and splendid testament.[96]

Among Owen's papers was the famous preface (quoted in the Prologue, p. 7), which indicates how he himself interpreted the role of 'war poet'. The 'anti-war' note was not sounded in his poetry until he had reached Craiglockhart and made the acquaintance of Sassoon, and what we read today is largely the work of two years at most.

The first 'war poem', 'Has Your Soul Sipped?', is about the death of a young boy. Here the real event has stiffened and focused the verse. The shock of the directness of the phrase 'On a boy's murdered mouth' emphasises his innocence ('no threat/ On his lips') and makes 'murder' for the first time part of the lexicon of English war poetry. The influence of Sassoon was immediate and very quickly Owen had abandoned the archaic diction of his juvenilia and discovered how to use colloquial dialogue in a poem. Few as these poems are, a substantial number, like the powerful sonnet 'Anthem for Doomed Youth', have become classic anthology pieces and will be familiar to readers. In 'I Saw His Round Mouth's Crimson' he achieves an effective analogy between the dying man and a sunset, the sensuousness of the verse in tension with the truth-telling imperative, true to the purported wish in the preface to avoid the capitalised notion of 'Poetry' in the interests of conveying the reality of war, and the poet's duty to warn.

At their best when most ambivalent, poems like 'Strange Meeting' are the most affecting. In that poem, in another subterranean excursion, this time to Hell, the poet in a dream encounters another ('I am the enemy you killed, my friend') who may have now escaped the war, but who has the 'undone years' to regret as well as 'the truth untold,/ The pity of war, the pity war distilled'. He is a German. They lost the chance, both of them, to tell the truth about the pity of war, the poem seems to say, and so they died and lived in vain. Another much anthologised poem, 'Futility', reverses Julian Grenfell's 'Into Battle' by showing how the sun's renewing force is negated by war, where Grenfell saw natural processes as moving hand in hand with the valiant warrior's fighting spirit. Others are harsher, more angry, like 'Mental Cases' which shows the full horror of the shell-shocked: 'Pawing us who dealt them war and madness'. Or 'The Send-Off', a sombre poem about the send-off with flowers, from England, of soldiers whose return, if there is indeed a return, will be muted, for they 'May creep back, silent, to village wells'.

Graves greatly admired the poem 'Disabled', about a man who lost his legs and an arm in action and is now back from a conflict in which camaraderie was stronger than any hatred of Germans: 'Some cheered him home, but not as crowds cheer Goal.' In 'A Terre', a monologue by a wounded soldier, the poet is represented as being akin to a journalist or war reporter: '"My glorious ribbons? – Ripped from my own back/ In scarlet shreds. (That's for your poetry book.)"' In 'Exposure', Owen paints a very spare picture of war's futility but also includes a stanza that achieves a more ambivalent tone:

Since we believe not otherwise can kind fires burn . . .
Therefore, not loath, we lie out here; therefore were born,
For love of God seems dying.

Just as the preface made a virtue of witness – as opposed either to aestheticising or polemic – so the best of Owen's poems draw their primary strength from their authenticity of feeling and perception of war's actuality. They are poems of their unique historical moment and for that reason will always be read as a means of understanding these crucial years of conflict.

The third member of the Craiglockhart group of poets was Robert Graves whose 1929 autobiography *Goodbye to All That* is one of the best prose memoirs of the War – sharper and wittier than Sassoon and richer in specific detail and anecdote. No one, for example, has given a better description of No Man's Land:

I looked at the German trenches through a periscope – a distant streak of sandbags. Some of these were made of coloured cloth, whether for camouflage or from a shortage of plain sacking, I do not know. The enemy gave no sign, except for a wisp or two of wood-smoke where they, too, were boiling up a hot drink. Between us and them lay a flat meadow with cornflowers, marguerites, and poppies growing in the long grass, a few shell holes, the bushes I had seen the night before, the wreck of an aeroplane, our barbed wire and theirs. Three-quarters of a mile away stood a big ruined house; a quarter of a mile behind that, a red-brick village – Auchy – poplars and haystacks, a tall chimney, and another village – Haisnes. Half-right, pit-head and smaller slag heaps. La Bassée lay half-left; the sun caught the weather-vane of the church and made it twinkle.[97]

Graves's specifically war poetry is not extensive, though he had the opportunity, like Sassoon, to reflect and look back on his war experience. Surviving until 1985, Graves seems not to have wished, understandably, to be forever categorised as 'war poet' and his writing career blossomed in many different directions in the decades after the War. He also distanced himself from his war poetry.

Like the veterans of the War, the last of whom died while the current book was being written, Graves was a great survivor whose image, setting aside the popular historical novels that are perhaps his most-read work now, was of a kind of shamanistic poet-sage, a self-mythologiser, a votary of the White Goddess, and a lover of women. He was also a controversialist in his dismissal of many of the poets thought to be the leading figures of his epoch and, in the end, became an increasingly isolated figure, as is inevitable to some extent when one has survived so long.

Born in 1895 in Wimbledon in Surrey[98] to an Irish father and a German mother, Robert von Ranke Graves was brought up in a literary and artistic ambience – his father was a poet – but also in a very orthodox religious atmosphere, which was waiting to be kicked against by the growing young poet. He was educated at various preparatory schools before entering Charterhouse in 1909. He would remain there until he joined the Army in 1914.

A crucial encounter for the sixteen-year-old Graves was with Edward Marsh when the latter visited a friend at Charterhouse in 1912. When Marsh later began to compile the Georgian anthologies the precocious poet was consulted – and in exchange Marsh criticised his early poems, pointing out, for example, their outworn poetic vocabulary. Graves would write to him again from the Royal Welch regimental depot in Wrexham in January 1915, thoroughly bored, to ask him what he thought of his newest verses: 'Be as cruel as you like as I wrote them here where lack of criticism leaves me in doubt of their worth . . . I have bought Rupert Brooke's *Poems* of which I had only seen a very few before: I think he is really good. What a torture his sensitiveness must always be for him, poor fellow!'[99] He accepted that he was still under the influence of Victorian models but declared: 'However, I am still in my teens and when this ridiculous war is over, I will write Chapter II at the top of the new sheet and with the help of other young Georgians to whom I trust you will introduce me, will try to root out more effectively the obnoxious survivals of Victorianism . . . Well, *au revoir*, till after the War, if the Gods are kind: I know I am a prig but three years' misery at Charterhouse drove me into it, and I am as keen as you for the regeneration of poetry.'[100]

Goodbye to All That begins in May 1915 when Graves first arrived in France, and his first letters to Marsh are full of the same witty and carefree spirit. His first experience of the trenches involved a 'violent artillery duel going on above my dug-out' which failed to wake him – but 'a very persistent lark' did:

I feel here exactly like a man who has watched the 'Movies'
for a long evening and then suddenly finds himself thrown on
the screen in the middle of scalp-hunting Sioux and runaway
motor cars: and rather surprised that I am not at all frightened, and that the noise doesn't disturb me at all yet . . . So
far I have been let down very lightly but of course no one
expects to dodge everything and the best I can hope for is to
'do the Blighty touch', i.e. get a wound serious enough to
qualify me for England. There are three touches: the Base
Touch, the Blighty Touch and the Six-foot Touch (*absit
omen*). It's hard to know if you're alive or dead with Busy
Berthas booming over head.[101]

In September Graves took part in the Loos offensive and,
although he felt keenly the lack of congenial intellectual company, he persisted in his passion for poetry and, shortly after
being gazetted as a special reserve captain and transferred to
the 1st Battalion at Locon, near Cambrin in the Pas-de-Calais,
he met Siegfried Sassoon, who had just arrived in France.
They were not at first very keen on each other's poetry. Graves
thought Sassoon's work a bit 'eighteen ninetyish' and Sassoon
for his part warned Graves that 'war should not be written about
in such a realistic way'.[102] Graves told him that he would soon
learn. He was just discovering the work of Charles Hamilton
Sorley and much later concluded that Sorley, Isaac Rosenberg
and Owen were the three most important poets to be killed
in the War. The latest *Georgian Poetry* anthology had been
published in November 1915 and for Graves it was 'perhaps
the most treasured possession I have out here'.[103] He loved
nearly everything in it, he told Marsh, with the exception of
Gordon Bottomley.

At Fricourt on the Somme in March 1916 he was back in the
trenches, and it is clear that he never shared quite the same attitude to the War as his fellow poets:

It's rather trying, having to go back into trenches after a three months' holiday . . . there are a lot of new terrors since last December. The *spécialité* here is 'canisters', round, tin, barrel-shaped trench-mortars filled with about twenty pounds of the highest explosive. About ten or twelve times as much stuff is handed round now than when I first came out, but I always enjoy trenches in a way, I must confess: I like feeling really frightened and if happiness consists in being miserable in a good cause, why then I'm doubly happy. England's is a good cause enough and the trenches are splendidly miserable: my company firing-line averages 30 yards from the Bosches, the mud is *chronic*, there are few parts of the trench where one can stand upright without exposing oneself, and not a single canister-proof dug-out. If only it was blowing sleet and a gas attack was due tomorrow my cup of happiness would be full.[104]

Graves now found that Sassoon's verses were getting better than the first crop he saw, much freer and more 'Georgian' as he put it: 'What a pity he didn't start earlier! I suspect [Edmund] Gosse of being his retarding influence – "keeping me to my moons and nightingales and things," as S.S. put it himself yesterday.'[105] It was difficult, however, for the two poets to talk about poetry together because the other officers became curious and suspicious. They had to pretend to be swapping recipes for rum punch rather than discussing verse technique in order to avoid being thought odd for not concentrating on the proper topic of smut.

Soon Graves was separated from Sassoon by having to have a nose operation (as the result of a boxing injury), which sent him back to England and convalescence at Harlech. While he was there his first book of poems, *Over the Brazier*, was published – luckily for him, because high paper costs since the War were causing many such books to be postponed. Graves felt depressed at being separated from his fellows and guilty at sitting in a small white-walled Merionethshire cottage at 'an especially nice small round beechwood table'[106] writing poems. He was still in his transient public-school homosexual phase (he later called it 'pseudo-homosexual') and exchanged gossip with Sassoon about Sorley, asking if that poet had been, as he put it gnomically, 'so'. Graves concluded that he must have been because he had reached the age of twenty without penning any conventional love lyrics.

Towards the end of May, Graves's poetic interlude was over and he was back with the Royal Welch in camp at The Huts, Litherland, which he found boring and squalid, preferring instead the prospect of the trenches. His Charterhouse friend Peter Johnstone had now been banned from speaking to him after his mother found some compromising letters: 'so I am now widowed, laid waste and desolate'. Peter said in his last letter 'he'd never forget me'.[107]

Graves was then sent to France in time for the Somme offensive on 1 July and on the 20th he was so badly wounded in the attack on High Wood that he was mistakenly reported dead. He had been hit by a shell fragment while his company was retreating from a barrage and he describes the incident in *Goodbye to All That*: 'I heard the explosion, and felt as though I had been punched rather hard between the shoulder-blades, but without any pain. I took the punch merely for the shock of the explosion; but blood trickled into my eye and, turning faint, I called to Moodie: "I've been hit." Then I fell.'[108] He was taken to a disused German dressing station in Mametz Wood to be left to die and his name was entered in the official casualty list and a letter of condolence written. In fact, he survived the night in extreme pain and was taken to hospital in an excruciating train journey to Rouen. The wounds turned out to be mostly superficial except for some damage to the right lung.

Graves was sent back to England to recover and, a little later,

Sassoon was sent back with lung trouble so the two had the chance to convalesce together at Harlech before reporting back to Litherland in November, where they shared a hut. Graves was very impressed with Sassoon's daring exploits, which earned him the nickname 'Mad Jack' from his comrades. He told the poet Robert Nichols that Sassoon was 'a most extraordinary good man ... and says what he means very courageously. No Union Jack flapping or sword waving, but just a picture of France from the front trench and our "brutal and licentious soldiery". He's not musical, always, but it's good stuff, original too and not redolent of Masefield as is so common these days and contains no ode either to Kitchener or Rupert Brooke.'[109] Graves was slow to recuperate, and his long periods of convalescence in England and Wales made him think guiltily of Sassoon and others. In March 1917, after returning from France yet again, he wrote to Sassoon, telling him that he had been to Oxford where he had seen 'a lot of the Garsington people who were charming to me, and of the young Oxford poets, Aldous Huxley, Wilfred Childe and Thomas Earp – exceptionally nice people but a trifle decayed, as you might say'.[110] He was also in London, seeing 'the Half Moon Street set', but was glad to get back to 'good old Cymraeg [Wales]'. He hoped to get a job as instructor in No. 4 Officer Cadet Battalion in Oxford.

He told Sassoon he was looking forward to his book of poems, *The Old Huntsman*: 'I don't see why it shouldn't be awfully successful, with all the reviewers and literary patrons squared.'[111] Graves was very shrewd about literary politics and claimed to have got to the people who mattered for the reception of the book. It was unlikely now that he would go back to France for a fourth time, given the state of his health, 'and if it wasn't for you being out there again I'd feel this was too good to be true'. Graves was making frequent visits to 'Lady Utterly Immoral' at Garsington and comparing notes with Sassoon on how much they got for their poems. Thirty shillings was the going rate on the well-paying *Nation*, 'i.e. 3 shillings a line, pretty good going'.[112]

Graves, however, was starting to get worried about Sassoon's attitude to the War: 'I want to know what characteristic devilment this is. Are you standing as pacifist M.P.? That's the most characteristic thing I can think of next to your bombing Lloyd George.'[113] But when Sassoon eventually made his protest statement on 30 July Graves told him he was 'magnificently courageous'. At the same time, though, he believed he couldn't physically endure court martial and imprisonment, and the gesture was futile as no one in either country would follow his example. He wrote to Eddie Marsh, suggesting that he might have been able to prevent it had he known in advance what Sassoon proposed to do and say:

About Sassons first. It's an awful thing – completely mad – that he's done. Such rotten luck on you and me and his friends, especially in the Regiment. They all think he's mad: and they'd be prepared to hush it up if the Army Council don't get to hear of the bomb shop incident,* but I don't think S.S. will let them hush it up. I don't know what on earth to do now. I'm not going to quarrel with Sassons: I'm so glad you realize that he's not a criminal which was the line I was afraid you'd take. Personally I think he's quite right in his views but absolutely wrong in his action . . . It would be true friendship for me to heap coals of fire on the head of the dog that bit me by turning pacifist myself but you can be quite assured that I'm a sound militarist in action however much of a pacifist in thought. In theory the War ought to

---

* Francis Meynell at the Pelican Press had printed the statement, which was distributed from Henderson's bookshop in Charing Cross Road – known as 'the bomb shop' for its stock of peace propaganda.

stop tomorrow if not sooner. Actually we'll have to go on
while a rat or a dog remains to be enlisted and the remains
of the famous Kilkenny cats will look nothing remarkably
small compared with ours . . . This S.S. business has taken
me at a very bad time, nervous breakdown, and again today
the worst possible news about my friend Peter who appears
to have taken a very wrong turning and to have had a mental
breakdown. I only wish I'd known about S.S. in time: it
would never have happened if I'd been there but I've not
seen him since January.[114]

Graves's mood was darkened further by the news that Peter
Johnstone had been caught propositioning a Canadian corporal
stationed near Charterhouse, an occurrence that so deeply
shocked Graves it appears to have at a stroke terminated the
'pseudo-homosexuality' of his Charterhouse days. He nonetheless pulled himself together and wrote to Litherland asking
the colonel to be sympathetic to Sassoon. He also wrote to his
old friend Evan Morgan, private secretary to the Minister of
Labour, to persuade the War Office not to press the matter
of a disciplinary case but instead to give him a medical board.
'I've smoothed it all down,' he reported to Marsh, 'and he's
going away cheerfully to a home at Edinboro'. I've written to
the pacifists who were to support him telling them that the
evidence as to his mental condition given at his Medical Board
is quite enough to make them look damned silly if they go
on with the game and ask questions in the House about his
defiance. I'm quite knocked up.'[115]

Graves, who attended the Board, had actually been in a nervous state, breaking down three times in tears while giving his
statement and being told he ought to be before the Board himself. He was supposed to be Sassoon's escort but he missed the
train and Sassoon reported to Craiglockhart without him. Later,
he told Sassoon:

Well, you are notorious throughout England now you silly old thing! Everybody here who's been to France agrees with your point of view, but those that don't know you think it was not quite a gentlemanly course to take: the 'quixotic-English-sportsman' class especially. But you have accomplished something I suppose. Now that you have been immortalized in the columns of the *Daily Mail* and *The Times* I suppose strings of newspaper reporters are surging round the doors of Craiglockhart and the inmates seething within? What a ridiculous business! I hope it won't injure your poetry: and that old Gosse won't think better of celebrating his protégé in the *Edinburgh Review*.[116]

The one good thing about Craiglockhart was that Sassoon was writing again:

Stick to it and show me something good before New Year. Try, now you've got such good clarity of expression, to cut down the slang as much as possible: personally I don't mind because I know what you're at, but one or two people have not been overcome by the 'Dead Officer' as it ought to make them, because they've been put in the wrong mood by the telephone metaphor – the ideal is to use common and simple words which everyone can understand and yet not set up a complex by such vulgarities but to make the plain words do the work of the coloured ones – badly put, still.[117]

Graves also tried to defend himself against Sassoon's charge that he was more interested in 'good form' than in supporting his friend's principled protest. Graves insisted that the ordinary soldiers, 'who are the exact people whom you wish to influence and save by all your powers', would think that changing his mind 'in the middle of the war, after having made a definite contract', was bad form:

You can only command their respect by sharing all their miseries as far as you possibly can, being ready for pride's sake to finish your contract whatever it costs you, yet all the time denouncing the principles you are being compelled to further. God knows you have 'done your bit' as they say, but I believe in giving everything. Thus you'll be able to do more good both now and after the war than anything you are likely to do through your present means . . . Sorry you think that of me – I should hate to think I'm a coward. I believe though in keeping to agreements when everybody else keeps them and if I find myself party to principles I don't quite like, in biding my time till I have a sporting chance of rearranging things . . . Your conscience is too nice in its discernment between conflicting forces . . . But as you say, I wish to God our people could state definite peace terms.[118]

Graves tried to lighten things by reporting a meeting with a bomber, on leave from Passchendaele, who said that 'Mr Sarson [sic] never got the wind-up . . . we'd follow him anywhere. It's different with an officer like that somehow: we could trust him.'[119]

And then, in a letter to Robert Nichols, a close friend now and a poet he greatly admired, Graves revealed: 'I think I have found a new poet as yet unfledged. One Owen, subaltern in the 2nd Manchester Regiment.'[120] Owen attended Graves's marriage to Nancy Nicholson on 23 January 1918 at St James's, Piccadilly, the occasion described amusingly (though tinged with some retrospective score-settling) in *Goodbye to All That*. It was a very society occasion and the reception afterwards at Nancy's studio at Apple Tree Yard, St James's, was attended by senior publishers, smart friends of Nancy's parents, and the poet Harold Monro. Sassoon was unable to be present, though this might have been a tactical absence to show disapproval of Graves's enthusiastic adoption of heterosexuality. Certainly there was a *froideur* of some kind between them. Edward Marsh and Robbie Ross, however, turned up to make up for Sassoon. A lot of champagne flowed and Mrs Graves took a breath when her new daughter-in-law walked into the reception wearing breeches and a smock with a red scarf around her neck.

Graves would not now fight again because of his poor health and in the early months of 1918 he worried about Sassoon, in Palestine now, fearing that his friend might not live to see the young couple's new child, due at the end of the year. But whether from marital happiness or neglect he failed to keep up correspondence with Sassoon for several months, which provoked a disgruntled protest from his fellow poet. Sassoon also implied that Graves's poetry was going soft. Graves countered:

Old boy do you want me to stop writing altogether? I can't write otherwise than I am now except with hypocrisy for I am bloody happy and bloody young (with only very occasional lapses) and passionate anger is most ungrateful. And I can't afford to stop in these penurious days and anyhow my 'antique silk and flower brocade' continue to please the seventeen-year-old girls and other romantics for whom they are intended: and why not? Worrying about the war is no longer a sacred duty with me: on the contrary, neither my position as a cadet instructor nor my family duties permit it. I am no longer fit to fight and I am out to get as healthy as possible for the good I can do in England. Curse me to hell: I shall hate it: but I must be honest according to my lights however dim they have grown. As [J. C.] Squire said in his last review of you, you seem to think that there are more people who love War than there really are in this fifth year of war with our 3½ million casualty list. And poetry shouldn't be all propaganda because a war is on.[121]

That last remark of Graves seems hard to quarrel with, and his own war poetry is certainly less propagandist than that of most of his contemporaries. One of his earliest poems of war, written in July 1915 when he was only twenty, is called 'Big Words'. A young soldier finds

> a faith in the wisdom of God's ways
> That once I lost, finding it justified
> Even in this chaos

and is prepared to die, but the poem's concluding couplet signals an abrupt change of mood:

> But on the firestep, waiting to attack,
> He cursed, prayed, sweated, wished the proud words
>   back.[122]

A year later he wrote at the Front a grimmer poem, 'A Dead Boche', about coming across a German corpse in Mametz Wood (also described in *Goodbye to All That*). The horrifying physicality of the description of the corpse is offered as 'A certain cure for lust of blood'.[123] Also in late 1916, he wrote 'Goliath and David', dedicated to Sassoon's lover David Thomas, who was killed at Fricourt in March 1916. It suggests that the young boy, loved both by Sassoon and by Graves, was brave but vulnerable in an unequal contest, and it ends with Goliath in the shape of a German soldier 'spike-helmeted, grey, grim' straddling his young victim.[124] A slightly later poem, 'The Legion', reflects Graves's pride in his regiment, the Royal Welch, who are here compared with Caesar's troops in Gaul, waging war against the barbarians. It implies that the present-day troops are 'slovenly' and lack the imperial discipline of the Roman legions, but the struggle is the same.[125] His poem 'Two Fusiliers' is about himself and Sassoon, both invalided home in the spring of 1917, the pair uniquely bound together by their experience of conflict, 'the wet bond of blood', and through facing death:

> we faced him, and we found
> Beauty in Death
> In dead men breath.[126]

Neither Sassoon nor Owen, one feels, could have written in that way. After the War, Graves continued to write about the experience and one of his retrospects, written in 1920, 'Haunted', as its title suggests, is about seeming to meet the ghosts of long-lost comrades in the street, the guilt of the survivor: 'Dead, long dead, I'm ashamed to greet/ Dead men down the morning street.'[127]

After demobilisation in 1919 Graves went to St John's College, Oxford, to read English but, struggling with recurring bouts of shell-shock and the difficulty of making ends meet, he failed to complete the degree – though he subsequently garnered a B.Litt, in 1925, after which he took up a post as professor of English literature at Cairo University. Here his relationship with the American poet Laura Riding developed and became crucial, through her criticism, to his subsequent career. In 1929 he and Laura moved to Majorca and he started to write the popular *Claudius* novels. The Spanish Civil War disrupted this sojourn but he was back after the Second World War and wrote there his most original work, *The White Goddess* (1948). He lectured and wrote about poets as well as continuing to write his own poetry and from 1961 to 1966 was Oxford Professor of Poetry. By the time he died in 1985 he had published more than 135 books, but the last ten years were difficult and dependent. He is buried in the churchyard of Deyá in Majorca.

5

Transcripts of the Battlefields:
Isaac Rosenberg

I never joined the army for patriotic reasons. Nothing can
justify war. I suppose we must all fight to get the trouble
over.[1]

ISAAC ROSENBERG

The best single poem of the First World War, in my view, is
Isaac Rosenberg's 'Break of Day in the Trenches'.[2] Of all the
poets considered in this book Rosenberg is the most 'anti-war'
in personal disposition, yet his poetry is neither satirical nor sen-
tentiously anti-war in the manner of the more famous anthology
pieces. It merely reflects what he saw and felt, and his fine
poem derives its strength from a subtle balance of wry observation with poised acceptance of things as they are. An ordinary
soldier, not an officer like so many of the other poets,
Rosenberg had a rougher war than Sassoon or Owen, doing
manual work such as unloading wire in the middle of the night
for which, as an 'artist and poet' – as he is described simply on
his tomb in the little British war cemetery at the corner of a flat
field on the outskirts of Arras – he was clumsily ill suited.

The poem begins at dawn with the observation that the only live thing apart from himself stirring is a 'queer sardonic rat'. The poet makes a light gesture of plucking a poppy from the parapet to stick behind his ear. The poppy gains extra symbolic force when the poem is read immediately after its predecessor, 'In the Trenches', which describes the poet taking two poppies and giving one to his companion who is killed while Rosenberg escapes:

> I am choked . . . safe . . . dust blind – I
> See trench floor poppies
> Strewn. Smashed you lie.[3]

In the second poem the poet addresses the rat (like the ubiquitous lice, an omnipresent curse of trench life) as 'Droll rat' whom 'they would shoot' if his 'cosmopolitan sympathies' were known. The ambiguity of 'they' (which side?) subtly suggests the indiscriminate nature of war's slaughter, and the cancelled line immediately following (deleted after its first magazine publication) which we can read in the drafts – 'And God knows what antipathies' – reinforces the point. The poet's decision to delete the line perhaps flowed from his reluctance to be too obvious here. The simple, sensual immediacy of the lines 'Now you have touched this English hand/ You will do the same to a German' after the rat has crossed 'the sleeping green' of No Man's Land, draws attention to the queer human intimacy of trench warfare. The rat, seen as 'droll', 'sardonic', prone to 'inwardly grin', is proxy for the dispassionate observer of war who struggles to see sense in the universal slaughter of those who are

> Bonds to the whims of murder,
> Sprawled in the bowels of the earth
> The torn fields of France.

The poet interrogates that witness, demanding to know what he sees in the eyes of the contending armies: 'At the shrieking iron and flame/ Hurled through still heavens?' Poppies – and Rosenberg could not have known the powerfully expressive iconic future that lay in wait for that flower as a symbol of the battlefields of Flanders – are said to have 'their roots in man's veins', blood-red. Like the fallen soldiers, they 'Drop, and are ever dropping'. The closing lines express Rosenberg's sense that he has witnessed these things through the eyes of his droll, neutral observer and can simply say that he is here, unillusioned, humanely sentient, able to survive a little longer than those other poppies (less than two years, as it turned out), and able to add nothing more in the way of judgement or condemnation:

> But mine in my ear is safe –
> Just a little white with the dust.[4]

Rosenberg's poem was written in June 1916 and carefully dated by him in his typescript. It was a week or two before the beginning of the Somme offensive. A couple of months earlier, a regular critic of German literature, Alec Randall, was writing in *The Egoist* about contemporary German poetry in a piece headed 'Poetry and Patriotism':

> Some misguided people, I believe, still hold that war is a good thing for the arts; even this machine-made, absolutely unromantic war has not convinced them of the contrary. They may still be found writing to *The Times* letters full of panegyric nonsense on young heroes such as Rupert Brooke, whose death was a far greater poem than his life. And the same letters almost invariably conclude with remarks on Prussian militarism, as if the two attitudes were not in every respect alike. The German militarist is a man

who has exalted war into a thing of beauty, whereas nine people out of every ten in this country believe it to be in its essentials an unmitigated horror or, at least, a very regrettable necessity.[5]

Randall went on to report that a German critic had claimed that during August 1914 about 50,000 poems a day were written and that during the first twelve months about 600,000 were notched up. He went on: 'The poets who have been to the war are better, if less patriotic in the usual sense. War-patriotism is proved to be a very barren emotion, unless brought into relation with the "grim realities". Then some approach to true art may be looked for.' He reported that some young German poets 'have been producing work of greater poetic value than most of the romantic, easy, oratorical efforts of stay-at-homes', and certain poets such as Stefan George 'have done good work, not by writing reams of patriotic poetry, but by maintaining the international and essentially peaceful character of all true art'. He went on to say that 'all art, should be regarded as superior to national quarrels, and so they continue, in the face of much unpopularity, in their work of reconstruction. And in this work shall we not wish them well?'

In December, the month that 'Break of Day in the Trenches' was published in *Poetry* magazine in Chicago, *The Egoist* returned to the theme of war poetry with a piece by John Gould Fletcher headed 'On Subject-matter and War Poetry'. Fletcher began with a defence of the Imagists against the charge that their poems were not 'about' anything: 'it is not the subject which is important, for it may be only a trifle, it is the emotion contained in that trifle which is important'.[6] He identified the key question for war poetry at the end of the second year of the conflict as being: 'Has a poet a right to make use of the war as a subject? And if so, how should it be treated?' He answered:

The fact is, that no artist creates his subject-matter. The trouble why most poems that have been written on this war are so hopelessly banal is due to the wave of national hysteria which struck Europe at the outset and which is now just slackening. The poets devoted themselves to giving the Allies laurels and the Germans a black eye, or the reverse, as the case might be, never pausing to reflect that the war might have some significance beyond the mere question of which side was going to win, and that with some slight changes of uniform and colour, the same scenes of drilling and leave-taking etc. were taking place in both Berlin and London. Now with another winter campaign facing us and no definite conclusion in sight, with Mr. Lloyd George and [Field Marshal] Sir William Robertson both declaring that no one can predict how much longer it may take, it is time that some one seriously took up in poetry the issue of the war – not of one side or the other, but of the whole business – or of such part thereof as he has access to. Mr. [Charles] Nevinson has already done an efficient and workmanlike job in his pictures, of giving us feelings, emotions concerning war; now why should not a poet try his hand at the same thing, pray? I do not despair of seeing some decent war poetry in the English language, some poetry that puts the reader face to face with the imaged reality, perplexing, horrible, and yet at times curiously beautiful. So far this poetry has not yet made its appearance – we must go to prose to find out what the war is like, or else swallow the soothing syrups of Masefield's 'August 1914', or Brooke's *Sonnets* – charming soothing syrups but not within a million miles of the stern crushing reality. Whatever way we look at it, the need for good war poetry is more acute now than ever. For if war is of any use, we must understand what war is like before making use of it. And if wars are useless and should be abolished it is again for the poet to show why. This is why it seems to me that it is reserved for some Imagist or the other to write (if the censor doesn't interfere) the only straightforward and truly honest views of this war we are ever likely to possess.

Rosenberg's poem surely met the demand for 'poetry that puts the reader face to face with the imaged reality, perplexing, horrible, and yet at times curiously beautiful'.

By this crucial point, late 1916, many anthologies of war poetry had appeared. The most notable, published in September 1916, was edited by Galloway Kyle and issued under the aegis of the *Poetry Review*. 'I think the writers should be hung, or the Editor rather. They may be good soldiers but they're poor poets,'[7] thought Rosenberg of this periodical. The *Poetry Review* anthology, *Soldier Poets: Songs of the Fighting Men*, was so popular that it was reissued in November and December and was also made available in a 'trench edition'; and Erskine MacDonald, the publisher (actually Kyle using a pseudonym), was described by the periodical *London Opinion* as 'the unofficial publisher in general to the poets of the British Army'. According to the editor, the poems 'define, record and illustrate the aspirations, emotions, impressions and experiences of men of all ranks and branches of the Army, and they reveal a unity of spirit, of exultant sincerity and unconquerable idealism that makes the reader very proud and very humble'.[8] He added that these were 'essentially war poems, revealing the soul of the soldier going into battle', and that the whole volume 'represents the soldier as poet rather than the poet as soldier'. He claimed that most of the poets had been serving since the outbreak of war, rather than being reluctant recent conscripts, with the result that 'The note of pessimism and decadence is absent, together with the flamboyant and the hectic, the morose and the mawkish. The soldier poets leave the maudlin and the mock-heroic, the gruesome and fearful handling of Death and his allies to the neurotic civilian who stayed behind to gloat on imagined horrors and inconveniences, and anticipate the uncomfortable demise of friends.' Warming to his theme, Kyle continued:

> When the history of these tremendous times comes to be written, the poetry of the period will be found to be an illuminating index and memorial. And the historian will be least able to neglect the poetry of the camp and the battlefield, which reflects the temper and experiences of our great citizen army. The spirit that has turned our soldiers into poets is the spirit of the V.C. – brave and debonair, but neither melancholy nor mad . . . the braver spirits were shocked into poetry and like the larks are heard between the roaring of the guns – the articulate voices of millions of fighting men, giving to poetry a new value and significance.

Scores of slim volumes from men in the Army had been gutted to fill the new anthology, and a typical poem would be this by Rifleman S. Donald Cox CLR, London Rifle Brigade:

To My Mother – 1916
If I should fall, grieve not that one so weak
   And poor as I
   Should die.
Nay! though thy heart should break
Think only this: that when at dusk they speak
   Of sons and brothers of another one,
Then thou canst say – 'I too had a son;
   He died for England's sake!'

Also available were volumes such as *The Day of Battle: An Epic of the War* by Arthur Thrush, priced at one shilling.

The *Poetry Review* anthology was so successful that in December 1917 *More Songs by the Fighting Men* (Soldier Poets:

Second Series) appeared. The publishers this time declared: 'The national spirit would be fortified if every adult and every adolescent were acquainted with this book. Order it now and see that every friend and every school knows about it. A big Public School edition is in preparation.' The same year saw the publication by John Murray of *The Muse in Arms: A collection of war poems, for the most part written in the field of action, by seamen, soldiers, and flying men who are serving, or have served, in the great war.* The editor, E. B. Osborn, determined to present a heroic conception of war poetry, explained:

> The object of this Anthology is to show what passes in the British warrior's soul when, in moments of aspiration or inspiration, before or after action or in the busy days of self-preparation for self-sacrifice, he has glimpses of the ultimate significance of warfare. To some extent the selection (which can claim to be fairly representative of the verses written by those who are serving, or have served, in the present world-war) presents a picture of the visible imagery of battle as mirrored in his mind. As such it illustrates his singular capacity for remembering the splendour and forgetting the squalor of the dreadful vocation in which he was so suddenly engaged – a capacity at the root of that infinite cheerfulness which was such a priceless military asset in the early days of disillusion and disaster.

Writing after the Somme, Osborn ignored the poems of disillusion (publishing Brooke, Robert Nichols, Gurney, Grenfell, Graves, early Sassoon, Sorley, but not Owen) and praised the 'open and sunny joyousness which is eternally expressed in the wonderful lines entitled "Into Battle" by Julian Grenfell', adding:

> The poems here collected give, it is true, a stirring picture of the outward and visible semblance of modern scientific

warfare. But modern battles are so vast and so extended in both space and time that composed battle-pieces, such as have come down to us from the far-off centuries of archery and ballad-making, may no longer be looked for. The thread on which all such pictures are strung . . . is the insular conception of fighting as the greatest of all games, that which is the most shrewdly spiced with deadly danger. The Germans, and even our Allies, cannot understand why this stout old nation persists in thinking of war as a sport; they do not know that sportsmanship is our new homely name, derived from a racial predilection for comparing great things with small, for the *chevalerie* of the Middle Ages.

Getting into his stride, he continued:

But it is as an efflorescence of the spirit that this collection of war poetry by those who know war from within is most engrossing. There has been nothing like it before in the history of English literature, nor, indeed, of any other literature. Even the long agony of the Napoleonic Wars, so fertile in picturesque episodes which stand out in the flux of indistinguishable incident, gave us only two or three poems by soldier poets. The celebration of its great days and personalities was left to the professional poets, who wove out of hearsay their gleaming webs of poetic rhetoric.

For Osborn this anthology was 'the first coherent picture of the British warrior's moods and emotions in war-time which has ever been painted by himself. For that reason it is far more valuable than all the huge harvest of war poetry by civilian verse-makers.' He even described it as 'this offensive in rhyme'. He noted interestingly that a distinguishing characteristic of 'the new soldier-poet' was 'the complete absence of the note of hatred for a most hateful enemy . . . Of the many hundreds of his pieces (one in three of them unpublished) I have considered only six were addressed to Germany or the Germans; and, of these six, not one was abusive or argumentative. All seemed to be written rather in sorrow than in anger.' He gave the obvious instance of Sorley's 'To Germany', exemplifying 'a mood that so seldom becomes articulate . . . No civilian poet, not being a Pacifist by profession, would have dared to write these lines.' He noted the absence of rancour which meant that 'invective is left to the non-combatant versifier, who has not the safety-valve of action in arms for his tumultuous feelings'. What is more, 'The tenacity of the British people in warfare is largely due, no doubt, to their faculty of economising emotions in a crisis, of avoiding all the excesses in word and thought which make for nervous exhaustion in a nation or an individual.' Another distinguishing characteristic of the soldier-poets was an absence of explicit patriotism, which for Osborn mean that 'only the patriotism which serves in silence counts'.

Acknowledging that the poets mainly preferred traditional forms, he concluded rhetorically:

The symbolism in which love of country is shadowed forth in the true English war-poetry assumes many forms in this Anthology. It is variously shown, this dominant emotion, in abiding memories of sights and sounds and odours of the green country-side, the turmoil and clangour of great cities, the historic towns inscribed with the 'frozen music' of unravished centuries, the curious laws and quaint customs of famous schools and ancient universities, the more humane games which teach an unselfish discipline, the treasured books which are a mirror of the past that flashes light into the future. Now and again, also, there is a glimpse of the certainty that the dread glittering visage of war is what it has always been – that, as we are but guests of England's dead in

their serried patience, so we go out to fight, or come back
with thanksgiving, accompanied by ghostly comrades.

By the time the last of the big anthologies appeared in 1918,
Poems Written During the Great War 1914–1918, it was impossible
to exclude the anti-heroic poets. This anthology is an important
turning point for it is the first major collection that tried to
define a different view of what war poetry was about. In his
preface, the editor, Bertram Lloyd, wrote:

> The contributors to this collection, several of whom either
> have been or actually now are at the Front, represent widely
> divergent and even fundamentally opposed points of view as
> to the value, necessity, and results of 'civilised warfare'. Some
> are believers in this war but in no other, some are believers
> in other wars but not in this one, while some have no faith at
> all in any war. Their only common point of agreement can
> probably be best described as hatred of the cant and ideal-
> ization and false glamour wherewith the conception of war is
> still so thickly overlaid in the minds of numbers of otherwise
> reasonable people. This is frequently quite unconscious, and
> is doubtless also often no more than the natural heritage of
> thousands of years of tradition. It might be supposed that the
> present war must have given the death-blow to such feelings;
> but they still exist, and, to judge from the language of our
> newspaper-warriors at any rate, even flourish in many quar-
> ters.[9]

He claimed in addition: 'We are to-day at last beginning to work
out a new synthesis of war, and . . . both its superficial and its
radical causes are being subjected to a far more general, if not
actually more penetrating, analysis than has ever been the case
in the past.' He also noted: 'One of the most significant features
of the present war has been the disgust and revulsion of Youth

at beholding itself goaded and driven by Age, usually under the ancient traditional catchwords of Glory and Duty, into utter disillusionment and cynicism. Not unnaturally this feeling is specially noticeable among the poets.' He felt that another outstanding feature of the war was

> the fact that the moral bankruptcy of the professional diplomatists, politicians, and statesmen as a class has become apparent to a degree never possible before. This fact also is profoundly influencing the minds of great numbers of thinking people throughout the world. It is indeed reported that even that shadowy personage the Man in the Street – invented, owned, and controlled though he is by our Captains of Journalism – is growing restive and beginning to question the wisdom and judgement of his Directors in the making, conducting, and ending of wars.

We can see here the template for future interpretations of the poets of the Great War tentatively beginning to take shape.

Isaac Rosenberg, though always a stubbornly individual figure, was certainly part of this reaction against the rhetorical tradition, disliking, as we have seen, the 'begloried sonnets'[10] of Rupert Brooke. Born in Bristol on 25 November 1890, the second child of poor Lithuanian immigrants, his father, a pedlar, having fled, initially to Leeds, from conscription into the Russian army – a fact that accounts in large measure for Rosenberg's instinctive anti-militarism – Isaac moved with the family to Cable Street in Stepney in the East End of London in 1897.[11] He was educated first at St Paul's School, St George's in the East, then at Baker Street board school in Stepney East where his artistic gift was encouraged by the headmaster.

The Rosenbergs were so poor that Isaac found his first canvases to be the East End pavements where he drew in chalk, but in 1902 he started to attend special art sessions at Stepney

Green Art School. He was also taken by his sister, at the age of eleven, to meet the librarian of Whitechapel Public Library, Morley Dainow, who encouraged the boy to read poetry. In 1905, the poet was apprenticed to a firm of engravers in Fleet Street called Carl Hentschel. He met around this time Winifreda Seaton, a schoolteacher, who was another who encouraged the uncertain young man. He wrote to her about his apprenticeship and 'the fiendish mangling-machine' to which he was bound, 'without hope and almost desire of deliverance'.[12] He complained to her, 'I can't look at things in the simple, large way that great poets do.' His parents thought that this apprenticeship might be the route to an eventual career as a painter but the young boy hated it, seeking solace in poetry, especially the work of William Blake, and in attending evening classes in painting at Birkbeck College in Bloomsbury. When his apprenticeship finished in 1911 he was lucky enough to find himself patronised by three well-off Jewish women, who supported him by paying his fees at the Slade School of Fine Art. Lily Delissa Joseph had spotted him copying in the National Gallery and subsequently introduced him to her sister, Mrs Henrietta Lowy, and Mrs Herbert Cohen. To Henrietta Lowy he wrote in March 1912 about poetry and painting: 'Nothing is rarer than good poetry – and nothing more discouraging than the writing of poetry . . . Circumstances and other considerations have prevented me from applying myself assiduously, and also diffidence.' He added: 'I have a dread of meeting people who know I write, as they expect me to talk and I am a horrible bad talker. I am in absolute agonies in company.'[13]

The Slade nonetheless opened Rosenberg's horizons and he made the acquaintance there of the outstanding painters Mark Gertler, David Bomberg, William Roberts, Charles Nevinson, Dora Carrington, and Stanley Spencer. He had also joined a group of East End Jewish artists and writers who frequented the Whitechapel Library and Art Gallery and who were known as the Whitechapel Boys. Writing to his patron, Mrs Cohen, in October, he claimed that the Slade had taught him that 'Art is not a plaything, it is blood and tears, it must grow up with one; and I believe I have begun too late.'[14]

In 1912 Rosenberg started to correspond with the curator of Prints and Drawings at the British Museum, the poet Laurence Binyon. In an introductory memoir to the first posthumous publication of Rosenberg's work in 1922, Binyon wrote:

One morning there came to me a letter in an untidy hand from an address in Whitechapel, enclosing some pages of verse on which criticism was asked, and signed 'Isaac Rosenberg'. It was impossible not to be struck by something unusual in the quality of the poems. Thoughts and emotions of no common nature struggled for expression, and at times there gushed forth a pure song which haunted the memory ... At my invitation Rosenberg came to see me. Small in stature, dark, bright-eyed, thoroughly Jewish in type, he seemed a boy with an unusual mixture of self-reliance and modesty. Indeed, no one could have had a more independent nature. Obviously sensitive, he was not touchy or aggressive. Possessed of vivid enthusiasms, he was shy in speech. One found in talk how strangely little of second-hand (in one of his age) there was in his opinions, how fresh a mind he brought to what he saw and read. There was an odd kind of charm in his manner which came from his earnest, transparent sincerity.[15]

Binyon explained that Rosenberg showed him an autobiography that he had written which 'has perhaps been destroyed ... [it] was the story of a youth, mentally ambitious, consumed by secret desires for liberation and self-expression'. Binyon realised how liable to take offence the young poet and painter could be: 'with his sensitive artist's pride and jealous independence of spirit, he was not always easy to understand; and those, with the sole desire to help him, who advanced his circumstances sometimes felt that their efforts did not seem to be appreciated'. He felt that Rosenberg was a poet rather than a painter at heart and also that the modernism of his Slade generation was not really to his taste: 'Had he been born half a century earlier, he would have been an ardent disciple of Rossetti. But he could not escape from the mental atmosphere of his own generation, in which so "literary" a conception of painting was bound to wither in discouragement.' He told Binyon that he admired the work of the poet Francis Thompson: 'In fact that is the sort of poetry that appeals most to me – richly coloured without losing that mysteriousness, the hauntingness which to me is the subtle music – the soul to which the colour is flesh & raiment.'[16] On another occasion he told Binyon, 'I don't know whether I have quite followed your advice about being more concrete – I'm afraid my mind isn't formed that way – I believe, though, my expression is more simple. My muse is a very conventional muse, far away & dreamy, she does not seek beauty in common life.'[17]

More recent critics have questioned the usefulness of established poets like Binyon, Lascelles Abercrombie and Gordon Bottomley to an original spirit like Rosenberg. In his edition of *The Collected Works*, Ian Parsons wrote: 'They were the leading members of the academic poetic "establishment" of those days, and Rosenberg, whose letters show clearly how impressed he was by their works, came increasingly under their influence. It was not a very beneficial one.'[18] Parsons considered that if his mentors had been fellow war poets like Wilfred Owen he might have written more poems of personal experience and less 'verse drama built round grandiose biblical themes'.

In the summer of 1912 Rosenberg published his first collection of poems, *Night and Day*, a twenty-four-page pamphlet issued in a limited edition of fifty and printed by his friend

Reuben Cohen at the printing works of Israel Narodiczky in the Mile End Road. Rosenberg was lucky in his contacts but a prickly subject to handle and, after disagreements with his three patrons, he started to receive funds in 1912 from the Jewish Educational Aid Society until completing his Slade studies in 1914. In 1913 Gertler introduced him to yet more useful contacts: the Imagist poet T. E. Hulme and Edward Marsh. Marsh bought some of his paintings and encouraged him in his poetry. In May 1914 Rosenberg had work shown in the Whitechapel's exhibition of twentieth-century artists.

But in spite of this support, he was poor, jobless, and not in good health so he decided to sail to South Africa where his sister, Minnie, was living. He painted there and lectured on art but, in March 1915, he came back to the East End. He published another pamphlet of poems, *Youth*, and sold some paintings to Marsh, but was struggling. In September he started evening classes in blockmaking but there was still no prospect of a job, so in October he enlisted (because of his short stature) in the Bantam Battalion of the 12th Suffolk Regiment, 40th Division. 'I wanted to join the R.A.M.C. [Royal Army Medical Corps],' he wrote to the author Sydney Schiff, 'as the idea of killing upsets me, but I was too small.'[19] Binyon recalled: 'No one could have been less fitted for a military life. He suffered not only from physical disability, bad health, and sensitiveness, but from the absent-mindedness of one whose imagination was possessed by his poetic schemes.'[20]

Rosenberg's military career confirmed this. To Edward Marsh he had written four days after war was declared: 'Know that I despise war and hate war.'[21] In June when he was still not sure of what he would do he told Schiff, 'I am thinking of enlisting if they will have me, though it is against all my principles of justice – though I would be doing the most criminal thing a man can do – I am so sure my mother would not stand the shock that I don't know what to do.'[22] Rosenberg was torn between wanting to have a steady job – which is what enlisting would mean with its 'separation allowance' for the family back home in the East End – and dismaying his family, who hated war as much as he did. He eventually left without telling anyone and his mother was indeed distraught when she eventually found out he had joined up.

Overcoming his sense of 'the immorality of joining with no patriotic convictions',[23] Rosenberg set off for the 12th Suffolks' training camp at Bury St Edmunds where there were extra burdens on top of the marches and unwelcome military discipline: 'My being a Jew makes it bad amongst these wretches.'[24] He felt the Bantams were a 'horrible rabble' but he had Donne's poems and Sir Thomas Browne's *Religio Medici* to console him, even if it was hard to write and he couldn't even lay his hands on a box of watercolours. He told Schiff philosophically, 'One might succumb, be destroyed – but one might also be renewed, made larger, healthier.'[25] Like Ivor Gurney, Rosenberg saw that combat might have its own therapeutic value, but he still believed 'This militarism is terrorism to be sure.'[26] Interestingly, he told Edward Marsh at the end of 1915, 'I believe in myself more as a poet than a painter. I think I get more depth into my writing.'[27]

Rosenberg acknowledged that he was clumsy and largely inept as a soldier. Very quickly he ended up in a military hospital after he slipped on some mud and gravel and cut his hands rather badly, and although he claimed to be managing to cope with the drill and general discipline he was bullied by the officers, including one 'impudent schoolboy pup'.[28] He told Marsh, 'I find that the actual duties though they are difficult at first and require all one's sticking power are not in themselves unpleasant, it is the brutal militaristic bullying meanness of the way they're served out to us.'[29]

Sending Marsh the poem 'Marching – As Seen from the Left File', he told him, 'But it is something else I want to write about. I never joined the army for patriotic reasons. Nothing can justify war. I suppose we must all fight to get the trouble over.'[30]

In early January 1916, Rosenberg was transferred to the 12th South Lancashires and was in training camp at Farnborough – where he reported that he got very little food and sometimes none at all. He found himself 'amongst the most unspeakably filthy wretches, it is pretty suicidal', and he told Abercrombie, 'Believe me the army is the most detestable invention on this earth and nobody but a private in the army knows what it is to be a slave.'[31] He sent off two poems, 'Spring 1916' and 'Marching – As Seen from the Left File', to two papers – 'as they are war poems and topical but as I expected, they were sent back. I am afraid my public is still in the womb. Naturally this only has the effect of making me very conceited and to think these poems better than anyone else's.'[32] He hated the stupidity of the army camp routines and the 'puny minds' that controlled it but he made things worse for himself by dreaming about poetry when he should have been concentrating on the matter in hand and was sometimes punished for not following orders. Thinking about his verse play *Moses* was a prime cause of abstractedness. He was making plans to have it published by one of his Jewish printer friends in Stepney, 'as I felt this would be the safest way of keeping my best work if anything should happen'.[33] He was worried that his writing might suffer in quality from the terrible conditions in which it was written.

On 3 June 1916 Rosenberg finally arrived in France. He told Winifreda Seaton, 'We made straight for the trenches, but we've had vile weather, and I've been wet through for four days and nights ... We've had shells bursting two yards off, bullets whizzing all over the show, but all you are aware of is the agony of your heels [he had lost his socks].'[34] He was still, however, writing and thinking about poetry: 'People are always telling me my work is promising – incomprehensible but promising, and all that sort of thing, and my meekness subsides before the patronising knowingness.'[35] He was able, however, to bask in the praise of Gordon Bottomley, one of those poets like Lascelles Abercrombie for whom he had what looks today like an exaggerated reverence.[36] He was less enamoured of some poems by an (unnamed) soldier printed in *Poetry Review* which he found commonplace in their phrasing. Rosenberg's view of Brooke's begloried sonnets has already been noted.

As for his own poetry, Rosenberg sent Marsh his 'Break of Day in the Trenches', adding that it was 'surely as simple as ordinary talk'.[37] He was conscious of how difficult it was to write in the trench conditions. And he had no country house like Sassoon to take refuge in during periods of leave:

> You know the conditions I have always worked under, and particularly with this last lot of poems. You know how earnestly one must wait on ideas (you cannot coax real ones to you) and let as it were, a skin grow naturally round and through them. If you are not free, you can only, when the ideas come hot, seize them with the skin in tatters raw, crude, in some parts beautiful in others monstrous. Why print it then? Because those rare parts must not be lost. I work more and more as I write into more depth and lucidity, I am sure. I have a fine idea for a most gorgeous play, Adam and Lillith. If I could get a few months after the war to work and absorb myself completely into the thing, I'd write a great thing.[38]

By August 1916, however, Rosenberg was forbidden by the Army to send any more poems back home 'as the censor won't be bothered with going through such rubbish'.[39] He was working as a salvage officer and was short of reading matter. Sometimes he tore pages out of the bibles he found in dead men's clothes. The poet and translator R. C. Trevelyan began to correspond with him at this point and the poet was happy that he liked his work, especially as 'very few people do, or, at least, say so; and I believe I am a poet'.[40] He told Marsh, 'I have too much to write about . . . My exaggerated way of feeling things when I begin to write about them might not have quite healthy consequences.'[41] In a letter to Laurence Binyon around November he wrote:

Winter has found its way into the trenches at last, but I will spare you & leave to your imagination, the transport of delight with which we welcomed its coming. Winter is not the least of the horrors of war. I am determined that this war, with all its powers for devastation, shall not master my poet-ing – that is if I am lucky enough to come through all right. I will not leave a corner of my consciousness covered up, but saturate myself with the strange extraordinary new conditions of this life & it will all refine itself into poetry later on . . . I am not decided whether truth of period is a good quality or a negative one. Flaubert's 'Salambo' [*sic*] proves perhaps, that it is good. It decides the tone of the work, though it makes it hard to give the human side and make it more living. However it is impossible now to work and difficult even to think of poetry, one is so cramped intellectually . . . If I get the chance I'll write a sequence of poems of trench life which I mean to be a startler. You know all that goes on so I won't worry you with my experiences now, but they the poems will be pysological [*sic*] & individual & I hope interesting.[42]

At the end of 1916 Rosenberg, now twenty-six years old, started to plan in his head a book of war poems but, apart from Wilfrid Gibson's 'Battle', he was not impressed with what was being written under that rubric: 'The Homer for this war has yet to be found – Whitman got very near the mark 50 years ago with "Drum Taps".'[43] He thought Gibson's poem 'the best thing the war has turned out. Personally, I think the only value in any war is the literature it results in.'[44] In the new year of 1917 his health declined and he was assigned to a works battalion behind the lines, repairing roads. He had abdominal pains and the practice of 'dumping' lice-ridden clothing had, he surmised, left him more vulnerable to cold and damp. 'I wonder if Aeschylus as a private in the army was bothered as I am by lice,'[45] he asked Bottomley. The poem 'Louse-Hunting' – 'an amusing little thing'[46] – was written at this time. As the spring advanced, his health got no better (though it meant he was out of the firing line) and, acknowledging Marsh's praise of his *Moses* play, an extract of which would appear in late September in the new *Georgian Poetry* anthology, he observed ruefully: 'His creator is in a sadder plight; the harsh and unlovely times have made his mistress, the flighty Muse, abscond and elope with luckier rivals, but surely I shall hunt her and chase her somewhere into the summer and sweeter times.'[47]

In May something of those 'sweeter times' came back and he felt able to send Marsh the poem 'Dead Man's Dump' – 'some lines suggested by going out wiring'.[48] Rosenberg accepted some of Marsh's criticisms but stressed 'the absolute necessity of fixing an idea before it is lost, because of the situation it's conceived in'.[49] As for its metre he confessed, 'Regular rhythms I do not like much ... I think that if Andrew Marvell had broken up his rhythms more he would have been considered a terrific poet.'[50] He was able to write infrequently – 'only when we get a bit of rest', adding that when 'the others might be gambling or squabbling I add a line or two'.

Describing to Marsh a poem he was working on, he realised 'I fancy poetry is not much bothering you or anybody just now. I've heard of the air raids and I always feel most anxious about my people. Yet out here, though often a troublesome consolation, poetry is a great one to me.'[51] He was working on unloading barbed wire and so had the morning to sleep 'unless

I happen to be doing some punishment for my forgetfulness' (seven hours' pack drill being his recent punishment for forgetting to go out wearing his gas-mask).

In spite of these harsh conditions, the sense that poetry was central to Rosenberg's life at this moment is powerfully felt: 'I have a way, when I write, to try and put myself in the situation, and I make gestures and grimaces,'[52] he wrote to Marsh, which reminds us of the intense physicality and sense of the human self that his best poems seem so often to embody. He knew the dangers of his situation and the fragility of an art practised in such conditions: 'I must take any chance I get of writing for fear another chance does not come . . . My great fear is that I may lose what I've written which can happen here so easily. I send home any bit I write, for safety.'[53] Evidently he had now decided to ignore the censor's instruction not to send poems home. To Schiff he wrote, 'things are so tumultuous and disturbing . . . I managed to jot down some ideas for poems now and then . . . they are actual transcripts of the battlefields'.[54] He continued to think about poetry and its best means of expression. Some of his poetry is close-wrought, opaque and even downright obscure, a fact that worried even his closest admirers, but the best is beautifully direct and lucid. He insisted to Marsh, 'I think with you that poetry should be definite thought and clear expression however subtle; I don't think there should be any vagueness at all; but a sense of something hidden and felt to be there.'[55]

In mid-September Rosenberg had ten days of leave in Stepney but he was uneasy and could do none of the reading and writing he might have expected: 'I feel so restless here and unanchored. We have lived in so elemental a way so long, things here don't look quite right to me somehow.'[56] It was almost as if he needed the turmoil of the battlefield to make his 'transcriptions'. Not long after he returned to France he was admitted to the 51st General Hospital with influenza. He stayed there until December and, from his hospital bed, wrote to Winifreda Seaton with some observations about poetry and his long artistic struggle to get it right:

> I think anybody can pick holes and find unsound parts in any work of art . . . It is the unique and superior, the illuminating qualities one wants to find – discover the direction of the impulse. Whatever anybody thinks of a poet he will always know himself: he knows that the most marvellously expressed idea is still nothing; and it is stupid to think that praise can do him harm. I know sometimes one cannot exactly define one's feelings nor explain reasons for liking and disliking; but there is then the right of a suspicion that the thing has not been properly understood or one is preju-diced. It is much my fault if I am not understood, I know; but I also feel a kind of injustice if my idea is not grasped and is ignored, and only petty cavilling at form, which I had known all along was so, is continually knocked into me. I feel quite sure that form is only a question of time.[57]

Rosenberg, aware of the fragility of his position, began to be more anxious not just about preserving his manuscripts, but about getting poems published. He wrote to his East End friend Joseph Leftwich: 'I have written a few war poems but when I think of 'Drum Taps' mine are absurd. However I would get a pamphlet printed if I were sure of selling about 60 at 1s each – as I think mine may give some new aspects to people at home – and then one never knows whether you'll get a tap on the head or not: and if that happens – all you have writ-ten is lost, unless you have secured them by printing.'[58]

At the end of January 1918 he was back in the trenches, 'which are terrible now', with 4th Platoon, A Company, 11th King's Own Royal Lancasters. He told Marsh, 'We spend most of our time pulling each other out of the mud . . . I am not strong.'[59] It was not merely the external battle-landscape that was oppressing Rosenberg's spirit. He could see the damage it was doing to him as an artist. He explained to Winifreda Seaton that there was 'no chance whatever for seclusion or any hope of writing poetry now. Sometimes I give way and am appalled at the devastation this life seems to have made in my nature. It seems to have blunted me.'[60] To other correspondents at this time he expressed his anxiety about writing and about the futility, for an artist, of being unable to create properly under the duress of murderous conditions: 'I feel stupefied. When will we go on with the things that endure?' He told Gordon Bottomley, 'Since I left the hospital all the poetry has gone quite out of me. I seem even to forget words, and I believe if I met with anybody with ideas I'd be dumb. No drug could be more stupefying than our work (to me anyway), and this goes on like that old water torture trickling, drop by drop unendingly, on one's helplessness.'[61] Again to Bottomley: 'If only this war were over our eyes would not be on death so much: it seems to underlie even our underthoughts.'[62]

So desperate was Rosenberg that he put in for a transfer to the Jewish Battalion fighting in Mesopotamia, where Jacob Epstein was serving. Instead he was moved nearer to Arras for training with his present battalion, and reported to Marsh, 'We are very busy now and poetry is right out of our scheme . . . I've seen no poetry for ages now . . . My vocabulary small enough before is impoverished and bare.'[63] On 19 March the battalion moved into the front line near Arras and on the 21st a major spring offensive was launched by the German Army, sending the battalion back to Fampoux close by. On 31 March Rosenberg was sent off on a wiring patrol. The next day, 1 April 1918, he failed to return. His remains were later found with eleven other comrades and buried in the cemetery at Fampoux, to be re-interred at Bailleul Road East British Cemetery outside Arras. Today, a few yards away, in a small wood, are the rows and rows of iron crosses of a much larger German war cemetery – together with a small handful of German Jewish graves.

Rosenberg's poetry was first collected in 1922 by Gordon Bottomley with a memoir by Laurence Binyon attached. Then in 1937 a collected edition of his poetry, prose, letters and drawings was issued with a foreword by Siegfried Sassoon. It was a perceptive summing-up and stressed the originality of the work:

> I have found a sensitive and vigorous mind energetically interested in experimenting with language, and I have recognised in Rosenberg a fruitful fusion between English and Hebrew culture. Behind all his poetry there is a racial quality – biblical and prophetic. Scriptural and sculptural are the epithets I would apply to him. His experiments were a strenuous effort for impassioned expression; his imagination had a sinewy and muscular aliveness; often he saw things in terms of sculpture, but he did not carve or chisel; he *modelled* words with fierce energy and aspiration, finding ecstasy in form, dreaming in grandeurs of superb light and deep shadow; his poetic visions are mostly in sombre colours and looming sculptural masses, molten and amply wrought. Watching him working with words, I find him a poet of movement; words which express movement are often used by him and are essential to his natural utterance.[64]

For Sassoon, Rosenberg was not consciously a 'war poet'.

> But the war destroyed him, and his few but impressive 'Trench Poems' are a central point in this book. They have the controlled directness of a man finding his true voice and achieving mastery of his material; words and images obey him, instead of leading him into over-elaboration. They are all of them fine poems, but 'Break of Day in the Trenches' has for me a poignant and nostalgic quality which eliminates

critical analysis. Sensuous front-line existence is there, hateful and repellent, unforgettable and inescapable. And beyond this poem I see the poems he might have written after the war, and the life he might have lived when life began again beyond and behind those trenches which were the limbo of all sane humanity and world-improving imagination. For the spirit of poetry looks beyond life's trench-lines. And Isaac Rosenberg was naturally empowered with something of the divine spirit which touches our human clay to sublimity of expression.

A more recent critic, Jean Liddiard, argues that 'the other war poets (and the Georgians) like Owen, Edmund Blunden and Edward Thomas, still hold to the Romantic view of a beautiful natural universe, quickened with spiritual power shared by man. Rosenberg stands aside from this tradition ... For Rosenberg, humanity with its "fierce imaginings" is central, and he asserts the human value of the destroyed life, not, like Owen, by mourning the beauty of men deformed by death, but characteristically by celebrating the energy of "their dark souls".'[65]

Rosenberg himself said in the summer of 1916, 'Simple *poetry* – that is where an interesting complexity of thought is kept in tone and right value to the dominating idea so that it is understandable and still ungraspable. I know it is beyond my reach just now, except, perhaps, in bits. I am always afraid of being empty. When I get more leisure in more settled times I will work on a larger scale and give myself more room, then I may be less frustrated in my efforts to be clear, and satisfy myself too.'[66] But all his poetic aspirations and aesthetic values were wrought from the terrible conditions of war and his particular experience of it as, in effect, a navvy or labourer, which is what privates such as he were: 'I don't suppose my poems will ever be <u>poetry</u> right and proper until I shall be able to settle down and whip myself into more expression. As it is, my not being able to get poetry out of my head & heart causes me sufficient trouble out here.' He insisted that these obstacles 'will never break the ardour of my poetry'.[67]

Perhaps Rosenberg's first 'war poem' was 'Lusitania',[68] inspired by the sinking of the passenger ship on its homeward voyage from New York on 7 May 1915. One thousand one hundred and ninety-eight people died, including a hundred Americans, a fact which accelerated America's entry into the War. The poem talks of the 'Soulless logic, inventive enginery' of the means of destruction of 'the peace-faring Lusitania' and uses the word 'chaos', which occurs several times in these pre-combat poems of Rosenberg and which reflects the way his writing situates war as a felt physical reality in the universal scheme of things. Invited to contribute an introduction to his poems in 1922, Yeats declined, claiming that the work was 'all windy rhetoric',[69] but the poet's early work, like that of Yeats, draws beauty precisely from its seeming imprecision or 'windiness', even if his best poems, again like Yeats's, are tauter, more spare, more direct. The first of the latter was 'The Troop Ship':

> The wet wind is so cold,
> And the lurching men so careless,
> That, should you drop to a doze,
> Wind's fumble or men's feet
> Is on your face.

But it was with 'In the Trenches', a poem composed immediately before 'Break of Day in the Trenches', that Rosenberg started to achieve directness.

His poem 'The Dying Soldier', which shows a fatally wounded man crying out for water and delirious, is simply presented with no commentary, no underlining, no insistence. The same apparently neutral tone – letting the facts speak for themselves – is there in the poem 'In War', which describes a soldier digging a grave without realising until the priest reads his brother's name for whom it is dug. Like his famous trench rat 'sardonic' and 'droll' in many of these poems, Rosenberg conveys an unvarnished sense of the war in a poem like 'The Immortals', about louse-hunting, with his special signature of grim lightness. His poetic mentors approved of this evolution of his art. Gordon Bottomley said of 'The Destruction of Jerusalem', 'I like its vigour and directness; it gives me the comforting feeling that you are learning to say what you want to say in a straighter, swifter, more economic way than you did formerly.'[70] Like Sassoon, Rosenberg was acutely alive to the beauty of nature in proximity to war's horrors and one of his most beautiful short poems is 'Returning We Hear the Larks', about a party of men, dog-tired, wearily treading a 'poison-blasted track' back to camp for 'a little safe sleep' when they encounter the 'strange joy' of larks singing:

Death could drop from the dark
As easily as song –
But song only dropped . . .

'Dead Man's Dump' is a poem with affinities in subject matter to Owen's 'Dulce et Decorum Est' but without its explicit protest. A wagon is dragged along, crushing dead bodies ('Earth has waited for them/ All the time of their growth/ Fretting for their decay:/ Now she has them at last'), and they are imagined as having reintegrated their human essences into the earth. The poet uses a strange image for the fatal weaponry: 'When the swift burning bee/ Drained the wild honey of their youth'. The density of this longer poem, the poet's wrestle with expression, have made some critics compare his poetry to sculpture, the very physical sense of a chiselling-out of form. The poem climaxes with a dying man waiting for the stretcher bearers to come, but he is dead on their arrival: 'And our wheels grazed his dead face.' Rosenberg's work is characterised by an objectivity that is just as eloquent and effective as the more pointed poetry of protest. He himself thought 'Daughters of War' his best poem but readers are unlikely to agree. Very mythological in tone, it is powerful in expression but lacks that vibrant dramatic realism of his best verse.

The last poem Rosenberg wrote, 'Through These Pale Cold Days', was enclosed in a letter to Edward Marsh, arriving after the poet had been killed in action. It is beautiful and poignant, about the soldiers' wild eyes burning in shared suffering through 'the pale cold days'. Their spirits 'grope/ For the pools of Hebron again' and 'They see with living eyes/ How long they have been dead.'

6

The English Line: Ivor Gurney, Edward Thomas and Edmund Blunden

English literature, like other literatures, is full of battle-poems, but it is worth noticing that the ones that have won for themselves a kind of popularity are always a tale of disasters and retreats ... The most stirring battle-poem in English is about a brigade of cavalry that charged in the wrong direction. And of the last war, the four names which have really engraved themselves on the popular memory are Mons, Ypres, Gallipoli and Passchendaele, every time a disaster. The names of the great battles that finally broke the German armies are simply unknown to the general public.[1]

GEORGE ORWELL, 1941

We may have no great poets, but poetry so saturated with the spirit of England has not been written before.[2]

IVOR GURNEY

If critics like the former Poet Laureate Andrew Motion are right about the corpus of British poetry of the First World War constituting 'a sacred national text',[3] then we should be looking in the work of its practitioners for some sign that it embodied more than just the inevitable agglomeration of war experience in verse, a record of its progress, a commemoration of its heroic passages. Those who perceive an 'English line' that withstood the assault of twentieth-century international modernism and instead connected modern English writing more squarely with the English poetry of the past find, in the poetry of the War, evidence of that English tradition (and for once precision demands 'English' not 'British' here) whose superficial indicators are a love of nature, a note of pastoral lyricism or topographical *tristia*, expressed, for preference, in traditional forms that honour tried poetic craftsmanship rather than revolutionary innovation. It is certainly one way – and a fruitful way – into the work of several of the poets.

Ivor Gurney – whose first book of poems published in 1917 was called *Severn and Somme* – far more than Isaac Rosenberg and for fairly self-evident reasons, was a poet rooted in a particular landscape: his native Gloucestershire. His passion for the county permeates his poetry before, during and after the War: 'There was such beauty in the dappled valley/ As hurt the sight, as stabbed the heart to tears,' he writes, typically, in 'There Was Such Beauty'.[4] The landscape of Gloucestershire, the River Severn, the Cotswolds, the Malvern Hills, possessed his mind in Flanders, constituting a kind of reference point, a pastoral counterweight to the blasted trees and churned mud, smashed spires, and damaged villages of the battlefields.

Ivor Bertie Gurney was born in Gloucester on 28 August 1890,[5] the eldest son of a Gloucester tailor. Like Rosenberg's painting, Gurney's musical composition was one of the twin strands in his creativity sometimes displacing, sometimes being displaced by, the poetry. Gurney was educated at the King's School, Gloucester, and was a chorister at the cathedral and later articled to the cathedral organist as a pupil. In 1911 he won a composition scholarship to the Royal College of Music under

Sir Charles Stanford. Like Rosenberg, he was lucky in his artistic patrons. His godfather, the learned bachelor Revd Alfred Hunter Cheesman, vicar of St Matthew's Church, Twigworth, near Gloucester, opened his library to the young musician in these formative years.

Gurney originally tried to enlist in 1914 but was rejected because of his poor eyesight. He tried once more in February 1915, while still a student at the Royal College of Music, and was this time accepted. On the 9th of that month he sent a postcard to his friend, Edward Chapman: 'Private Gurney (5th Gloucester Reserve Battalion) sends you greetings.'[6] In training he started to read the first *Georgian Poetry* anthology when it appeared and told his friend F. W. Harvey, 'Our young poets think very much as we, or rather as we shall when body and mind are tranquil . . . Meanwhile there is a most bloody war to go through. Let's hope it'll do the trick for both of us, and make us so strong, so happy, so sure of ourselves, so crowded with fruitful memories of joy that we may be able to live in towns or earn our living at some drudgery and yet create whole and pure joy for others. It is a far cry for me, but who knows what a year may do?'[7] It is an interesting comment which suggests that Gurney approached the war as an experience that would make him, transform him, a feeling that a great many young men enlisting must have experienced. Gurney seems to have needed and greatly appreciated the company and comradeship of his fellows in B Company of the Gloucesters' 5th Reserve. Although he was

hard-worked and, apparently, able to stand about 7 hours a day drill . . . It was an experience worth the writing about, when we recruits stood at ease in the dusk while the 5th Gloucesters crowded around us with cries of welcome and recognition and peered into our faces to make sure of friends. It gave me a thrill such as I have not had for long enough. I have already changed billet, and the chaps here are very nice indeed. Good men, which is a great point. But in this new democracy almost everyone is jolly, or tries to be.[8]

To another correspondent he wrote, 'Well, here I am; a soldier of the King, and the best thing for me – at present. I feel that nowhere could I be happier than where I am, (except perhaps at sea) so the experiment may be called a success . . . It is indeed a better way to die; with these men, in such a cause; than the end which seemed near me and was so desirable only just over two years ago.'[9] These comments hint at the underlying psychological instability that would become the tragedy of Gurney's life but for which the experience of soldiering seemed, for now, therapeutic. Drill was hard, but 'I hang on and hope for the best. I think I shall come through . . . I think there is no danger of my breaking down, and a large prospect of my becoming much better, thank the Lord, and paid a bob a day for it, too!'[10] Gurney described himself as a neurasthenic, the term of the day, and he felt that he was looking physically better in spite of the poor food in camp. To Herbert Howells, the composer and an old friend from the King's School, however, he offered a more nuanced self-diagnosis:

As to whether I like soldiering. I am convinced that had I stuck to music, complete health would have been a very long job. This life will greatly help. Secondly, supposing I had not joined, and never attained my high aim in music – I could not have forgiven myself. *Thirdly*, that if I get shot, it won't matter to me what my possibilities (with health) might or might not be. *4thly*. That the life, though hard, and the food scant and coarse, makes me as happy as I can be made without a yacht and money. It is hard, and always I am tired, but struggle through in a very much happier frame of mind than that I have had for some time – probably 4 years.[11]

Gurney's war was, like most of the poets', confined mainly to one small space in the larger theatre of war. He served from 25 May 1916 in France as a private with the 2nd/5th Gloucesters. He received a minor bullet wound on Good Friday 1917 and more serious gas injuries on or about 10 September 1917 during the third Battle of Ypres at Passchendaele, after which he spent time in various war hospitals in England. Here signs of mental instability began to surface and he attempted suicide on 19 June 1918. He was finally discharged from the Army that October. He was one tiny cog in the great machine of war but his observations are nonetheless pointed and often full of fascinating detail about the business of fighting.

Gurney admired the way the men never spoke about not wanting to fight or being in the trenches: 'Their attitude is – we don't want to fight, but someone must do it – the best attitude of all.'[12] He also admired the popular poetic responses to the War, judging Masefield's 'August 1914' the best of the war poems and being convinced that Rupert Brooke had left 'two sonnets which outshine by far anything yet written on this upheaval. They are as beautiful as music.'[13]

As well as feeling that enlisting had invigorated him as a man, Gurney also felt, what many of the poets felt, that at the same time his artistic gift might be the casualty of war. He seems to have possessed an unusually strong sense of his special vocation as an artist which, once or twice in his letters, comes to seem excessive or grandiose, but mostly was under control. To his lifelong musical friend Marion Scott he wrote in June 1915, 'My health is slowly improving; and as my mind clears, and as the need for self-expression grows less weak; the thought of leaving all I have to say unsaid, makes me cold. Could I only hand on my gift! . . . The war, however, seems like lasting a year . . . Still, I chose this path, and do not regret it; do not see what else I could have done under the circumstances.'[14]

This same month Gurney was moved to another camp,

Wintry Farm in Epping, and the work was hard with a reveille at five in the morning and no rest until lights out at 9.45. He had been thinking more about Rupert Brooke and revising his initial enthusiasm: 'It seems to me that Rupert Brooke would not have improved with age, would not have broadened, his manner has become a mannerism, both in rhythm and diction. I do not like it. This is the kind of work which his older lesser inspiration would have produced. Great poets, great creators are not much influenced by immediate events; those must sink in to the very foundations and be absorbed. Rupert Brooke soaked it in quickly and gave it out with as great ease.'[15] Gurney was perhaps chastened by the bulk of the special war poetry supplement of *The Times* of 9 August.

He would not be disappointed to leave Epping: the endless parades, the horrible 'shackles' (stewed meat), execrable tea, and stale bread. Gurney always liked his food and spent any surplus cash on boosting his consumption of meat. He had of course been put in the band, where he played the baryton, a bass cornet, and he stuck to his view that this was all doing him good and that the neurasthenic's days were numbered. It seemed that he was soon to be sent to France and he thought he would apply for a commission on the very sensible grounds that 'It is best to get paid for taking risks.'[16] But first he had five grateful days of leave, returning from which made him feel that 'Gloster's delicate colours, long views and sea breezes are the whole breadth of England away. That soil bore me and must ever draw my dreams and for ever be home to me. It is to be torn up by the roots for me to live flatly in a flat marsh like Essex, where the air is stagnant and unalive.'[17] He thought of getting a job in railway transport but was feeling the lack of intellectual stimulation, as he explained to Herbert Howells: 'I *must* have something to think about . . . You can imagine, too, what the hope of being able to praise England and make things to honour her is in me, as in yourself. You can imagine too what a conflict there is between that idea and warfare . . . to suffer all this in the thought-vacuum in which the Army lives, moves, and has its being, is a hard thing.'[18]

Rediscovering Walt Whitman and reading Wordsworth's *Prelude* kept him sane, though he felt Milton was crabby and mean-spirited. In spite of 'the feeling of utter futility and waste of time that is the average thought of any educated man in Army life'[19] he felt his health was constantly improving: 'I am fit for double as much as when I joined 9 months ago. My mind escapes from itself a little.' Summing up his view of himself at the end of 1915, he wrote, 'I pass with my comrades as one who is willing to be friendly with almost anybody; looks depressed, but makes more jokes than anyone else round here. One who can play the piano above archangels, who can read anything at sight, and makes (O wonder) classical music interesting; but has an itch, a positive mania for arguing, and discoursing on weird and altogether unimportant subjects. A good card-player, a good goal-keeper, a first-rate liar, (on occasions needful) and a friend of the 1/5 D.C.M.*'[20]

At the end of January 1916 Gurney's battalion moved from Epping to huts on Salisbury Plain which were a vast improvement on the tents. 'We are firing and marking for a fortnight, which is an interesting and cushy job. It would tax Shakespeare's mind to conceive the monotony of eternal bayonet fighting, squad drill, and fatigue.'[21] In May the Gloucesters finally shipped to Flanders and Gurney began to gauge what it might mean to be at the Front at last: 'The only thought that disturbs me ever, is that all my continual striving and endeavour to become a fit and full man, ('full man' is Shakespeare) [actually he was wrong, it was Francis Bacon] may be ended by a German bullet or bayonet.'[22] In reality it was the tedium of Army life that was beginning to get to him: 'But O, O, O to get

* The 1st Battalion of the 5th Gloucester Regiment.

back to my music, and time for books and walks. All manifestations of energy are hard for me, but I'd manage more work now than ever before in my nerve-ridden existence.'[23] Just before he left for France, he expressed the wish that his friend Howells had been writing – 'Something clear and English I hope'[24] – and reminded him of their joint love for 'that Severn county of ours'.[25]

Although Gurney was bored by Army routine, his first reactions on arriving in the trenches were positive. He was passionate about the comradeship of his fellows, especially the Welsh regiments, in a way that is matched nowhere else in the recorded comments of other poets of the War:

> But O what luck! Here I am in a signal dugout with some of the nicest, and most handsome young men I ever met . . . I did not sleep at all for the first day in the dugout – there was too much to be said, asked, and experienced; and pleasure in watching their quick expressions for oblivion. It was one of the notable evenings of my life . . . War's damned interesting. It would be hard indeed to be deprived of all this artist's material now; when my mind is becoming saner and more engaged with outside things. It is not hard for me to die, but a thing sometimes unbearable to leave this life; and these Welsh God makes fine gentlemen. It would seem that the War is one of His ways of doing so.[26]

He was earning five francs a week pay, and gratefully biting into decent French bread: 'excellent – in great round slabs. Very grateful after the drier Army bread is its dampness and yielding quality. The chocolate is excellent, and the people very kind.'[27]

In June 1916 Gurney had what he called 'the most amazing experience, it may be, in my life'[28] which combined everything that mattered to him: music, poetry, good fellowship, and love of the border counties and of Wales. He had been sent through 'interminable communication trenches' to get instructions from a Welsh battalion. At the end of this difficult journey he eventually crawled into a dugout:

> Not high but fairly large, lit by a candle, and so met four of the most delightful young men that could be met anywhere. Thin faced and bright eyed their faces showed beautifully against the soft glow of the candle light, and their musical voices delightful after the long march at attention in silence. There was no sleep for me that night. I made up next day a little, but what then? We talked of Welsh Folksong, of George Borrow, of Burns, of the R.C.M.; of – yes – of Oscar Wilde, Omar Khayam, Shakespeare and of war. Distant from us by 300 yards snipers were continually firing, and rockets – fairy lights they call them; fired from a pistol – lit up the night outside. Every now and again a distant rumble of guns reminded us of the reason we were foregathered. They spoke of their friends dead or maimed in the bombardment, a bad one, of the night before, and in the face of their grief I sat there and for once self forgetful, more or less, gave them all my love, for their tenderness, their steadfastness and kindness to raw fighters, and *very* raw signallers.[29]

And they sang, Welsh and English songs. It was this experience which inspired the poem 'First Time In', describing 'the Welsh colony' who

> Sang us Welsh things, and changed all former notions
> To human hopeful things.
> And the next day's guns
> Nor any line-pangs ever quite could blot out
> That strangely beautiful entry to war's rout.[30]

Gurney was struck by how, at the Front,

Everything goes on as usual behind, and only just behind, the firing line. The children move gracefully, the farmers tend their fields, coffee is sold and beer in large quantities; and at evening soldiers stroll about under the lime trees in the shadow of ruined churches and roofs long ago wrecked – usually in a blind rage, it seems, by our neighbours the Bosches, only a few hundred yards away from where I write. This is a queer war though. Guns are going in the distance, and every moment there is the chance of a strafe (we have had one, not a bad one) yet the note of the whole affair is boredom. The Army is an awful life for an artist, even if he has such experiences as we had with the Welsh. Either it is slogging along uselessly with a pack or doing nothing but hang about after – or boredom or hell in the trenches. Very little between.[31]

One morning he heard a cuckoo while standing outside a dugout cleaning mess tins and it made him think once more of the Gloucestershire countryside:

This Welshman turned to me passionately. 'Listen to that damned bird', he said. 'All through that bombardment in the pauses I could hear that infernal silly "Cuckoo, Cuckoo" sounding while Owen was lying in my arms covered with blood. How shall I ever listen again . . .!' He broke off, and I became aware of shame at the unholy joy that had filled my artist's mind . . . By God, I want to come out of this safe, discipline my nerves and mind into a normal sanity, and do my best in some symphony to praise these men as they deserve; if it were possible.[32]

Once again there is a very particular quality of human empathy in Gurney that is not so evident in any of the more high-profile war poets. He was not a poet of protest but he had the aspiration to witness, to 'praise these men as they deserve'.

About this time he confessed, 'I am indeed proud of my steady quiet comrades. Who vanish one by one notwithstanding, while the rest of us wait our turn.'[33]

A matter of days now before the Somme offensive, Gurney seems to have got it into his head that the war would not last much longer and that he would get back, rejuvenated, to the work of composing music 'for which I am more fit, more eager than ever in my life'.[34] He thought it would all be over by September. In the meantime he tried to define what the war meant to him as a man and an artist, conveniently setting it out as a series of numbered points:

(1) It is a weird queer war – this, against unseen enemies.

(2) That I have really no part in it. I wake up with a start from my dreams of books and music and home, and find I am – here, in this!

(3) That I have as little fear as anyone I have seen around me. Partly because I am more or less fatalistic; partly because my training in self-control not yet finished, has been hard enough. Partly because I possess an ingrained sense of humour. (A whizzbang [88mm German shell] missed me by inches over my head and exploded ten yards from me – and the impression it gave and gives me now is chiefly of the comic.)

(4) The conviction that prayer is no use to me.

(5) The fineness of the men. (The officers *may* develop.)

(6) My increasing love of music.

(7) An absolute belief (not so very old) that once out of the Army I can make myself fit . . .

(8) The conviction also, that in a hand to hand fight I shall be damned dangerous to tackle. A useful one to have; but I hope to God that He has a nice blighty ready for me and that there will be no need of such vulgar brawling – greatly against my taste as it is.[35]

Gurney felt 'I might be a good soldier could I forget music and books . . . A sense of beauty is every hindrance to a soldier; yet there would be no soldiers – or none such soldiers had not men dead and living cherished and handed on the sacred fire.'[36] He longed for a piano and was seriously bored rather than frightened, 'but I would not willingly give up such a memory of such a time'.[37] He never shaved in the trenches and wore old sandbags around his legs against the mud, which earned a reprimand. The sergeant major accused him of looking like a scarecrow: 'Come, come, Gurney, look more like a soldier for the Lord's sake.'[38] And, in spite of it all, the beauty of the June countryside of France: 'And O the Somme – the valley of the Somme round Amiens! A delight of rolling country, of a lovely river, and trees, trees, trees.'[39]

He kept reading whatever he could lay his hands on: Paul Claudel's *Trois Poèmes de Guerre*, copies of the *Times Literary Supplement*, Palgrave's *Golden Treasury* (which annoyed him) and whatever contemporary verse came his way. 'There is no verse pleases me better than the best of present day stuff though. We may have no great poets, but poetry so saturated with the spirit of England has not been written before.'[40] And he never lost his keen eye for his fellow men: 'Men behaving kindly to one another. Strained eyes and white faces yet able to smile. The absence of swank of any sort – among the men. The English virtues displayed at their best and least demonstrative.'[41] For himself he felt that 'Every day my mind gets less sick and more hopeful someday of sustained effort.' But one thing he would probably not be doing was writing an avant-garde concerto capturing the noise of war: 'I wonder whether any up to date fool will try to depict a strafe in music. The shattering crash of heavy shrapnel. The belly-disturbing crunch of 5.9 Crumps and trench mortars. The shrill clatter of rifle grenades and the wail of nosecaps flying loose. Sometimes buzzing like huge great May flies, a most terrifying noise when the thing is anywhere near you.'[42] To Howells he insisted, 'All nonsense about the rhythm of war . . . Some of the guns have a fine noise; but nearly all is of an insensate fury – too savage and assertive to be majestic.'[43] And to Marion Scott he speculated, 'it is better to live a grey life in mud and danger, so long as one uses it – as I trust I am now doing – as a means to an end. Someday all this experience may be crystallized and glorified in me; and men shall learn by chance fragments in a string quartett [sic] or a symphony, what thoughts haunted the minds of men who watched the darkness grimly in desolate places.'[44]

Gurney expressed to Howells his view of the value – or likely efficacy – of war poetry: 'Against a huge evil there has risen up a huger force of good, and the world, knowing itself to be saved, must endure the utmost misery for the sorrow necessary in and inevitable to the fighting of evil. It is doubtful whether artists can gain a full enough view of all this drama for generations yet.'[45] He also worried about the ethics of war poetry. 'Do you think there is too much regret in mine,' he asked Marion Scott, 'too much the confession of being unwillingly a soldier? Is there too much of a whine? I would not be out of it – right out of it – for anything; this gives me a right to talk and walk with braver men than myself and an insight into thousands of characters and a greater Power over Life, and more Love.'[46]

September came and went and his predictions of an early end to the War also vanished. Winter was coming on and he was having to survive on around three hours' sleep a day. For his old friend Marion Scott he produced a useful summary of a day in the life of a soldier-artist on the Western Front:

I promised to tell you something of life in the trenches. Our last orders were as follows. – From Stand to 5.30. Stand Down, clean rifles 6.0. Breakfast 7.30. Work 8.30 – 12.30. Dinner 1. Tea 4.30. Stand to 5–5.30. Stand Down. Then Ration fatigue. Listening Post. Sentry. Wiring-Party. Some of these last all night. One is allowed to sleep off duty – but not in dug outs. And the average, now the cold weather has come, and rain, is about 3 hours sleep. Out of trenches, there are parades, inspections, chiefly for shortages; and fatigues. R.E., Pioneer, and Ration fatigues for battalions in the line. The life is as grey as it sounds, but one manages to hang on to life by watching the absolute unquenchability of the cheerier spirits – wonderful people some of them.[47]

This didn't mean he didn't relish a little leave in London when it now came: 'Hot baths – breakfast in bed – tablecloths – books – late reading – Bach – Great walks – Renewing friendships – Talks of books – hunting second hand bookstalls – a sight of St Pauls again and to lose oneself in being in London'.[48] The winter was harsh in the early months of 1917 and, despairing of finding the materials to compose music properly, Gurney decided to concentrate on poetry. On one bitterly cold night in February he wrote the poem 'Firelight' in a room, fourteen feet by ten, containing eight people. Meanwhile the RSM seemed to be softening towards him, telling the colonel after an inspection, 'A Good man, sir, quite all right. Quite a good man, sir, but he's a musician, and doesn't seem able to get himself clean.' But shortly afterwards he recanted: 'Ah Gurney, I'm afraid we shall never make a soldier of you.'[49]

Early 1917 also saw Gurney trying to prepare his first volume of poems, some of which had been published in the Royal College of Music magazine in the past by Marion Scott. Several of his songs had been performed also at the College. He was drafting versions of the preface and one sentence is unsurprising: 'Most of the book is concerned with a person named Myself, and the rest with my county, Gloucester, that whether I die or live stays always with me.'[50] He explained to Marion Scott, 'All the verses were written in France, and in sound of the guns.'[51] He also tried to describe to her the mindset of his fellow soldiers and his own rather more complex attitude, which was neither Sassoonish protest nor simple patriotism: 'In the mind of all the English soldiers I have met there is absolutely no hate for the Germans, but a kind of brotherly though slightly contemptuous kindness – as to men who are going through a bad time as well as themselves . . . The whole thing is accepted as a heavy Burden of Fate. I have never been able to accept anything that way myself, and can only envy those who have such an attitude.'[52]

His aim with the poetry book was, as he put it, '(1) To leave something definite behind if I am knocked out. (2) To say out what Gloucester is, and is to me; and so to make Gloucester people think about their county. (3) To have *some* good stuff in it, whatever one may say about the whole. (4) To make people realise a little what the ordinary life is.'[53] That last phrase is ambiguous. Did he mean the 'ordinary life' of the trenches in particular or, more widely, the provincial life of western England?

Gurney knew that trench conditions were not ideal for writing poetry and felt that so much more could have been achieved had he had some peace and tranquillity, but this is always what writers feel, forgetting that sometimes adversity is itself a form of stimulus. His letters from the Front at this time give more insight into this tension than those of any of the other soldier-poets. Two things he believed his war experience had taught him: 'first, that the price of almost anything that one desires worthily is only Pain . . . and the knack of getting on with people, which I have developed out here to a much greater extent than heretofore'.[54] Increasingly, he was feeling that he needed to feed his life as an artist: 'I need modern verse now. It is difficult in these circumstances to live out of the thought of the present day, and Milton is absolutely impossible.'[55] And in one of those striking phrases in which the grandeur of his ambition is glimpsed he said that he was possessed by a 'fear of not living to write music for England; no fear at all of death'.[56]

And then on 6 April 1917, Good Friday, near Vermand in Picardy, he was wounded in his right arm just below the shoulder. The bullet went clean through the arm and he was sent to hospital at the 55th Infantry Base Depot at Rouen. This was not, alas, the 'blighty' that would have ensured a passage home. And he was luckier than his fellow poet, Edward Thomas, who was killed three days later at Arras: 'So Edward Thomas is dead,'[57] he observed laconically. He dreamed of what would happen if he really did catch that wound: 'If the Bosches hit an arm off me I will get the largest pension I can and go tramping the country, sleeping rough or with strange and wonderful tales attracting hospitality. And the first walk I shall take shall be Dymock, Newent, Ross and into Wales, to end at Chepstow after meeting names met in Malory.'[58]

Difficult as it was to live as an artist in these conditions, he was cheered by the acceptance by Sidgwick & Jackson of his book, and after recovery from his wound he was transferred to No. 1 section of 184 MGC as a machine gunner, his reputation as an excellent shot having gone before him. Gurney's own opinion of *Severn and Somme* was candid and it disperses some of the ambiguity referred to earlier:

Where it will fail to attract is that there is none, or hardly any of the devotion of self sacrifice, the splendid readiness for death that one finds in Grenfell, Brooke, Nichols etc. This is partly because I am still sick of mind and body; partly for physical, partly for mental reasons; also because, though I am ready if necessary to die for England, I do not see the necessity; it being only a hard and fast system which has sent so much of the flower of England's artists to risk death, and a wrong materialistic system; rightly or wrongly I consider myself able to do work which will do honour to England.

Such is my patriotism, and I believe it to be the right kind. But how to write such poems as 'If I should die' in this mood? (Also, I am not convinced that poets believe what they write always. Brooke was a sincere exception, but then, he was lucky; he died early in the war. So often poets write of what they wish to believe, wish to become, as one prays for strength and virtue not yet obtained.)[59]

Gurney sounds a rare note of dissent from the War's purposes here. He also expressed his admiration for Sassoon and his 'candour', but with pointed reservations. He felt that Sassoon was 'one who tries to tell Truth, though perhaps not a profound truth', and although Sassoon's poem 'They' contained things that 'need to be said', it was nonetheless 'journalism pure and simple'.[60] Cuttingly, he added that Sassoon was 'half-poet, the borrower of magic'. On another occasion he called him, damningly once more, 'a neat picturesque interesting writer who occasionally reaches poetry'.[61] But mercifully Sassoon did not belong to the poetic avant-garde: 'As for the Imagists – I hate all attempts at exact definition of beauty, which is a half-caught thing, a glimpse.'[62] And what was the point of such high aesthetic discourse on the battlefield near Passchendaele? 'Ruined tanks in front of me against a flaring west of tomorrow's wind and rain. A country like the last Hell of desolation. And to write verse, and abstract perfection!'[63] Sometimes the tension was almost too much, though he also knew that suffering was the catalyst of great art:

Why does this war of spirit take on such dread forms of ugliness, and why should a high triumph be signified by a body shattered, black, stinking; avoided by day, stumbled over by night, an offence to the hardest? . . . What consolation can be given me as I look upon and endure it? Any? Sufficient? The 'End of War'? Who knows, for the thing for which so great a price is paid is yet doubtful and obscure . . . God should have done better for us than this; could He not have found some better milder way of changing the Prussian (whom he made) than by the breaking of such beautiful souls? Now *that* is what one should write poetry upon. I have made a book about Beauty because I have paid the price which five years ago had not been paid.[64]

In early September, Gurney was involved in a gas attack at St Julien which, though he did not realise it immediately, was the end of the line for his military career. At first it was just an irritating feeling in the throat like catarrh, but soon he was transferred to Bangour War Hospital near Edinburgh where, in ward 24, he discovered that 'Only slowly and uncertainly is the conviction leaking in through the strong covering of frost and use that I am *really* in Blighty.'[65] At last he could play the piano and feel that his joy in doing so, the concentrated pleasure, showed that his neurasthenia was now a thing of the past. He saw with absolute clarity that 'War is simply a necessary but horrid nuisance, and my aim is work in Art, not a medal or a ribbon.'[66] Though not an anti-war poet, Gurney was, as we have seen, without illusions: 'Men at last do things not from courage or for their Country, but because of discipline (as I was told in 1914 and more still in 1915, but refused to believe). It is that which revolts one, and makes one long for the finish.'[67]

In the hospital no one cared much for Gurney's sort of music and there was nothing to read. He was forced to be the accompanist to drawing-room ballads and to yield to 'the universal clamorous desire for ragtime'.[68] He reported to Marion Scott that he had on one occasion played Beethoven at last, 'and for one golden minute my wandering mind was fixed and could see stars; I forgot the restraint that so long has been partly self-imposed on myself and flew free . . . Perhaps some songs may come from me before I return, but there is a lot to do before my mind will freely conceive anything. You simply don't know what France means, not in horror, but in everyday trial.'[69]

It was in Bangour, too, that he met Annie Drummond, a volunteer nurse, who would later be the dedicatee of his poems, but he was discharged from there in November and went to Northumberland for a signalling course. By February 1918, however, he was back in hospital, in Newcastle and then Durham. Signs of an incipient nervous breakdown appeared and in the summer he made threats of suicide and was treated for shell-shock, until in October he was discharged from the Army with a small pension and returned to Gloucester to work in a munitions factory. The blighty had not yielded its promise and, at the end of November 1917 from hospital, he had confessed, 'Yes there *were* good things in that bad time a year ago; good things. One feels far more fed up here than in France, as a general thing. It is good to go to one's limit, and good to see men facing hardships well and coolly facing vile Deaths.'[70]

War had indeed bound the disparate parts of Gurney's psyche together and in peace they would, once more, fall apart: 'O, if I were out of the Army and free, how I could write, but now all my courage and strength is needed to live as much as I do.'[71] The doctors marked his file 'Debility', and he was certainly behaving strangely. He had a dream in which he felt that he was in touch with the spirit of Beethoven. It was 'the strangest and most terrible spiritual adventure'.[72] Beethoven spoke to the poet, telling him 'That I should probably not write anything really big and good; for I had started late and had much to do with myself spiritually, with much to learn'. The doctors, he felt sure, would say he was insane but Gurney thought otherwise: 'No, it is the beginning of a new life, a new vision.' He was beginning to feel that, after the War, music would be his main ambition, telling a friend, 'Still, Music is my real game, and sooner or later I shall chuck verse altogether.'[73]

After the War he did indeed compose most of his best-known

and loved songs and the years 1919–22 were very productive, but after 1922 there were increasing signs of mental disturbance and in the autumn of that year he was committed to an asylum for the first time. He wrote from Barnwood House, Gloucester, many harrowing letters, some almost too painful to read, over the next fifteen years, until his death in the City of London Mental Hospital in Kent on 26 December 1937. One of these letters, from December 1922, reads: 'Death would be rest from torment . . . Hoping for chance of death. Rescue me I pray . . . It is Ivor Gurney calls for help and release.'[74]

Gurney's reputation as a poet has grown steadily – and his musical reputation, not considered here, has also risen – with one critic, John Lucas, writing that, after initially seeing him as little more than a minor Georgian, his *Collected Poems* in 1982 'left me gasping, knowing beyond doubt that I was in the presence of genius . . . Gurney is one of the most original, extraordinary, and *essential* of twentieth-century poets.'[75] As we have seen, his refusal, like Rosenberg, to propagandise is the reason why both of these poets may endure longest of all the 'trench poets', possibly coming to eclipse the more obvious and celebrated names.

Gurney's first volume, *Severn and Somme* in 1917, had on its title page the simple words 'Ivor Gurney, Private, of the Gloucesters', and in its preface he thanked 'my comrades of two platoons of the Gloucesters, who so often have wondered whether I were crazy or not'.[76] He also wrote:

All these verses were written in France, and in sound of the guns, save only two or three earlier pieces. This should be reason enough to excuse any roughness in the technique. If more reason is required, people of home, and most of all, people of Gloucester, may well be indulgent to one who thought of them so often, and whose images of beauty in the

mind were always of Gloucester, county of Cotswold and
Severn, and a plain rich, blossomy, and sweet of airs – as the
wise Romans knew, who made their homes in exile by the
brown river, watching the further bank for signs of war.

Gurney's first modern editor, P. J. Kavanagh, suggested that,
although attached deeply to Gloucestershire, he was 'sparing of
topography' and more interested in seasons and sky effects. 'If
he is to be given a locality, he could with more justice be called
a sky-poet.' Army censorship was a real problem for him in this
regard because he was a poet who liked to name names: 'It is
the poetry of a particularized, not a generalized humanity, of the
flesh and nerves rather than of the intellect.' Kavanagh suggests
that while Owen and the protest poets were indignant at the
War, 'and tell us truths we ought to have guessed, Gurney gives
us pictures we would not have imagined'.

The early poems in the 1917 volume express a sense of
regretful severance from his Gloucestershire roots, as in 'The
Fire Kindled' with its couplet 'God, that I might see/ Framilode
once again!' Although he had reservations about Rupert Brooke,
Gurney could produce, if he wanted, a heroic poem, as in 'To the
Poet Before Battle' where he addresses the young soldier-poet:

Now, youth, the hour of thy dread passion comes;
Thy lovely things must all be laid away;
. . .
. . . they must know we are,
For all our skill in words, equal in might
And strong of mettle as those we honoured; make
The name of poet terrible in just war,
And like a crown of honour upon the fight.

Another poem, 'Strange Service', again stresses this sense of
War's dislocations:

Little did I dream, England, that you bore me
Under the Cotswold hills beside the water meadows,
To do you dreadful service, here, beyond your borders
And your enfolding seas.

'The Mother' talks of how 'We scar the earth with dreadful engin'ry', and in another, 'Song and Pain', he declares: 'Out of my sorrow have I made these songs.' There are poems about 'the horror of war' as painful as anything in Owen –

Men broken, shrieking even to hear a gun.
Till pain grinds down, or lethargy numbs her,
The amazed heart cries angrily out on God.

– but none that challenge it in the way Owen and Sassoon did. In his second war volume, *War's Embers* (1919), 'De Profundis' imagines again the lost Arcadia of Gloucestershire:

We are stale here, we are covered body and soul and
     mind
With mire of the trenches, close clinging and foul,
We have left our old inheritance, our Paradise behind,
And clarity is lost to us and cleanness of soul.

But there is also an element not so prominent in the work of other war poets, a sense of comradeship and fondness for his fellows. In the poem 'To the Prussians of England' he recalls the 'plain heroic strength' shown at Ypres, then reads 'the blither written by knaves for fools' in praise of English soldiers:

Who purely dream what England shall be made
Gloriously new, free of the old stains
By us, who pay the price that must be paid.

Gurney found beauty as so many of the poets did, intermittently on the battlefields, as in the lovely short poem 'Memory Let All Slip' which urges:

Memory, let all slip save what is sweet
Of Ypres plains.
Keep only autumn sunlight and the fleet
Clouds after rains.

Many of these poems were written between 1919 and 1922, Gurney being one of those, like Sassoon and Blunden and David Jones, who had the survivor's privilege to remember. A poem like 'Possessions', for example, regrets the trees that were felled on Witcombe hill for war purposes. And 'Strange Hells' is a bitter poem about war's legacy: 'There are strange Hells within the minds War made,' he writes, recalling some Gloucester soldiers singing defiantly under an enemy attack:

Where are they now, on State-doles, or showing shop-
    patterns
Or walking town to town sore in borrowed tatterns
Or begged . . .

Another poem, 'Mist on Meadows', expresses unusual anger, at neglect of soldiers after the war.

But nothing could be as horrifying as Gurney's own descent into madness after the War. A poem written sometime in the mid-1920s is addressed 'To God' and asks, 'Why have you made life so intolerable/ And set me between four walls?' And in another, 'The Interview', in his asylum he longs for the death he outfaced in France. He also recalled, in 'On Somme', the special kind of courage demanded by trench warfare:

No flame we saw, the noise and the dread alone
Was battle to us . . .
Courage kept, but ready to vanish at first touch.
Fear, but just held. Poets were luckier once
In the hot fray swallowed and some magnificence.

One of the late poems is particularly poignant, 'Song', which regrets that war prevented truly great work emerging, that something was lost: 'But where are such verses/ That in my heart burned?'

In one of his letters from the Front he referred to the work of Edward Thomas, whose poetry, we might feel, had a natural affinity to his, but Gurney was sensing something else in the poems: 'Very curious they are, very interesting; nebulously intangibly beautiful. But he had the same sickness of mind I have – the impossibility of serenity for any but the shortest space. Such a mind produces little.'[77] For Gurney, 'a sense of imperfection, of a veil between him and his object continually haunts me in reading him'.[78] He was right, in one sense, that Thomas, who came late to poetry and whose life was snatched away before very much even of that could be written, has left a relatively small body of work, and of that written while at the Front, little of it fits into the 'trench poet' category.

Thomas was indeed a complex and emotionally unstable personality. He found it difficult to relate to people, once telling the poet Gordon Bottomley, 'Social intercourse is only an intense form of solitude.'[79] He struggled to make a living and his early life was very difficult. His wife, Helen, who also struggled to help him to maintain his hold on life, referred to the 'hateful hackwork books' he had to write to live as failing to satisfy his own creative impulse, 'the damming up of which contributed largely to his melancholy'.[80] Another friend commented, 'He seemed to be a born poet. He loved and understood poetry as few men of his time did. He longed to write it himself. But it would not come. It was, I think, the conditions of his life that made it impossible. There was no peace, no rest.'[81] The dark moods of despair, self-loathing and doubt about the value of the writing that circumstances compelled him to produce in such furious abundance, interacted with his hypersensitive nature and tendency to melancholy to create a man in torment. As with Gurney, war was, in some sense, a kind of solution.

Philip Edward Thomas, whose name is so often thought of in connection with the English countryside, was born in Lambeth in London in 1878[82] of Welsh ancestry and educated at Battersea Grammar School and St Paul's, leaving the latter in 1895 to take, under family pressure, the Civil Service examinations, when he really wanted to be a writer in the spirit of Richard Jefferies (1848–87). A year later he published his first book of nature writing, *The Woodland Life*. He also began a relationship in 1896 with Helen Noble, whose later autobiographies such as *As It Was* (1926) paint a vivid picture of him, and she was pregnant when they married on 20 June 1899. Thomas was an Oxford undergraduate at this time and in 1900 his poor degree, coupled with his decision to become a writer, merely increased his father's disapproval. In 1901 the family moved to Rose Acre Cottage at Bearsted in Kent and he threw himself into the life of a literary hack, living on less than £2 a week. They frequently moved house, always in the country, and he churned out reviews of poetry, criticism, and books about the countryside, wrote essays and edited anthologies, guidebooks and collections of folk-tales, as well as more substantial critical studies of writers such as Maeterlinck, Swinburne and Pater. The tension between this literary drudgery and his deep creative need caused repeated breakdowns and at one point he came near to suicide.

It was not until December 1914, after the War had been declared, that Thomas first turned from prose to poetry and wrote his first poem, 'Up in the Wind'. A year earlier he had met

Robert Frost and by praising him in England he helped to make Frost's reputation in his native America where, incredibly, he was at that time unknown. The friendship was an important one and Thomas at one point thought of following Frost to America if the War had ended earlier. Frost saw the poetic elements in some of Thomas's intensely felt prose and encouraged him in poetry. Thomas had already tried to come to terms with the War in prose, in *In Pursuit of Spring* (1914), and, finding fewer outlets in wartime for his usual work, he devoted more time to poetry. In January 1915 he confessed to a friend, 'I have even begun to write verse, but don't tell a soul, as if it is to be published at all it must be anonymously.'[83] To another friend, the poet Gordon Bottomley, he described this new venture in writing: 'Perhaps it is only like doing the best parts of my prose in verse & leaving out the connecting futile parts.'[84] The influence of Frost was palpable and he told Bottomley that his American mentor stressed the importance of speech rhythms, which Thomas's poetry was to derive great strength and distinctiveness from: 'All he insists on is what he believes he finds in all poets – absolute fidelity to the postures which the voice assumes in the most expressive intimate speech.'[85] Although he was paranoid about being identified as a poet, through the agency of Bottomley eventually he shyly produced a selection under the name 'Edward Eastaway' for *An Annual of New Poetry* (1917). These were the only poems Thomas ever saw published in his lifetime.

In July 1915, in spite of being much older than the run of recruits, Thomas enlisted with the Artists' Rifles. In April he had written to his aunt, Margaret Townsend, setting out his apprehensions at taking this step:

> I have been thinking a good deal from time to time, trying to decide whether to try to enlist or not. I don't want to: only I feel that is the only thing to do if a man is able-bodied and

has nothing else to do. And who can do anything else much
now? The war must probably last many months, more than a
year, longer. The only satisfaction I get is in realizing that so
many men in a civilized age are capable of this kind of extrav-
agant courage and endurance. I can't imagine that as men are
at present, and as I imagine they will long remain, a nation is
of much use that is not capable of this violent folly, when the
body and whatever of the mind can work with the body pre-
vails and boosts itself.[86]

Thomas was sent in November 1915 to Hare Hall Camp in
Gidea Park, Essex, at the same time as another new Artists'
Rifles recruit, Wilfred Owen. There is no evidence that the two
ever met, though Owen's biographer, Dominic Hibberd, spec-
ulates that Owen could have been in one of Lance Corporal
P. E. Thomas's map-reading classes at Romford.[87] Not as out-
going and clubbable as Ivor Gurney seems to have been,
Thomas nonetheless claimed to enjoy his training and got
along with people better than he had expected to. 'It is all like
being somebody else,' he told Frost, 'or like being in a dream
of school.'[88] Thomas's tasks included, as well as map-reading,
teaching field sketching, the use of compass and protractor, and
making a map on the ground with and without the compass, for
which he was paid a shilling a day. This also involved taking
the men out on exercises on Hampstead Heath once a week to
make maps, ending with a swim in the Hampstead ponds. In
his spare time he continued to write poems and he came near
to inclusion in the new *Georgian Poetry*, but seemingly Harold
Monro, whom Thomas had met in London and found rather
bumptious and provocative, edged him out. The only things he
cared for in the anthology were by de la Mare and W. H.
Davies.

In March 1916 Thomas was promoted to corporal and
applied for a commission in the Royal Artillery in June, in order,

he said, that a better pension would be available for Helen. He was accepted in July and trained as an officer cadet in London. 'From 6 a.m. to 7.30 p.m. except for meals, I am being lectured to about levers & pulleys and fuses etc . . . It is school again & I am far from the top of the class,'[89] he told Bottomley. He was commissioned as 2nd lieutenant in November and posted to 244 Siege Battery, Royal Garrison Artillery, in Lydd, Kent. In December he volunteered for service overseas, speculating that he might be sent to Salonika, but on 29 January 1917 he finally embarked from Southampton for France. He gave Bottomley a brisk summing-up: 'It will be a change to be in France & be judged simply by what one does or doesn't do. I have a good pair of fieldglasses & my ears can stand the racket, so I can only fail because I couldn't succeed. I have practically no chance of promotion.'[90] All this activity put paid to reading anything other than the service manual and his writing was also on hold, but at least he had enough to put together a draft volume of *Poems* for Selwyn & Blount, which would be published posthumously in 1917.

The Allies had been coordinating a major advance in early 1917 and, in April, the British would push forward in the Battle of Arras, and in July would again join battle at Ypres (Passchendaele), where mustard gas would be seen for the first time. This was the military context in which Thomas arrived at Dainville near Arras in the first week of February 1917, and after a spell at headquarters he rejoined 244 Siege Battery whence he reported to Bottomley:

We have been out a month but it took us over a week to crawl up to the front on snowy roads & sleeping in trains & tents & other cold places. But I enjoyed most of it. I like the country we are in. It is open hilly chalk country with great ploughed fields & a few copses on the hilltops. The ruined villages of brick & thatch and soft white stone have been beautiful. Of course one does not stroll about here, but the incidental walks to Observation Posts or up to see my battery are often very pleasant, both in the frost & in the sunny weather which has begun at last . . . One gets – I mean I get – along moderately well, or even more, with all sorts of uncongenial people, & I have nothing to complain of except lack of letters & parcels.[91]

Towards the end of March, at his observation post, Thomas watched the flashes of enemy guns at night and froze. He meditated on fear on the battlefield:

Fear too, I have discovered – to that point where the worst moment is when you find you have survived & that all your fear was useless. You screw yourself up for a second to bear anything & nothing comes – except a curious disappointment which I suppose is also relief. Sometimes at night I have been in this state a hundred times, but partly through inexperience, not knowing what might mean harm. Still, I shall never like the shell that flaps as it falls, or the one that suddenly bounces into hearing & in a second is bursting far off – no sooner does it open the gate than it is right in the door, or even the small one that complains and whimpers & is called a 'pipsqueak' or a 'whizzbang', & flies into that ghastly village all night long like flights of humming birds.[92]

Yet in spite of these terrors, Thomas decided he was happy to look at the villages, and the ruined city of Arras and 'the larks in the bloody dirty dawn, the partridges, the magpies floating about among shellfire & once a bat, & a hundred different houses, in city, suburb, & village'.[93] Thomas was a countryman and a writer about country things and never lost his appetite for landscape. On 4 April he wrote to Gordon Bottomley:

It is the end of a beautiful sunny day that began cold with snow. The air has been full of aeroplanes & shells & yet there have been clothes hanging up to dry in the sun outside my window which has glass in it, though whether it will tomorrow not even the Hun knows. The servants are chatting outside in their shirtsleeves & war is not for the moment dirty or ugly – as it was this morning when I was well in front & the shining sun made ruins & rusty barbed wire & dead horses & deep filthy mud uglier than they are in the stormy weather or in the pale cold dawn. I am muddy to the waist now, but not going to change till I go to bed, for we have a big woodfire supplied by the ruins of the neighbouring houses & today is not a busy one.[94]

Five days after writing these words, on 9 April 1917, during the first hour of the Battle of Arras, Edward Thomas was killed at his observation post by a direct hit from a shell. There are no more details of what happened, just the brutal abruptness of the fact of death, as with so many of the other poets who died in action. He was buried in Agny military cemetery on the outskirts of Arras. He had not lived to see published any of his work in *Poems* (1917) under the pseudonym Edward Eastaway, to be followed by *Last Poems* in 1918.

His old friend Eleanor Farjeon wrote shortly afterwards to Bottomley: 'They said in the Battery they looked on him as a sort of Father, because he was the oldest of them.'[95]

When the poems of 'Edward Eastaway' were published early in 1917 in *An Annual of New Poetry*, the anonymous *Times Literary Supplement* reviewer said, 'At present, like most of his contemporaries, he has too little control over his eyes.' The comment infuriated Thomas because seeing, observing, was what he did, in prose and in poetry. Like Thomas Hardy he was 'a man who used to notice such things', and he shared his anger with Bottomley: 'Why do the idiots accuse me of using my eyes? Must I only use them with fieldglasses & must I see only Huns in these beautiful hills eastwards & only hostile flashes in the night skies when I am at the Observation Post?'[96] But Thomas's best poetry is more than mere photographic observation of nature. Like Frost he deployed the natural speaking voice in his poems and had a directness and fluency that contrast with, for example, Gurney, with his dense, sometimes opaque style.[97] One of Thomas's shortest poems, written in April 1915, illustrates perfectly the nature of his gift, its enviable ease, and its defiance of commentary, in this instance, to add anything useful at all:

In Memoriam
The flowers left thick at nightfall in the wood
This Eastertide call into mind the men,
Now far from home, who, with their sweethearts, should
Have gathered them and will never do again.

The poem is instantly graspable. It expresses a simple but moving truth, and says more about the nature of war, its violation of natural processes and proper human rituals, than any more laboured or accusatory poem of denunciation of war's horrors or futility could do. The strained attempt by some critics to make those unplucked lovers' flowers into symbols of fallen soldiers is redundant. The poem does not need that kind of over-egged decoding.

Shortly after this, Thomas wrote another poem which explored his complex personal feelings about the war, 'This is no case of petty right and wrong'. Containing the line 'I hate not Germans', the poem rejects the jingoistic patriotism that some of Thomas's friends – and his father – resorted to. In an unpublished notebook containing his compressed thoughts on war poetry, while he was still debating with himself whether or not to sign up, he wrote, 'Some writers can't go on with old work but no reason why they should at once be able to admit war into subject matter. Poetry excepting cheapest kind shows this dark chaotic character. People expressing all sorts of <u>views</u> and trumping up old canting catchwords, but not yet the compact essential real truth to this occasion alone. Statesmen may say "No price too high when honour and freedom are at stake" etc. But it can't be translated into poetry.'[98] The issue was the extent to which subject matter could be allowed to get the upper hand in the war poem, but there was another question for a poet who had not yet decided whether to enlist: what kind of poetry could be written if the War were refused? How could one simply go on writing what one had been used to in that context of world war, when others were fighting, when that powerful reality was pressing on the writer's consciousness, combatant or non-combatant? There was really no escape from the question.

Thomas was not naively patriotic nor was he one of those who believed in innate national superiority. Like Brooke or Sorley, he could not support the ridiculous notion that an Englishman was superior to a German. His patriotism was not about hatred or suspicion of the foreigner, it was about love of the place he knew and its traditions. England was not a bulwark against the foreigner, but

> She is all we know and live by, and we trust
> She is good and must endure, loving her so:
> And as we love ourselves we hate her foe.

In a much quoted reply to a question from Eleanor Farjeon about whether he knew what he was fighting for, 'He stopped, and picked up a pinch of earth. "Literally, for this." He crumbled it between finger and thumb, and let it fall.'[99]

The patriotism, the 'Englishness' of this half-Welsh poet, was about attachment to the landscape and the cyclical rhythms of the countryside. It was nothing to do with the militant jingoism of the wartime media. And it was clear-sighted, as in another poem of early 1916, 'February Afternoon', which finds the poet in a stretch of English ploughland, hearing 'the roar of parleying starlings', and feeling that this will all continue even though 'men strike and bear the stroke/ Of war as ever'. But there is scant consolation to be derived from religion, for God looks down on the scene 'stone-deaf and stone-blind'. That juxtaposition of pastoral and the immanence of war is present in another poem of May 1916, 'As the Team's Head Brass', which is set in the Essex countryside, Thomas in dialogue with a ploughman about the War and its impact. Many young farm-boys have gone to France and been killed: 'Only two teams work on the farm this year.' Even the fallen elm on which the poet sits is there only because there are no hands to move it. And two lovers are seen disappearing into the wood. This is not, however, sweet escapist pastoral; it is a dialogue about the sharp impact of war on the life of the countryside. The short poem 'No one cares less than I' juxtaposes a quatrain made up to match the raucous morning reveille of the bugle at the Gidea Park camp. The quatrain is about 'Whether I am destined to lie/ Under a foreign clod' and the alien noise of the bugle is a comment on the military world's indifference to the individual's fate. Thomas was not a Sassoon but nor was he a Brooke.

Speaking in 1974 at the memorial service in St Bride's, Fleet Street, for the poet Edmund Blunden, Rupert Hart-Davis declared, 'It is interesting, if unprofitable, to wonder whether he would have remained a purely pastoral poet if he and his whole generation had not been engulfed in catastrophe.'[100] Blunden was only seventeen when the War broke out, 'But the Armistice brought no respite to his mind, and for the rest of his long life he continually thought, wrote, and dreamed of the horror of the trenches.'

For the poets who survived, as opposed to those like Owen, Rosenberg or Sorley whose poems are fresh dispatches from the Front, the long aftermath of peace – punctuated for Graves, Blunden, Sassoon, and David Jones by yet another world war – brought mixed benefits. Time to reflect and put in order the poets' sense of what they had been through conflicted with the sense of being haunted by an experience from which there was no release. 'I must go over the ground again,'[101] wrote Blunden in the opening pages of his *Undertones of War* (1928). He felt that he would be doing so until he died.

Blunden was a very traditional poet, uninterested in the work of the literary modernists. He too was a lover of the English countryside and its traditions and it was war's violation of rural tranquillity and peaceful order that pained most his imaginative world. Had it not been for the War he would probably have been remembered as a minor pastoral poet but instead he became a poet of memory who gave expression to the haunted feelings of the survivors. He was a small, quick man with darting movements, whom Sassoon once referred to as 'perching' on a bed: 'He always reminds me of a bird,' he wrote.[102] Though his commanding officer in the army referred to him as 'Rabbit'.

Blunden spent longer at the Front than any other British war poet, yet his poems are seldom about the actual front-line experiences that made so many of the classic poems of the War. His two years of service, from 1916 to 1918, involved him in some of the most serious fighting of the conflict. He was at Ancre and Thiepval Wood in August 1916 and was awarded the Military Cross for his performance at the Schwaben Redoubt on 13 November that year. He was also involved in the third Battle of Ypres that began on 31 July 1917.[103]

Edmund Blunden was born in 1896 in Tottenham Court Road, London, the eldest of nine children of parents who were schoolteachers. At the age of four he left the city centre for

Yalding in Kent, where his love of the countryside was planted. Clever and precocious, he won a scholarship to Christ's Hospital in Sussex, the public school where Coleridge and Lamb had been pupils, but in his final year war was declared and he was commissioned in August 1915 as a 2nd lieutenant in the Royal Sussex Regiment. Early in 1916 Blunden was sent to Flanders: 'I was not anxious to go. An uncertain but increasing disquiet had been upon me, and when, returning to the officers' mess at Shoreham Camp one Sunday evening, I read the notice that I was under orders for France, I did not hide my feelings.'[104]

The seventeen-year-old pastoral poet went straight from Victoria to Étaples, to a dismal base with its notorious 'Bull-Ring', which he called a 'thirsty, savage, interminable training-ground'.[105] He was relieved when eventually he was sent on to Béthune: 'The long and slatternly train, scarcely in motion for the past twelve hours, stopped dead, and the carriages in succession gave that sudden backward mule-kick which gives troop-trains one of their unique charms, jolting us out of our singularly horrible counterfeit sleep. Yawning and rusty, we collected our trappings and jumped out on to the track. I had no more idea than the man in the moon how far we were from the line – from one to thirty miles I decided!'[106] Blunden records the impact of the war on a highly sensitive teenager, his first experiences of being under fire, and the macabre realities of trench life: 'At some points in the trench, bones pierced through their shallow burial, and skulls appeared like mushrooms . . . One of the first ideas that established themselves in my enquiring mind was the prevailing sense of the endlessness of the war. No one here appeared to conceive any end to it.'[107]

His descriptions of the battlefield are often vivid: 'The red sparks of German trench mortars described their seeming-slow arcs, shrapnel shells clanged in crimson, burning, momentary cloudlets, smoke billowed into a tidal wave, and the powdery glare of many a signal-light showed its rolling folds. The roarings and cracklings of the contest between artilleries and small-arms sometimes seemed to lessen as one gigantic burst was heard.'[108] The trenches themselves 'were merely cast-up ridges of earth held in place by stakes, wire, hurdles, and wooden framework. Underneath their floors of boards and slats, water welled and stagnated, and an indescribable nocturnal smell, mortal, greenweedy, ratty, accompanied the tramp of our boots to and fro.'[109] In 1916 steel helmets were issued and Blunden saw this as significant: 'The dethronement of the soft cap clearly symbolized the change that was coming over the war, the induration from a personal crusade into a vast machine of violence, that had come in the south, where vague victory seemed to be happening.'[110]

Before Blunden set out for Flanders he had left with a publisher 'a trifling collection of verses' which he had forgotten about until his colonel appeared saying that the young platoon commander was wanted at battalion HQ: 'A review of my poems has been printed in the *Times Literary Supplement* (a kind review it was, if ever there was one!), and my Colonel is overjoyed at having an actual author in his battalion. How rosy he looks!'[111] In fact, Blunden didn't want to be transferred to battalion HQ and its 'lordly style'. 'But all to no purpose; that book of verse had done its work; and the same evening I was at dinner in [Colonel] Harrison's presence, afraid of him and everyone else in that high command, and marvelling at the fine glass which was in use there.'[112]

Soon, however, he left Givenchy, where his battalion had been based since its move from Festubert (his first experience of the trenches), in order to occupy the Neuve Chapelle area in preparation for the Battle of the Somme. 'I passed good men of ours, in our front line, staring like men in a trance across No Man's Land, their powers of action apparently suspended ... All was in ominous discommunication ... The day was hot outside, glaring mercilessly upon the burned, choked chalk trenches . . . No one could say what had happened or what was happening.'[113] Blunden's vivid and immediate picturing in his reminiscences contrasts with a vagueness about the bigger picture – the conditions of trench warfare preventing anyone from seeing that larger, informed perspective on strategy – with the result that the confusion and noise and terror of the battlefield seem all the more intense. Some days later, in the trenches round about Thiepval Wood, he saw a Scottish soldier dead but kneeling, facing east: 'Death could not kneel so, I thought, and approaching I ascertained with a sudden shrivelling of spirit that Death could and did.'[114] In October 1916, towards the end of the Somme offensive, after an attack on Stuff Trench, he was awarded the Military Cross.

Blunden's account of the War is largely neutral in political tone, but in May 1917 he recorded a discussion at the colonel's table in HQ where 'I began to air my convictions that the war was useless and inhuman'.[115] In response 'a highly conservative general' asked him why he wasn't in that case fighting for the Germans, 'to which I answered with all too triumphant a simplicity that it was only due to my having been born in England, not Germany'. He seems not to have been reprimanded for this and it was clearly not unknown for such thoughts to be expressed. Reading Sassoon for the first time in the *Cambridge Magazine*, Blunden approved his 'splendid war on the war'.[116] Reflecting a little later on some casualties in the Ypres offensive he recorded, 'These losses I felt, but with a sensibility blurred by the general grossness of the war.' He felt 'the uselessness of the offensive' and detected 'a mood of selfishness. We should all die, presumably, round Ypres.'[117] When he was moved to a new front during this period he discovered his 'enormous' indebtedness to the poet Edward Young, who wrote 'Night Thoughts', and 'felt the benefit of this grave and intellectual voice, speaking out of a profound eighteenth-century calm'.[118]

After the publication of *Undertones of War* in 1928, Blunden made two further attempts to record and take the measure of the experience on which he had brooded so long. The first of these was the release in 1930 of an account (actually written in 1918) called *De Bello Germanico*. Blunden had carried with him in his knapsack the original Latin work of Julius Caesar and claimed that, in the intervening period, his own manuscript had 'slept with cobwebs and dust'. Unlike *Undertones*, which 'has the mellowness of time and experience', the earlier version 'gives more attention to the very small detail which a young soldier was sure to notice, and indeed made his day and night'.[119] This is true up to a point but it has the same sense of the author being totally enclosed in an experience of immediate horror, often without the reference points of dates and firm geographical placing. At the same time, as suggested above, this is probably indeed what it was like to be there. *De Bello Germanico*, however, does contain a little more dialogue of the ordinary Tommy, as when Blunden arrived in Béthune in the spring of 1916: 'The countryside had a harmless, parcelled, thrifty look; but my incipient idyllic view of war (hope fathering thought) was shattered by the driver, who said, "Quartermaster were coming round this corner last night and Fritz sent over fifteen shells. Blew 'is 'orse onesided, one of 'em did."'[120]

Blunden, with his eye for landscape and the contour of the rural scene, always noticed how things actually looked when war was taken out of the equation: 'those rainy well-tilled lowlands checkered with red and white farms, colonnades of poplars and glistening shrines', or at the little hamlet of Le Touret 'where children and chickens peacefully engaged in the mud demonstrated how far we were from war's alarms'.[121] Actually, war's alarms were a good deal nearer than he thought, for very soon after arriving at the Front he met an officer who declared, 'The line's hell.' At this, wrote Blunden, 'the mercury in my courage thermometer dropped into the bulb'.[122] Hearing the new vocabulary of trench life he found that mention of duckboards 'led me to imagine a kind of archipelago with enclosures for ducks'.[123] He went into a local shop selling chocolate and pencils and the vendor said to him in broken English, 'M'sieu la guerre dure trop longtemps – zis war become too long izzent he?'[124]

Taking up his post at Festubert, Blunden soon noticed 'three or four insects of an unfamiliar kind whip past with a whining "Bizzz" – bullets!'[125] His new temporary home was 'a small and stuffy dugout', and when his bed was indicated he was warned of the presence of rats. The bed was 'a kind of burrow in the dugout wall, of sufficiently grisly appearance and a ratty odour'.[126] Food included a tin of Californian peaches and 'the inevitable trench savory – singed sardines on toast'. The dugout itself was 'Six feet by six, with every modern discomfort; hardly rainproof, but (by kindred fallacy with that of the hunted ostrich) accredited shelter from all Teutonic malice; fuggy, draughty withal, rat-stricken, primeval, crampt, and crowded, yet housing (as I soon recognized) stout hearts, good cheer, and unhesitating friendliness'.[127] Like Ivor Gurney, and in contrast to Sassoon, Blunden seems to have enjoyed the ordinary camaraderie of the trenches. His first night in the trenches at Festubert on his bed of sandbags, wrapped in an overcoat known as a 'British Warm', was comfortable.

The next morning he stepped out to be shown the ropes by an officer on watch:

The hot gold sun was already drowsy in the blue, and the war seemed to have slunk into a corner and fallen asleep. Old friends seemed to be all round; a skylark was floating and climbing steep above us, like his cousins over Sussex lands, with his fine melody let fall in prodigal enchantments. There was the growing drone of summer in the grassfields and

orchards behind, and on the broken hawthorn tree the blackbird was asking what war was; and did not see the
sparrowhawk hanging bloodthirstily over the stubbles. A
tabby cat came sleekly round a traverse and purred peace and
goodwill. My own idea of war improved wonderfully, till
presently a sickly breeze came by with history of the great
and murderous battle here a year ago [May 1915], and L——
pointed me out the skulls, jagging bones, and wooden crosses
with their weather-worn 'TO AN UNKNOWN BRITISH
SOLDIER' and 'R.I.P', on the side of the trench.[128]

Blunden soon discovered unburied skeletons in rotted uniforms, and his education in war accelerated:

These wooden crosses, gaunt, cynical, earthy, seemed utterly
unfriendly to the momentary peace and beauty, or perhaps
somewhat akin to the poems of Homer; the forlorn memorials of some far-off tribal bloodshed and horror not to be
encountered again . . . But I felt sure that this style of war was
utterly obsolete. This was another case of ignorance and
bliss . . . My impression of the trench (we were in the comfort of reserve positions) was now condensing into a glorified
ditch between two sandbag banks, lined with groups of sen-
tries; gloomy alcoves inscribed with witty names; lazer-holes
crammed with bomb boxes or ammunition; graves, lime, old
bayonets, braziers; and the saving grace of indolence over
all.[129]

As a young poet in love with the countryside Blunden was
struggling to reconcile the beauty of springtime Flanders with
the rumour of war: 'These placid early-summer days . . . were
to become my regretful dream a few months later', and he
represented himself as 'a humble Don Quixote facing war with
beautiful idiocy'.[130] His first really uncomfortable episode was

a scramble in moonlight to the front line in the course of which
he discovered how useless the British Verey lights were, so poor
in fact that the Germans would sometimes throw up lighted
matches from their trench in mockery. Blunden soon acquired
a batman who would be with him for the next two years and
found that his duties were to organise the digging of trenches
and censoring letters. One night he was suddenly caught in a
hail of fire that turned out to be caused by a torch in his pocket
accidentally coming on and giving a guiding gleam to 'Fritz'.

It was when the Company moved to the front line to defend
a position known as the Brickstacks that things started to get a
little more sticky: 'Of all battle-fields this was perhaps the most
grotesque and gripping.' A score or so of brickstacks rose up 'out
of a flat wilderness queasy with gamboge darnel and festering
heliotrope poppies'. These obvious forts had been fought over
and the Germans had some of them:

> Inside, stifling creep-holes twisted up to 'secret' machine-
> guns and look-outs, with painted instruction boards against
> the day of attack: below, muddy staircases opened into tun-
> nellers' and infantry dugouts, telephone centres and trench
> stores. From these nerve centres with more or less effrontery
> led forward or backward a series of boyaux, alleys half-
> choked with glutinous pudder of a filthy grey, crumbling,
> aromatic, tangled with signallers' wires. The front line itself
> was a mere ditch; with defects.[131]

And ahead of him 'An intolerable landscape . . . In front, like
the waste of dreadful days to come, stretched No Man's
Land, a blur, a curse to the eyes, gouged into great craters and
innumerable shell-holes, strewn with the apparatus of wire
entanglements.'[132]

Like Sassoon, Blunden liked nothing better than to walk out
into the surrounding countryside, still beautiful in spite of

everything that war could do to it. This contrast, of rural beauty, the stability of the earth and its seasonal changes, with the man-made destruction of the landscape through war, is one of the dominant themes of British war poetry. Unlike the Italian Futurists, for example, who saw war (at least in their paper manifestos) as an exciting construction of dazzling modernity and dynamic energy, the English poets adhered to an older pastoral script. One evening Blunden walked out 'to the reedy marshes beyond the houses, and almost became a pagan. The vast, serene summer sky, the deepening blue spaces and the silence only surer for the sad rustle of reeds in a little wind; but a death-liness, a poignancy, a sapping stagnancy lying on the mind, embittering the lonely beauty – these influences wove me in a spell. It was as though all nature knew of the war, and saw its future.'[133]

Blunden's third memoir, *The Mind's Eye*, appeared in 1934 and it found him reflecting in the preface:

How mysterious that after so many years, not inactive, not undramatic, nor passed without much delight and discovery in man and nature, I find myself frequently living over again moments of experience on the Western Front. The war itself with its desperate drudgery is not the predominant part of these memories – I need a more intense word than memories; it is Nature as then disclosed by fits and starts, as then most luckily encountered 'in spite of sorrow' that so occupies me still. The mind suddenly yields to simple visions. Pale light striking through clouds in shafts, like the sunrays of Rembrandt, beyond the mute and destined tower of Mesnil, continues inextinguishably to lure me . . . I think to pick up the rosy-cheeked apples fallen in the deserted, leaf-dappled, grassy gunpits in the orchards of Hamel. And then some word from my companion calls me to lose no more time with our bomb-boxes on the menacing village road.[134]

Break of day in the trenches.

The darkness crumbles away.
It is the same old Druid Time as ever,
Only a live think leaps my hand,
A queer sardonic rat,
As I pull the parapets poppy
To stick behind my ear.
Droll rat, they would shoot you if they knew
Your cosmopolitan sympathies,
(And God knows what antipathies).
Now you have touched this English hand
You will do the same to a German
Soon, no doubt, if it be your pleasure
To cross the sleeping green between,
It seems odd thing, you grin as you pass
Strong eyes, fine limbs, haughty athletes,
Less chanced than you for life,
Bonds to the whims of Murder,
Sprawled in the bowels of the earth
The torn fields of France.
What do you see in our eyes
At the boom, the hiss, the swiftness,
The irrevocable earth--buffet....
What rootless poppies drooping
But mine in my ear is safe---
Just a little white with the dust.

at the shrieking iron + flame
Hurld through still heavens?
What quaver — what heart aghast?
Poppies whose roots are in mans veins
Drop, + are ever dropping.

Isaac Rosenberg.
June. 1916.

A.R.

The typescript of Isaac Rosenberg's 'Break of Day in the Trenches',
one of the finest poems of the War

(© Imperial War Museum)

A self-portrait by Isaac
Rosenberg, 1916
(© Lebrecht Music and Art)

Isaac Rosenberg in France as a
private with the King's Own
Lancaster Regiment in 1917.
He had enlisted two years
earlier purely to assist his family
financially, and struggled to
keep his poetry alive: 'My not
being able to get poetry out of
my head & heart causes me
sufficient trouble out here'
(© National Portrait Gallery)

Edmund Blunden as
a young soldier
(© Imperial War Museum)

Blunden the survivor: 'Since 1918 hardly a day or night passed without my losing
the present and living in a ghost story.' He died in 1974
(© Imperial War Museum)

Edward Thomas and
his wife Helen
(© Imperial War Museum)

Edward Thomas, the young
poet and countryman, before
his enlistment in the Artists'
Rifles in July 1915
(© Imperial War Museum)

Above: Thomas at home in Steep, Hampshire, with his daughter Bronwen and a small friend

(© Imperial War Museum)

Right: Corporal Edward Thomas in 1916. At thirty-seven, he was much older than his fellow recruits

(© Imperial War Museum)

T. E. Hulme, flinty scourge of 'the Liberal school of opinion'
(© Getty Images)

Private Ivor Gurney of the 5th Gloucesters in 1915. He enlisted while he was a student at the Royal College of Music, and went to France in 1916
(© LF/Lebrecht Music and Art)

David Jones, poet and artist, in his studio. He survived to write his great war poem *In Parenthesis* in 1937, in which he calls himself 'Dai Greatcoat' – see picture left

(© Mark Gerson/National Portrait Gallery)

David Jones, in January 1915, aged twenty, after enlisting in the Royal Welch Fusiliers as a private soldier

(© The Estate of David Jones)

Brockley in April 1928, a watercolour by Jones. He was born in this London suburb and is buried in the local cemetery

(© Private Collection/ Susannah Pollen Ltd/The Bridgeman Art Library)

The grave of Ivor Gurney, poet and musician, in the churchyard at Twigworth, in his beloved Gloucestershire
(© Author)

The grave of Isaac Rosenberg, 'Artist & Poet', in the Bailleul Road British Cemetery at Arras
(© Author)

Blunden was well aware that something other than documentary reportage was going on here and even in his natural descriptions, such as 'Under a plank bridge carrying a trench tramway a nameless runnel whispered, with tiny fish revelling in their brief brilliant existence', he acknowledged 'the transforming clarity of such reperceptions'.[135] Time and memory were engaged in a dialogue with the past and complex 'reperceptions' were being enacted, continuously:

At such moments one's mortal franchise seems to be enlarged, and a new sphere of consciousness opened. I go a great distance in no time, and hear bells rung in secret. Why should the war leave such effects? God forgive me if they were the only remembrance of the Western Front still vivid to me; in fact they are the singular prologues to long and strenuous enactions of a drama beside which, even in partial and imperfect view, Mr. Hardy's *Dynasts* lacks profundity and appalment. They are the puzzling, unanticipated, and ever swiftly concealed side of the picture, and as such I note them, wondering whether ordinary life without the fierce electricity of an overwhelming tempest of forces and emotions could project such deep-lighted detail.[136]

Blunden reflected in his third memoir on the six months of the summer of 1918 he had spent in camp in Suffolk: 'It was a camp among ancestral trees, copses, meadows, cornfields bubbling with poppies . . . yet I screen my eyes from that summer. The delight of being away from France after almost two years of ruins and ever-spreading terror was not itself wholly good; youth, now certain of a short time to live, through some magic dispensation of the War Office, did strange things to a world which it had never had time to study.'[137] No sooner had he arrived in this camp than he applied to go back, in a psychological impulse familiar from the stories of Sassoon and Owen.

The doctor examined him and said he was unfit. 'I had the blank half of the warrant which carried me from France, only cancelled in copying pencil. I considered the necessary innocent forgery which offered no apparent difficulty.'[138]

Then he was ordered to assist at a military court of inquiry in Bury St Edmund's where he met and fell in love, at first sight, with a young local girl (she was eighteen, he twenty-one) called Mary Daines whom he married on 1 June 1918. Life in the camp itself, however, was less idyllic in spite of the glorious summer weather. Tensions existed between the veterans and those who had never 'been out' and there were suicides because of the brutal camp regime. When his orders finally came through to return to France, Blunden was ill with asthma and then the Armistice was declared: 'Nobody had expected an armistice, and nobody was excited by it.'[139] But he still was required to go to France where he had an overwhelming sense that he should have been throughout 1918. It was a strange time, with battlefields being looted and everyone waiting for the end. He was sent to Arras, feeling as if he was 'in a mental blind alley. This is Arras, full of the domestic echoes of our army, our armies; I was ever an antiquary, and searched the hummocks of Ypres like an Orientalist in Xanadu; I should be going about Arras and reading every syllable of her ancient and modern drama, the comic reliefs and the tragic impacts alike. But again, I am out of tune. It needs the old faces, voices, songs, jests, Colonel Harrison, the sequence and limitation of trench warfare.'[140] He was struggling:

Looking back over 1918 and this opening quarter of 1919, I became desperately confused over war and peace. Clearly, no man who knew and felt could wish for a second that the war should have lasted a second longer. But, where it was not, and where the traditions and government which it had called into being had ceased to be, we who had been brought up to it were lost men. Strangers surrounded me. No tried values existed now . . . the sunnier hours of my old companionship at Béthune, and even in the valley of the Ancre, with their attendant loyalties and acceptances, seemed like sweet reason and lost love.[141]

The Mind's Eye also contains a reflection on Blunden's experience of the Somme, written in 1929, called 'The Somme Still Flows'. In it he tries to recall the great battle but also to interpret it, and it is his most judgemental performance: 'It was a sunny morning, that of July 1st, 1916. The right notes for it would have been the singing of blackbirds and the ringing of the blacksmith's anvil. But, as the world soon knew, the music of that sunny morning was the guns. They had never spoken before with so huge a voice. Their sound crossed the sea. In Southdown villages the school-children sat wondering at that incessant drumming and the rattling of the windows.'[142] He recalled 'the once serene farmlands of Picardy' where the armies of the three nations 'had arrived at a wonderful pitch of physical and spiritual strength', an exceptional display of men and equipment compared with earlier armies, but they amounted to 'Such monstrous accumulations'.[143] For Blunden the outbreak of the Somme battle was

a tremendous question-mark. By the end of the day both sides had seen, in a sad scrawl of broken earth and murdered men, the answer to that question. No road. No thoroughfare. Neither race had won, nor could win, the War. The War had won, and would go on winning. But, after all the preparation, the ambition, the ideals and the rhythms of these contending armies, there could not be any stopping . . . Accordingly, what had been begun on July 1st became a slow slaughtering process; the Somme might have been a fatal quicksand into which division after division was drawn down.[144]

In the Battle of the Somme Blunden had been in a division far north of the battlefield which was sent on a 'minor operation' to keep back German troops and artillery from the real affair. '"Going South" was at first more like a holiday adventure than the descent to the valley of the shadow. I still make myself pictures of that march, and could not guess at any summer days more enchanting ... We marched with liberal halts through wooded uplands, under arcades of elms, past mill-streams and red and white farms; and, as we marched, we sang ... Every man knew his neighbour. Never was such candour or such confidence.'[145]

Eventually his division went over, on 3 September, and attacked and withdrew and the pattern was repeated, then they moved to a mud-field east of Thiepval, and then:

After this winter battle we left the Somme – but who were 'we'? Not those who had marched south in the time of ripening orchards; a very different body of men. We had been passed through the furnace and the quicksand ... There is no escape from the answer given on July 1st to the question of the human race. War had been 'found out', overwhelmingly found out. War is an ancient impostor, but none of his masks and smiles and gallant trumpets can any longer delude us; he leads us through the cornfields to the cemetery of all that is best. The best is, indeed, his special prey.[146]

After the War Blunden took up a scholarship at Oxford, then pursued a career as a poet and literary journalist. In 1924, to support his family he took up a post as professor of English at the Imperial University of Tokyo, until 1927. He became a Fellow and tutor in English at Merton College, Oxford, in 1931 but returned to full-time writing in 1944 and in 1945 joined the staff of the *Times Literary Supplement*, the same year in which he married for the third time, his two previous marriages having failed. In 1953 he again took up a professorship abroad, in Hong Kong, until his retirement in 1964. In 1966 he was a not entirely successful Oxford Professor of Poetry and eight years later he died of a heart attack at his home in Suffolk.

The War haunted Blunden throughout his life. He had nightmares. He felt guilty at having survived and even at not having been more directly engaged in the Battle of the Somme, calling himself in one poem a traitor. In November 1968 he told the *Daily Express*, 'I have of course wondered when the effect of the Old War would lose its imprisoning power. Since 1918 hardly a day or night passed without my losing the present and living in a ghost story. Even when the detail of dreams is fantasy, the setting of that strange world insists on torturing . . . I know, now that I am an old man, that I take with me something that will never yield to the restoratives of time.'[147]

Blunden was a pastoral poet in the English Romantic tradition, even though he was admired by the pope of modernist literature, T. S. Eliot. His first poems were privately printed in two collections in 1914 while he was still at school and a further four such collections appeared in 1916 while he was in training. After the War he published a full collection, *The Waggoner* (1920), and then *The Shepherd* (1922), *To Nature* (1923) and *English Poems* (1925). These titles seem to say it all. The complete war poems were published in 1996.[148] In a pamphlet about the poets of the First World War published in 1958 Blunden described how he wrote poems in France: 'In May and June 1916, in my notebooks, the grimness of war began to compete as a subject with the pastorals of peace. By the end of the year, when madness seemed totally to rule the hour, I was almost a poet of the shell-holes, of ruin and mortification. But the stanzas then written were left in the pocket-book: what good were they, who cared, who would agree?'[149] Although Blunden is in the end not a poet of the stature of Edward Thomas his war poems continue to appear in the anthologies, where they attract more interest than any 'pastorals of peace' might have done.

One of the poems from the trench pocket-books (almost all of which were lost) was 'January Full Moon, Ypres' written in January 1917, a description of an icy scene in the trenches with the pathetic fallacy of the moon looking down 'curious of evil'. In the same month, he wrote 'Les Halles d'Ypres' about the war-damaged Cloth Hall at Ypres, recalling its ancient dignity before 'this senseless rage' and the immemorial strutting of pigeons in the tower.[150] The simple oppositions between war and eternal nature deprive these poems of real complexity. But most of Blunden's war poetry was recollected in tranquillity, or in its absence, long after the War when the meaning of the experience, as in the prose, could be explored in richer ways. His poem 'Zero' from *Masks of Time* published in 1925 refers in its title to zero hour, the time of the attack at Hamel on 3 September 1916. The poet sees the incipient glory of dawn being prepared, but 'What is that artist's joy to me?' The murderous reality of war, a wounded soldier in front of him, displaces any contemplation of nature: 'It's plain we were born for this, naught else.'

This is Blunden's theme: the ravishment of pastoral calm and beauty by war's savagery. Shortly after the Hamel attack he and his battalion withdrew to Senlis, and the poem 'At Senlis Once' celebrates a moment of release for the men to come upon ordinary country life: 'With women chattering and green grass thriving.' They are able to relax and even 'ridicule their own sufferings'. Harsher is the poem 'The Zonnebeke Road' recalling trenches near Ypres in winter, and, once again, the mechanical unnaturalness of barbed wire that 'Rattles like rusty brambles or dead bine' is another violation of the natural order that a pastoral poet exists to celebrate. 'Rural Economy 1917' set in July of that year works the conceit of war as a cruel parody of farming: 'The sower was the ploughman too,/ And iron seeds broadcast he threw.' The dead provide 'bone-fed loam' for future harvests. The poem 'Pillbox' which incorporates scraps of common soldiers' speech is a more successful attempt at rendering the life and shared suffering of the trenches. A man is killed by a splinter of shell and his comrades pay tribute: 'All marvelled even on that most deathly day/ To see his life so spirited away.'

Some have judged Blunden's poem 'Report on Experience' his best, the poet suggesting that it was quite spontaneous and swiftly composed. Its regular metre and sardonic opening stanza (with a psalmic quality) have an echo of Sassoon, who became very friendly with Blunden after the War:

> I have been young, and now am not too old;
> And I have seen the righteous forsaken,
> His health, his honour and his quality taken.
>   This is not what we were formerly told.

The speaker has seen 'a green country, useful to the race/ Knocked silly with guns and mines, its villages vanished', a fact saluted with an ironic 'God bless us all'. These disillusions, he says, can be construed as God's 'curious proving' that He still does love humanity 'and will go on loving'.

The reader feels the question is left open.

7

Two Modernists: David Jones and T. E. Hulme

'For the old authors . . . the embrace of battle seemed one with the embrace of lovers. For us it is different . . .'[1]

DAVID JONES

For T. S. Eliot it was 'a work of genius',[2] for its author it was a piece of writing that 'has to do with some things I saw, felt, & was part of'.[3] David Jones's epic prose poem of the First World War, *In Parenthesis*, first published in 1937, is certainly one of the most remarkable attempts by a poet to render the War, but its status as part of that 'sacred national text' is more problematic. Most of the canonical poems of the War are read today in one or other of the countless anthologies, and the most popular are short, pointed lyrics of the kind in which Owen and Sassoon specialised. The complex and richly associative text of David Jones, with its profound reach backwards into British history of the post-Roman and early Welsh era and its sometimes perplexing allusions, with which readers less familiar with the sources of his poetic and historical imagination may struggle, is both challenging – and deeply rewarding – in itself and impossible to represent in the preferred anthology format. In consequence Jones is often overlooked. Yet his poem is centrally about those experiences of war – in his case the Western Front between December 1915 and July 1916 – that inform the celebrated poems of the First World War.

T. S. Eliot, who as poetry editor of Faber & Faber in 1937 first published *In Parenthesis*, felt it had an affinity with the work of the great early-twentieth-century modernists Joyce, Pound, and Eliot himself, the crucial difference being that Jones was the only one of that quartet to have fought in the War. Such a declaration of affinity, in the period in which it was published, and even more so today, did not ease its passage into popularity with readers. Yet this extraordinary text, mingling poetry and prose, past and present, high and low idiom, is unignorable. 'I have only tried to make a shape in words,' Jones wrote, 'using as data the complex of sights, sounds, fears, hopes, apprehensions, smells, things exterior and interior, the landscape and paraphernalia of that singular time and of those particular men'.[4]

Jones felt that the period his poem covers was highly significant. In December 1915 he went to France and, for the poet, July 1916, the date of the Battle of the Somme, 'roughly marks a change in the character of our lives in the Infantry on the West Front. From then onward things hardened into a more relentless, mechanical affair, took on a more sinister aspect.'[5] For David Jones the 'wholesale slaughter' of the later years and the introduction of a conscript army 'knocked the bottom out of the intimate, continuing, domestic life of small contingents of men' and ended a palpable historical link with the wars and conflicts of the past. 'In the earlier months there was a certain attractive amateurishness, and elbow-room for idiosyncrasy that connected one with a less exacting past.' The period of the individual rifleman or the 'old sweat' of the Boer War 'seemed to terminate with the Somme'. This was partly to do with a growing grim professionalism as the war became entrenched in 1916, and partly with a change in war's technology – 'all those new-fangled gadgets to master' – and the introduction of gas and chemical warfare:

> We feel a Rubicon has been passed between striking with a hand weapon as men used to do and loosing poison from the sky as we do ourselves. We doubt the decency of our own inventions, and are certainly in terror of their possibilities . . . the unforeseen, subsidiary effects of this achievement . . . Our perception of many things is heightened and clarified. Yet we must do gas-drill, be attuned to many new-fangled technicalities, respond to increasingly exacting mechanical devices; some fascinating and compelling, others sinister in the extreme; all requiring a new and strange direction of the mind, a new sensitivity certainly, but at a considerable cost.[6]

The cost could be computed as a loss of the immediate and humanly tactile, the sensory engagement with battle that made older war poets treat the embrace of battle as equivalent to the embrace of lovers. The consequence was that 'the Waste Land, the sudden violences and the long stillnesses, the sharp contours and unformed voids of that mysterious existence, profoundly affected the imaginations of those who suffered it. It was a place of enchantment. It is perhaps best described in Malory, book iv, chapter 15 – that landscape spoke "with a grimly voice".'[7]

This alienation was particularly hard for a poet and artist whose sense of connection to the past was powerful and mystical. It can be seen, for example, in the way in which Jones felt on his pulse 'the Celtic cycle that lies, a subterranean influence as a deep water troubling, under every tump in this Island, like Merlin complaining under his big rock'.[8] Written twenty years after the conflict itself – he marvelled at Owen's ability to write poems on the spot – *In Parenthesis* is able to draw, like so many other post-war works of poetry and prose, on reflection, meditation, imaginative reordering of the experience of war. Aware of the context into which it was launched in 1937, he insisted:

> I did not intend this as a 'War Book' – it happens to be concerned with war. I should prefer it to be about a good kind of peace – but as Mandeville says, 'Of Paradys ne can I not speken propurly I was not there; it is fer beyonde and that for thinketh me. And also I was not worthi.' We find ourselves privates in foot regiments. We search how we may see formal goodness in a life singularly inimical, hateful, to us.[9]

Finally, why 'in parenthesis'? Because 'for us amateur soldiers (and especially for the writer, who was not only amateur, but grotesquely incompetent, a knocker-over of piles, a parade's despair) the war itself was a parenthesis'. And although Jones was not an anti-war propagandist, he sensed, like so many other poets in the conflict, the essential absurdity of men being pitted against each other in war. His formal dedication to the poem therefore addresses 'the enemy frontfighters who shared our pains against whom we found ourselves by misadventure'.[10]

The poem is in seven sections, climaxing with the poet's being wounded in 1916 in Mametz Wood. It is hard to convey its flavour in any short extract but at its best it conveys the totality of the sensual experience of war in the trenches and, for all its apparatus of learning and footnotes (themselves a mixture of rare scholarship and fascinatingly down-to-earth explanations of the detail of trench life), it conveys a sense of rootedness in a shared and communal experience. It also, like Blunden's writing, expresses the engulfing nature of trench experience, the sense of working a small seam in ignorance of the wider picture:

You are moved like beasts are moved from upper field to pound, one hour carrying heaped-on weights, the next you delve in earth, or stand long time in the weather, patiently, a hitch in the arrangements; and now singly, through unfamiliar, narrow, ways. You don't know which high walls enclose your lethal yard, or what this tight entry opens on.[11]

Like Isaac Rosenberg, David Jones was a painter as well as a poet, and, like Edward Thomas, he was of mixed Welsh and English descent. His father came from the Welsh-speaking heartland of North Wales and his mother from Rotherhithe – where her father was a mast- and block-maker – beside the Thames. This London–Welsh ancestry is present in the poem in Jones's feeling both for the Cockney soldier and for the culture of Wales. He did not learn Welsh until later in life and regretted his distance from Welsh culture. He realised, as he later wrote of himself (in the third person, in *Dai Greatcoat*), that 'In spite of all David's attempts to Cambrianize his work, in spite of all he says with such pathos and eloquence, and in spite of his great devotion to a great Welsh myth, it was the English tradition that was most completely assimilated, and everything in his work that is most convincing, sincere, and based on real knowledge and understanding is English.'[12] He felt 'cut off from a Wales for which he had no more than a sentimental love . . . the Wales he loved ended with the death of Llywelyn ap Gruffyd on 11 December 1282 . . . of modern Wales he had little or no knowledge.'

An important point worth making here is that, as epigraphs to each of its seven sections make clear, *In Parenthesis* is shadowed by the great seventh-century Welsh war poem *Y Gododdin*. David Jones connected his poem to past battle poetry and it reminds us how rarely the other poets did this. This is surprising because war has always been a theme of poetry – *arma virumque cano*, 'of arms and the man I sing', Virgil began the *Aeneid* – from ancient epic through Homer, Anglo-Saxon poetry, the *Chanson de Roland* and beyond. It is as if the perception (shared by Jones, of course, to a great extent) that the First World War marked a wholly unprecedented change in war's very nature meant that no bridge could be built back to the earlier war imagery and language. The mechanisation of slaughter, perhaps, had ended the traditional ways of representing the battlefield and turning human conflict into song or brought about a permanent rupture in that tradition.

Jones decided to join up very soon after the outbreak of the war, and in September 1914 his father wrote to Lloyd George's private secretary asking about the formation of a London Welsh battalion of the Royal Welch Fusiliers. Jones later turned up a reply from the private secretary to his father, written the same month,

> which is damned funny to think of now. My father had evidently (unknown to me) written to Ll. G personally asking him when the Government were going to make official the proposed formation of a London Welsh battalion, as his son was anxious to enlist in such a formation and would otherwise enlist in some English regiment, which was not what he would prefer. The Secretary's letter was just a brief note saying that the War Office would shortly be authorizing this battalion as part of the Royal Welsh Fusiliers. It strikes me as bloody amusing, for it sounds as if Mr. Jones's son was anxiously waiting to be given some post of High Command, instead of merely, along with everybody else, attempting to enlist in the ranks of some regiment or other.[13]

Jones wrote of the 'illusions' that he shared with others of his generation, and spoke of being influenced by the posters that read 'Remember Louvain!'

He had been seriously concerned about what to do with

himself after art school so the War, as with so many others, came along at the right time. He tried to enlist in the Artists' Rifles, but was rejected 'as deficient in expansion of chest – they kept up the Regular Army standard very strictly and to the letter in the early months of the war'.[14] He really had wanted to join a Welsh regiment, and when he heard that a unit of cavalry was being raised, to be called 'The Welsh Horse', this attracted him, because he had always wanted to ride a horse. So he went to a recruiting base somewhere in the Inns of Court

> where I was taken before a perfectly round man wearing an eye-glass, and this followed: 'Can you ride?' 'No, sir.' 'Do you know anything about horses?' 'Well, not really, sir.' 'But y'r a Welshman, I take it.' 'My father is a North Welshman, my mother English.' 'I see, that's all right, Welsh enough, and we'd like to have you, but between ourselves, if you'll take my advice, you'll enlist in some infantry mob – Welsh by all means, but if you know nothing about horses this set-up is no place for you. We see to the care of mounts first and men second. You can please yourself, but I think you'll find it pretty tough – there'll be plenty of time and opportunity to join up, I assure you, and my advice to you is the infantry.'[15]

After enlisting on 2 January 1915 with the 15th (London Welsh) Battalion of the Royal Welch, Jones was sent to his ancestral homeland, North Wales, to the coast of Gwynedd, to train. He did squad drill on the esplanade at Llandudno. The men had substandard rifles and wooden bullets to train with, and the artillery at Pwllheli practised with telegraph poles mounted on old bus wheels.[16]

Jones was then sent to another training camp, at Winnol Down near Winchester, with the result that he spent most of 1915 in training. He remembered one of his companions of that time, a bandsman who played the large drum, Marx by name, middle-aged, with whom I shared a billet in Llandudno early in 1915. He was an inveterate drinker and I had to keep awake till he came in very late always smoking a cigar which he refused to put out before he was in bed and I feared that the ash from his cigar would get the bed on fire, but it was no use. When I thought he really was asleep I would walk across the room to where his corner was, but he always heard me and *would not* allow me to remove the cigar.[17]

Jones was finally dispatched to France on 1 December 1915, trained at Warne, eight miles south-east of St Omer, and then had his first spell in the trenches in the La Bassée sector, at the end of December. After six months in the trenches the division marched south through the hills of Artois towards the Somme. Jones later recalled: 'During this period [I] did small drawings in pocket-book in trenches and billets – none that survive have any interest as drawings and little as records, being feeble impressionistic sketches such as might appear in any second-rate illustrated paper. They are without any sense of form and display no imagination. But the War landscape – the "Waste Land" motif – has remained with me, I think as a potent influence, to assert itself later.'[18]

The various units of Jones's division took up positions astride the Estaires–La Bassée road, in the section of the Front with Laventie in the north, through Richebourg-l'Avoue and Festubert to Neuve-Chapelle and south to Givenchy. Units of the brigades that formed the division, and the four battalions that formed the brigades, took a 'tour in', and switched regularly from one sector to another. Jones remembered:

It was mostly as regular a routine as possible, so many days in the front-most trench, so many in the support trench (if there was one), so many days in 'reserve', which was less attractive than it may sound, for you could count on endless fatigues when in 'reserve'. Of course, this 'regular routine' was easily disrupted by all manner of happenings: heavy shelling, or raiding parties, or 'gas alerts'. A false alarm that gas was being used by the enemy could cause commotion right back at Divisional H.Q., or even over a whole Army area. It was those first six months in the trenches of the forward zone that I chose as the period and subject-matter in writing *In Parenthesis*, partly because it provided a convenient beginning and ending and demonstrated the varying pattern of our lives, and partly because those first six months could most easily be recalled in some detail, whereas later periods became much more muddled and less intimate, more wholesale and repetitive.[19]

On 5 July 1916 the London Welsh were given orders to enter the area below Mametz Wood, which was held by the Germans. They took over the front line between Bottom Wood and Caterpillar Wood and on 10 July the British assault on this stronghold began. Jones recalled this as a confused attack in the course of which he was wounded. He described in detail the experience of this wounding and what happened in its immediate aftermath, both in Part 7 of *In Parenthesis* and in later recollections. He later relived the experience:

Finding that I could not stand up or walk I crawled away in the opposite direction – that is in the direction of our own lines thinking that there might come some chance R.A.M.C. man. I don't know how far I crawled and my rifle with bayonet fixed I had somehow managed to sling over my shoulder and it hung a dead weight and somehow 'fouled', as sailors say, with my tin hat, but I did not want to be without my rifle, partly for the obvious reason that I had no other weapon, and after all for all I knew, there might well be groups of Germans about, though what I imagined I could do with my rifle under the circumstances I can't imagine – after a bit more crawling I found I should have to abandon it, which I did, still with a sense of shame and a feeling that can only be described as real affection . . . for what I was leaving. My gas mask I kept on grounds of sheer ungraced, pure utility. At some point I found myself looking at a corporal whom I recognized as of my own battalion – I did not know [him] at all well but I can see his kindly Welsh face – a countryman's face, even now. I can't remember what he said but recall only his lifting me up and carrying me on his back. We had not got far when in the darkness or half-darkness a tall figure emerged who happened to be a Major and 2nd in command of our battalion, a Major and a Welshman, much liked, and very able, good-looking, and I *think* in civilian life in the legal profession. He said, 'Is that you, Corporal X?' 'Yes, sir. I was trying to carry Pte. Jones a bit nearer the advanced dressing station or find some stretcher-bearers, sir.' 'Corporal X, you will no matter *who* he is, drop the bugger *here*. If every wounded man is to be carried from where he has chanced to fall, by a corporal or any other of the rank and file, we would double our loss of fire strength and that's not over much as it is. Put Pte. Jones (of 'B', I think?) down immediately. Stretcher-bearers will find him within a short time. Don't you know there's a sod of a war on?' (That last bit amused me, even at the time, for it was pretty obvious that a war was indeed on.)[20]

The bullet that wounded Jones passed clean through his left leg without touching the fibula or tibia,

but merely through the calf, it felt as if a great baulk of timber or a heavy bar of some sort had struck me sideways, in fact I thought a ponderous branch of one of the trees of the wood had been severed by shrapnel and had fallen across my leg but couldn't account for the *extreme violence and weight*. I did not realize it was S.A.A. [small arms ammunition] until I tried to stand up and felt the wetness seeping from the wounds, then I realized I'd been hit by a mere little bullet – but the disproportion of the smallness of the nickel projectile and the great bludgeoning weight of the impact astonished me even at the time.[21]

While awaiting transit to hospital, 'a jolly nice fair-haired nurse with a strong Canadian accent kissed me on the face and said, "You ought to be in a kindergarten, how did you manage to get attested?" – "Twenty last fall! You can't kid me!"'[22] He was taken to hospital in Birmingham and then to a nursing home to convalesce, near Shipston-on-Stour. He was back in France just before his twenty-first birthday in October 1916 where he found his unit was occupying positions on the extreme north flank of the British line, just north of the Ypres Salient:

I can only register a very considerable change of feelings and conditions on my return in late October: the piling-up of shells for guns of various calibre, with little attempt to camouflage them, and the bringing forward of heavy platformed howitzers, made one wonder. For one thing, continuous fatigue work was in progress, and defences were very evident, as though an impregnable line of sureness against an enemy attack, almost like German 'defence-in-depth', was in the mind of those in command. What it actually was, was the careful planning for an offensive against the enemy on a big scale. Anyway, the increased use of mechanical transport, and mechanization in general, made the whole 'feel' very different from the war I had known in the months before the Somme battle.[23]

Jones's division occupied this section of front for nearly a year, from October 1916 to September 1917, spending all the time consolidating or repairing and extending the trenches, and in particular the trench system, preparing for the British offensive launched at the end of July: 'The 38th (Welsh) Division with its numbers of labour companies of Welsh miners from the mining villages of south-east Wales were obviously of great use in all this building up period and it has been suggested by some that [it was] the reason or part reason for the Division's prolonged stay in one sector.'[24] Then his division was withdrawn to another sector away to the south of Armentières. But it had been involved in the first phase of the offensive, its objective being Pilckem Ridge, in the first days of August: 'From what I saw of that advance, I can't speak of the incredible nature of the warfare in the months to come, but I saw enough to guess something of the assaults over a terrain of churned-up mud, water-brimming shell-craters, not a yard of "dead ground", not a fold of earth the length of y'r body and sighted with his [the enemy's] usual accuracy his sweep of fire from narrow slits of concrete pill-boxes covering all the approaches, heavy mortars operating from behind each stark ridge.'[25]

In late July or early August Jones had been posted to a reserve group called 'Battalion nucleus', and as casualties mounted steadily

G.H.Q. formed groups of Battalion nuclei round which new men could be formed so that the life of the battalion or unit would retain its identity, and its life would not be wholly extinguished. But no one present at all in the terrain of battle could fail to feel the land bereft of its natural foliage and given over wholly to the desert of war – could altogether forget its feeling – the rain also made matters worse and by October one can well believe (what I was told later) that men were literally drowned in liquid mud. Those of us of my unit who had been in the contest in the woods of the Somme in July 1916 felt the great change that 'mechanization' in one form or another had unconsciously changed things quite a bit. Some, by a chance give-away word betrayed their feelings, their 'instress' that they would, if they could, bring back that sylvan terrain where so many Agamemnons had cried aloud.[26]

In 1964 a television documentary about Passchendaele 'gratified' Jones by using some extracts from *In Parenthesis*. He wrote to a friend:

We were involved only in the first bit and in late September or October moved into another sector. But we had been in that Boesinghe sector for a full year previous to the battle and were involved in all the preparations. There was hardly a moment's let up, and during the last part of the time the artillery on both sides were continuously active. Guns of every imaginable character were simply everywhere, and munition dumps rose like slag heaps on every available bit of ground – *more or less* camouflaged with bits of foliage.

He recalled their digging a new 'Assembly Trench' and

thinking of 'The wood of Birnam/ Let every soldier hew him down a bough.' I also recall how the C.O. walked up and down *in the open wearing no gas mask* but threatening blue murder on any man taking off *his* mask – the temptation was great for the masks at that date were ghastly to wear for very long, especially if one was exerting oneself – they became a filthy mess of condensation inside and you couldn't see out of the misted-over talc of the eye-vents . . . They were a remarkable breed of men, those Regular officers. I've forgotten his name . . . had that . . . outward calmness and immaculate attire as though he were paying an afternoon call in Belgravia, in which *I*, at all events, found a mixture of exhilarating morale-making and extreme amusement – also there was something *aesthetically* right about it . . . both consoling and, which is perhaps much the same thing, amusing, pleasing.[27]

Jones was then sent south to a part of the Front 'as astonishing in its quietness as north of Ypres was for its continuing and methodical activity. It was called the Bois Grenier sector: the communication trench had convolvulus and other floral creepers lending the revetment frames a positively festal feeling. A small French boy used to come along the road blowing a little metal horn of some sort, with packages of French newspapers such as *Le Matin* (now, I believe, extinct) for anyone who wanted to buy them.'[28]

According to Jones's friend René Hague, who compiled a life of the poet from post-war letters which reminisced about his war experiences, 'his four years in the army, the months in the trenches and the bloody battle of the Wood left him spiritually and psychologically unscarred and even invigorated: and for a short time at least ready for more soldiering. After demobilization he wished at first – until dissuaded by his father – to join the British forces in Russia.'[29] In a letter to Hague on Christmas Day 1930, Jones wrote: 'I came "out of the trenches" for the first time fifteen years ago today – it makes me feel incredibly ancient. I remember seeing field-artillerymen sitting astride the muzzle of a field-gun, singing carols (very badly!) on the La Bassée road.'[30] Hague was emphatic that Jones's 1933 mental breakdown was not caused by his war experiences:

David enjoyed the war. He loved soldiering and comradeship . . . His happiness in the ranks was largely due, I believe, to the absence of responsibility and of any need to take

decisions. What the private soldier has to do is always the eas-
iest thing: even if he has to overcome fear, he can only stay
where he is and do what he is told to do . . . I find confirma-
tion for this view in *In Parenthesis*. This is not an exposition
or condemnation of the horrors of war, even if it is concerned
with them. A careful reading of the Preface shows a pride and
delight in the type of war that, by David's reckoning, ended
in 1916; and the core of the book is the goodness of 'the intimate, continuing, domestic life of small contingents of men,
within whose structure Roland could find, and for a reasonable while enjoy, his Oliver'.[31]

Hague felt that in all the conversations he had with Jones and
in his letters the poet never showed any traumatic aversion
to what happened: 'There were no nightmares, no horrors that
could not be mentioned, no noises, smells, scenes that made
wounds bleed afresh. There was only pleasure in the search-
light of memory, the recapture of half-forgotten detail, the link
with tradition, the re-creation of personality, the analogy with
the problems of ordinary social and domestic life – and above all
humour.'[32]

Through Jones's letters we can trace the absorbing process
of retrospective exploration of what the War meant to him. On
2 July 1935, for example, he wrote to René Hague: 'On this
day nineteen years ago I heard read by the Officer Commanding B Coy a document, a rescript from G.H.Q. announcing the
initial success of the first attack on his trenches on the Somme.
We were permitted to cheer. I can't tell you the gnawing
thoughts as well up in your bosom at this memory.'[33] These
reminiscences included a rueful assessment of his soldierly
capability. He remembered that he was sacked from the Field
Survey Company after a few months 'because of my inefficiency in getting the right degrees of enemy gun-flashes'.[34]
Not long after celebrating his twenty-first birthday with rum

and bottled cherries, Jones was transferred in November 1916
to Battalion HQ: 'The Intelligence Officer, hearing that I had
been an artist, thought I might be useful in making some
maps and perhaps going on patrol with them and making
sketch drawings of the place where Jerry had put up some
new wire or other defences.'[35] It is clear from Jones's recollections, as well as from *In Parenthesis* itself that, like Ivor
Gurney, he relished the camaraderie of the trenches and drew
strength from it.

Jones was struck, years later, as noted above, by the fact that
Wilfred Owen was able to write his poems while actually in the
trenches.[36] But he seems to have had a quarrel with the theology ghosting Owen's poems, specifically the identification of
war's agony with the agony of Christ. Jones himself disavowed
any intention in *In Parenthesis* of making such an analogy. The
passion of Christ, for him, now a Catholic, was rather 'a unique
and profound Mystery of Faith'.[37]

Nonetheless, it was on the battlefield that Jones had a very
important religious experience:

> It was after the Somme, I think, so when I had returned to
> France from being wounded. Anyway when or where it was
> I can't exactly place. But as I was always cold, one of my
> main occupations was to hunt for any wood that was dry and
> could be used to make a decent fire. We were in some
> support trenches and I said to the people I was with, 'I'm
> going off to find some decent firewood'. Just a little way
> back that is between our support trench and the reserve line
> I noticed what had been a farm building now a wreckage in
> the main, owing to shell fire. No individual of any sort was
> about and I noticed that one bit of this wreckage a byre or
> outhouse of some sort still stood and its roofing appeared to
> be intact and its walling undamaged at least from a little
> distance.[38]

Guessing that there might be some firewood here to pilfer, Jones approached and put his eye to a crack in the timber:

> What I saw through the small gap in the wall was not the dim emptiness I had expected but the back of a sacerdos in a gilt-hued *planeta*, two points of flickering candlelight no doubt lent an extra sense of goldness to the vestment and a golden warmth seemed, by the same agency, to lend the white altar cloths and the white linen of the celebrant's alb and amice and maniple (the latter, I notice, has been abandoned, without a word of explanation, by these blasted reformers). You can imagine what a great marvel it was for me to see through that chink in the wall, and kneeling in the hay beneath the improvised *mensa* were a few huddled figures in khaki.

There were indeed only a few at this improvised mass because most of the London Welsh were nonconformist or Church of England,

> but there was a big-bodied Irishman and an Italian natural-ized Englishman, represented under the forms of Bomber Mulligan and Runner Meotti in *In Paren* . . . I can't recall at what part of the Mass it was I looked through that squint-hole and I didn't think I ought to stay long as it seemed rather like an uninitiated bloke prying on the Mysteries of a Cult. But it made a big impression on me. For one thing I was astonished how close to the Front Line the priest had decided to make the Oblation and I was impressed to see Old Sweat Mulligan, a somewhat fearsome figure, a real pugilistic, hard-drinking Goidelic Celt, kneeling there in the smoky candlelight. And one strong impression I had . . . for at that spying unintentionally on the Mass in Flanders in the Forward Zone I felt immediately that oneness between the Offerant and those toughs that clustered around him in the

dim-lit byre – a thing I had never felt remotely as a Protestant
at the Office of Holy Communion in spite of the insistence
of Protestant theology on the 'priesthood of the laity'.[39]

In February 1918, Jones became seriously ill with trench
fever which he said was 'like the worst imaginable type of flu',
and he spent several months at a field hospital behind the lines.
Not long after he returned to duty the London Welsh were sent
to Ireland where post-war political trouble was expected by
Lloyd George. Soldiers on guard duty at the barrack gates were
jeered at by local women. Stationed at Limerick, Jones had an
almost visionary experience prompted by 'an astonishing girl in
a red skirt driving a red cow in a red sunset – it was an
absolutely pre-historic Celtic sight'.[40] Jones's imagination was
always richly stimulated by anything that could speak to him of
the Celtic past, and the girl had also some of the mythological
aura of the 'eternal feminine':

It was a red sundown and I was coming with some other
fusiliers along a wet hill-road by a white-washed cabin and
we met a girl with a torn white shift of sorts with a red skirt
with a plum-coloured hem to the skirt which reached a bit
below the knee; and she had auburn hair floating free over
her shoulders and in the wind, and her feet and arms were
bare and she had a long stick; she was driving a red-coloured
cow before her and the evening sun bathed all these differ-
ing reds and bronzes ... For some reason that's another
image I associate with Troy – the red sunset on the red cattle-
girl in Munster ... cattle-raiders, horse-raiders, soldiers,
queens, queans, and the red as of flame – and the great dignity – well, *fuit Ilium*.

Although he never married, Jones was certainly not indifferent to women and, almost at the end of his life, he recalled his

period in hospital after the wound in Mametz Wood: 'I got into trouble for being seen having tea with one of the nurses and her mother on the lawn, trying to eat strawberries and cream *which I loathe*. But was far from loathing the heavenly nurse.' The daughter of the doctor running the place gave them away, such that 'even now nearly 60 years after, I harbour an unforgiving feeling towards her'.[41] The experience came vividly back to him when writing to a friend on 11 July 1958:

Forty-two years ago, yesterday and today, I was engaged in the operation in Mametz wood described in Part 7 of *In Parenthesis*. By this hour (the evening of the 11th July) I was comfortably in bed in a *very, very, very hot* tent, of some sort, ten miles, I suppose, from the scene of conflict. I can't remember much about that part of it or getting back there, except I do recall being in a motor ambulance. I was *very* tired and slept and dozed in a troubled sort of way rather, and after that I remember the hot tent – (It was really a large marquee, halfway between the Front and the Coastal Ports, a Casualty Clearing Station, I suppose, but out of the Forward Zone, for girls weren't allowed near the front in *that* war – I believe: at least not in 1916) – and (not unnaturally) the voice, the very English, very upper-class patrician 'decuriate' voice of a nurse of some sort . . . I remember I thought it was the nicest sound in the world. *Voices are extraordinary, I think*, they have almost limitless power to deject, repel, bore, or elevate, enchant, console, attract and all the rest . . . that particular voice was special for me, for I'd not heard an English woman's voice then since the previous December (1915), so I suppose that having come straight out of the 'bloody wood where Agamemnon cried aloud' and gone to sleep (and, I expect, injected with some opiate) and coming-to in the hot marquee, and being asked, in cultivated English, how I felt, left an indelible mark on me.[42]

After the War, David Jones had a long and productive life as an artist and writer. He worked at Westminster School of Art and then, after becoming a Catholic in 1921, with the sculptor Eric Gill at Ditchling in Sussex and Capel-y-ffin in the Black Mountains of Wales. He became engaged to Gill's daughter, Petra, but she broke off the engagement and married someone else. When *In Parenthesis* was published in 1937 it won the 1938 Hawthornden Prize and it was followed by *The Anathemata* (1952) and *The Sleeping Lord* (1974). His art ranged from engravings, paintings, and wooden sculpture to inscriptions and lettering. He was appointed CBE in 1955 and Companion of Honour in 1974, the year of his death.

Recollections of David Jones stress his charming, if occasionally distrait, personality, but the poet and critic T. E. Hulme was a far more astringent character who can perhaps be seen as the chief theorist of the Imagist school, his philosophical writings on art and society having a powerfully iconoclastic quality. His poetic output was relatively small, 'The Complete Poetical Works of T. E. Hulme' being published in the *New Age* (where many of the Modernists appeared) in January 1912, but his intellectual influence on the Imagists in particular and on the course of Modernism in general cannot be ignored. In his writings Hulme became the scourge of Romanticism, which was to him a spent force characterised by a sentimentality about the power of the individual and the possibility of progress, a stance which appalled Bertrand Russell who called him 'an evil man who could have created nothing but evil'.[43]

Hulme was undeflected by such criticism and continued to oppose Romanticism by praising its presumed antithesis, classicism, for its more realistic and limited notion of the nature of the human animal. Romantic poetry had to be got out of the way and he was convinced that 'a period of dry, hard, classical verse is coming'.[44] His complaint about Romantic poetry was that it yearned always for the infinite: 'I object to the sloppiness which doesn't consider that a poem is a poem unless it is moaning or whining about something or other.'[45] His poem 'Trenches: St Éloi' succeeds admirably in avoiding this vice. It is a perfect Imagist poem in its hard, clear, dry outline and its concentration on the image without feeling or commentary: men cleaning their mess tins behind a wall of sandbags or trudging,

> Making paths in the dark,
> Through scattered dead horses,
> Over a dead Belgian's belly.

The almost brutal indifference to the dead man contrasts with the way in which a poet like Owen would have handled this theme. The poem is so cool and collected that it could almost be a parody of the Imagist poem Hulme desired:

> The Germans have rockets. The English have no rockets.
> Behind the line, cannon, hidden, lying back miles.
> Behind the line, chaos:
> My mind is a corridor. The minds about me are corridors.
> Nothing suggests itself. There is nothing to do but keep
>   on.

Thomas Ernest Hulme was born on 16 September 1883 at Gratton in Staffordshire.[46] His father was a gentleman farmer who later went into business and the young Hulme was educated at Newcastle High School for Boys, where he won many mathematics and science prizes and from where he took an open mathematics scholarship to St John's College, Cambridge, in 1902. Hulme was a riotous and unconventional student and was sent down after two years for failing to do any work. His friends organised a mock funeral in farewell, an event which was so disorderly it attracted the attention of London newspapers. He enrolled at University College, London, but left after two years once again with no degree and set sail for Canada. His unconventional habit of philosophising in his own idiosyncratic way began at the time, as did the composition of his various notes on language, the nature of truth and other topics which were not published in his lifetime. In 1907 he returned from Canada to England, but soon left for Brussels to teach English for a year.

When he returned to England in 1908 he joined the Poets' Club, a group which met at the Eiffel Tower restaurant in Soho and wanted to remake English verse and cure it of its bad habits. The next year he formed his own group of poets including F. S. Flint and Ezra Pound, the nucleus of the Imagist poets. In 1912 Pound republished 'The Complete Poetical Works of T. E. Hulme' as an appendix to his own book of poems, *Ripostes*. At the same time Hulme renewed his philosophical explorations and became a student of the French philosopher Henri Bergson who seemed to him to offer a way out of the nineteenth-century intellectual and aesthetic decadence he saw around him. Hulme translated Bergson's *Introduction à la métaphysique* (1912) and also became interested in political theory. He was attracted to right-wing philosophers such as Georges Sorel and those thinkers associated with the journal *Action française*, liking their opposition to Romanticism. He set out his political beliefs in *A Tory Philosophy* (1912) and continued to advocate a 'classical' ideal opposed to ideas of human perfectibility or progress. Although he eventually became estranged from Bergson's philosophy the latter wrote a letter that helped to get Hulme readmitted to Cambridge in 1912. This renewed academic career was short-lived, however, because Hulme, a pursuer of young women throughout his short life, fled to Germany from Cambridge that summer when an angry don discovered he had been sending letters to his sixteen-year-old daughter at Roedean. In Germany he became

interested in contemporary art, finding in the sculptor Jacob
Epstein the possible embodiment of his ideas of hard-edged,
'classical' art.

And then the War broke out and Hulme, who had been living
since February 1914 in one of the rented rooms above Harold
Monro's Poetry Bookshop in Bloomsbury, enlisted on 10
August, less than a week after the declaration, as a private in the
Honourable Artillery Company at Finsbury Barracks in
London, still too bolshie to consider applying for a commission.
Richard Aldington, who came along with him to Finsbury, was
turned down by the selectors. Hulme was assigned to B
Company in the 1st Battalion of the HAC and sent for training
in Essex, then to France on 30 December.

It was a smooth crossing for the seven hundred troops in a
tramp steamer fitted out to carry cattle or horses: 'We slept in
the stalls, hurriedly whitewashed to make them clean, with a
notice painted over our heads "This is for urine only not for
dung". It sounds dreadful but it's really all right,'[47] he reported
to his family. On arrival the Company marched up a steep hill
for about four miles to a rest camp, deep in mud, where they
had to sleep twelve to a tent which made Hulme feel very
depressed. But he had liked the earlier stages in the journey,
'like being seen off at the dock . . . it's all very amusing – and
the girls at the windows'. Early in January he left the camp for
a job unloading supplies at the docks and then he was moved
to Rouen: 'We have had our fur coats issued to us – I have a
kind of goat or wolf skin, look like a bear, great long fur stretch-
ing out all over from me. I haven't had my clothes off since I left
Southampton.'[48] They had crossed the Belgian frontier into
France in cattle trucks and were eventually unloaded and billeted in 'a kind of greenhouse for grapes' where 350 men were
to sleep: 'It's a steel thing, looking like a small Olympia.'[49]
They were now close to the action: 'You can hear all the heavy
guns going off. It's like the sound of summer thunder a long

way off. We are only about 8 miles from the firing line here and
from the part of the trenches . . . every now & then on the hori-
zon, you see a flash, it's a kind of illuminating shell used to light
up things so that the artillery can fire at anything they see
moving. If you listen carefully you can hear from time to time,
quick firing by the men's rifles in the trenches.'[50]

The Company was soon off, marching with heavy equipment:

The roads are simply fearful with mud and you keep meeting supply motors and carts which push you to the side of the
road in the mud. All you can think of on the march, is various
ways of shifting the weight of your pack from one shoulder to
another, every now and then you rest and you bend down . . .
in order to save the weight of your pack on the shoulders. You
look reflectively at your feet & the patterns of the mud as you
do this, & that will be the predominant impression I shall
carry away from this war. The first thing that looked at all
characteristic of war (in the old Boer War scene) was when we
were overtaken by a transport wagon taking food, guarded by
men on horseback with rifles slung across their shoulders.[51]

On Friday 15 January 1915 a German shell dropped on them:
'You hear a noise like a train high up in the air appearing to go
very slowly, then you see a thick cloud of black smoke going up
where they have burst, then you hear the bang, then after that
the whistling noise seems to end.'[52] Hulme was applying in
prose his principles of clear focus on 'the image' in poetry and
his descriptions are often very vivid:

The only thing that makes you feel nervous is when the star
shells go off & you stand out revealed quite clearly as in daylight. You have then the most wonderful feeling as if you
were suddenly naked in the street and didn't like it. It isn't

that really but the impression it makes on you, as if you were walking across a flat heath or common at night & along a long line in front of you the lights were shooting off all the time silhouetting all the trees and bushes. It's really like a kind of nightmare, in which you are in the middle of an enormous saucer of mud with explosions & shots going off all round the edge, a sort of fringe of palm trees made of fireworks all round it.[53]

The military routine for Hulme and his comrades was at the firing line, forty eight hours on and four days off. For the latter they were billeted in villages, thirty-six to a room. They cooked meals on a village stove and were able to supplement their rations by buying eggs and local produce, the standard-issue bully beef giving people dysentery. One time they were billeted in a school chapel: 'It looks very curious to see a lot of troops billeted in a place like this, rifles resting on the altar, & hanging over statues of the saints, men sleeping on the altar steps.'[54] It was getting very cold so they lit a brazier in an old bucket with holes knocked in it, burning charcoal and coke, and one of the men went out and dug up some vegetables from a deserted garden and made a kind of stew without meat because they got no cooked meat in the four days.

Hulme was over six feet tall which created problems in the low-roofed reserve trench where he had to crawl on his hands and knees along a four-feet-high passage: 'You feel shut in and hopeless. I wished I was about 4 ft. This war isn't for tall men. I got in a part too narrow and too low to stand or sit & had to sit sideways on a sack of coke to keep out of the water. We had to stay there from about 7 p.m. till just before dawn next morning, a most miserable experience. You can't sleep & you sit as it were at the bottom of a drain with nothing to look at but the top of the ditch slowly freezing. It's unutterably boring.'[55] Boredom was the keynote of trench experience:

In reality there is nothing picturesque about it. It's the most miserable existence you can conceive of. I feel utterly depressed at the idea of having to do this for 48 hours every 4 days. It's simply hopeless. The boredom & discomfort of it, exasperate you to the breaking point. It's curious to think of the ground between the trenches, a bank which is practically never seen by anyone in the daylight, as it is only safe to move through it at dark. It's full of dead things, dead animals here and there, dead unburied animals, skeletons of horses destroyed by shell fire.[56]

By contrast, the four days of rest were relaxed, drinking wine outside a little inn, and imagining that the war was not on. Back at the firing line a German rifle trained on Hulme's section of the trench kept hitting the same spot on the parapet and scattering dirt over his bread and butter: 'It gets very irritating after a time & everybody shouts out "Oh stop it".'[57]

Although he was bored and frustrated by this kind of life he simply observed it, resisting the temptation to moralise:

The worst of shelling is, the regulars say, that you don't get used to it, but get more & more alarmed at it every time. At any rate the regulars in our trenches behaved in rather a strange way. One man threw himself down on the bottom of the trench, shaking all over & crying. Another started to weep. It lasted for nearly 1½ hrs and at the end of it parts of the trenches were all blown to pieces. It's not the idea of being killed that's alarming, but the idea of being hit by a jagged piece of steel. You hear the whistle of the shell coming, you crouch down as low as you can and just wait. It doesn't burst merely with a bang, it has a kind of crash with a snap in it, like the crack of a very large whip. They seemed to burst just over your head, you seem to anticipate it killing you in the back, it hits just near you and you get hit on the back with clods of earth & (in my case) spent bits of shell & shrapnel bullets fall all round you. I picked up one bullet almost sizzling in the mud just by my toe. What irritates you is the continuation of the shelling. You seem to feel that 20 min. is normal, is enough – but when it goes on for over an hour, you get more & more exasperated, feel as if it were 'unfair' . . . It was very curious from where I was; looking out and over the back of the trench, it looked absolutely peaceful. Just over the edge of the trench was a field of turnips or something of that kind with their leaves waving about in a busy kind of way, exactly as they might do in a back garden. About 12 miles away over the plain you could see the towers & church spires of an old town very famous in this war . . . You've got to amuse yourself in the intervals of shelling and romanticising the situation is as good a way as any other. Looking at the scene, the waving vege-tables, the white town & all the rest of it, it looks quite timeless in a Buddhistic kind of way and you feel quite resigned if you are going to be killed to leave it just like that.[58]

Hulme watched the reactions of the men in these wet, cold, muddy conditions of January 1915 at Kemmel in the Petit Bois area, then in February: 'It is curious how this continuing shelling and the apprehension of it has altered some men. They keep quiet all day long & hardly say anything.'[59] Although he could occasionally fix a detail like the night spent outside in a hard frost that made all the rifles white in the morning, Hulme was unable, he felt, to convey the full reality of trench warfare: 'It's very difficult to describe anything to you, to at all make you realize what it is *actually* like.'[60] The experience included carrying the corpses of his own men: 'This is a very unpleasant job when you have to go in pitch darkness a way you don't know very well over mud & ditches. I'm glad it wasn't a man I knew but it's very queer as you carry him down shoulder high, his face is very near your own.'[61]

On 14 April 1915, Hulme himself was shot and wounded in the vicinity of St Éloi by a bullet that passed through his arm and killed the man behind him. Five days later he was sent back to England to St Mark's College Hospital, Chelsea, where he shocked the nursing staff by openly reading German works of philosophy. He was visited by Ezra Pound who forced him to let his poem 'Trenches: St Éloi' be written down. Pound approved of Hulme's refusal, in the latter's words, to 'maudle in the rubbish of "war art"'.[62] Hulme also began to consider his future as a soldier and decided that the time had come to apply for a commission and leave the Honourable Artillery Company. He enlisted the influential help of Edward Marsh and, on 20 March 1916, he was commissioned to the Royal Marine Artillery as temporary 2nd lieutenant. He was in training in Portsmouth for the rest of 1916 and was not finally posted to Ostend until 19 May 1917.

During his convalescence in England, Hulme had not been idle and had contributed a series of commentaries on the War, which appeared in the *New Age* in seventeen instalments from November 1915 to March 1916. In them he took issue with the pacifists like Bertrand Russell and those, more generally, who in his opinion seemed not to grasp the true significance of the War. In the first of these pieces he wrote: 'The first remark of a foreigner visiting England to-day or of a soldier back from the front is that England does not yet realise that we are at war . . . Much less than the war itself are its issues realised; and since these, and not the event, are of the first importance, our failure to grasp the significance of the war may easily prove more disastrous than our failure to believe that a war is actually in progress.'[63] He went on: 'We are by nature one of the kindest people that ever lived, good-natured, sentimental and fundamentally amiable; and the contemplation of war, particularly in its realistic aspects, is naturally disagreeable to us. But this pleasing characteristic has unfortunately been flattered into something like a national vice by doctrines associated mainly with the Liberal school of opinion.'[64] These doctrines included a belief that the map of Europe is basically fixed and so minor disputes don't matter, but Hulme felt that Europe was 'in a continual flux of which the present war is a highly critical intensification ... Europe, in short, is a creation, not a blind evolutionary product; and nothing connected with its mental features is any more fixed than the present relations, as expressed in the trench-lines, between the Allies and the enemy.'

He also attacked the liberal assumption that progress is inevitable and naturally leads towards democracy, by inviting people to look at Germany which was not liberal in any way: 'In the matter of peril ... it is doubtful whether more than one in a thousand of our intelligent population has had his mind once crossed during the war by the thought that perhaps England is really in danger. And even fewer, I imagine, have once asked what are likely to be the consequences to the English of England's defeat. All that we mean by democracy will certainly take a second place in our lives if the Central Powers have their way. It cannot be otherwise.'[65] Hulme was exasperated by what he saw as complacency and wilful refusal to face the facts about the implications of the war for the future of Europe.

The philosopher in Hulme also disliked the media personalisation of figures like the Kaiser or Edith Cavell: 'Personalities, if they are allowed to become symbolic and to absorb the attention of the mind, disguise by diminution the magnitude of the super-personal issues at stake. Abstract terms would better express the combatants; only the abstract terms must be understood.' Hulme's 'War Notes' are an interesting mix of philosophical debate and strategic analysis. From his surely limited knowledge as a private in one entrenched sector of the Western Front he nevertheless asserted that the numbers of the enemy had been grossly underestimated and their casualties overestimated. But, in a comment that would have gained assent from Siegfried Sassoon, he maintained: '. . . the undeniable fact which ought to have been grasped after the first Ypres battle is this: that concentrated trench warfare is necessarily indecisive . . . Trench warfare, I repeat, conducted as it is being conducted at present, is not only a prolongation of the war, it is a prolongation to infinity. There is and can be no military conclusion to it.'[66] Nor was he impressed by the quality of the military leadership: 'There can be no doubt whatever that, in the bulk, our Staff work has been execrable, and that we owe to its badness the loss of thousands of lives as well as the prolongation of the war.'[67] But when it came to the pacifists only sarcasm was adequate for Hulme who proposed lumping them all together and calling them the 'No Conscription' Battalion. He claimed that it was impossible to shift a pacifist by argument and that what characterised them was a 'reluctance to recognise the dependence of *liberty* on *force*'.[68] Clive Bell, one of the more prominent Bloomsbury pacifists, he regarded as 'a contemptible ass'[69] and his pamphlet *Peace at Once* a piece of 'disgusting whining'.[70] He agreed to some extent with the argument of the pacifists that there would be social reconstruction in the post-war world: 'I admit that the new order of society will be different from the old; the old was breaking up before, the war did not cause the decay, it merely announced the fact on a hoarding.'[71] But when he attended a lecture by Bertrand Russell he felt his prospectus was soppy and irrelevant: 'This faded Rousseauism is based on an entirely false conception of the nature of man, and of the true hierarchy of values; the hierarchy is not objective, but is merely the result of an uncritical acceptance of the romantic tradition.'[72] In one of his last contributions Hulme defended heroic rather than liberal values: 'While humanitarian ethic attaches ultimate value to *Life* and *Personality*, true ethic can only value Life as a "bearer" of certain higher values, which themselves are quite independent of any relation to life.'[73]

In his new position as an officer in the Royal Marine Artillery, Hulme left England on 19 May 1917 to work with the Royal Naval siege guns, where residence in Barbara Camp on the Belgian coast near Ostend was far cushier than the grim life he had known in the trenches, in spite of the German shelling. 'I'd rather spend a year here than a month in the trenches I used to be in,' he wrote to his mother. 'I have plenty of time for my own private work.'[74] Fighting in this Nieuport and Lombartzyde area intensified throughout the summer, and when he returned from leave in September there was no let-up. On 28 September, four days after his thirty-fourth birthday, a direct hit from a shell ended his life. What was left of his body was buried in the Military Cemetery at Koksijde, West Flanders, in Belgium. On his grave is the inscription: 'One of the war poets'.

8

Other Voices

Your battle-wounds are scars upon my heart,
Received when in that grand and tragic 'show'
You played your part
Two years ago.[1]

VERA BRITTAIN

This book has been about the most prominent poets who
served in the British forces during the First World War, the
'soldier-poets' or 'trench poets'. As the Prologue regretted,
this choice excludes women – simply because in that era they
did not fight at the Front – but it also excludes many others
who wrote poetry during the conflict or afterwards. It leaves
out too those who were not British, in particular the German
enemy, as well as other European poets who had something
to say about the conflict. And there are also the prose writers
whose accounts have been just as influential as the work
of the poets in defining how the First World War is pictured
and remembered. And, finally, there is that vast pool – into
which we have dipped in earlier chapters – of the sincerely
felt, sometimes decently accomplished, verse produced by
serving British soldiers that was not destined to find lasting

readership in competition with the work of more distinguished talents.

Fortunately, there are many excellent anthologies of poetry
and prose, which fill out the picture of writing from the great conflict. Jon Silkin's *The Penguin Book of First World War Poetry* (1979)
has gone through many editions and is prefaced by a thoughtful
and challenging Introduction. He includes work by Thomas
Hardy, Herbert Read, Kipling, Edgell Rickword, Ford Madox
Ford and others to give a broader context to the war poetry of
this period. This volume contains, in addition to the poetry that
one would expect to see in such an anthology, the work of many
other European poets, from both sides of the conflict, in translation. Silkin notes a qualitative difference in the work of the
European poets, 'in that even before the War they wrote with
tense foreboding. Foreboding charges the work of Trakl, Heym,[2]
and Blok, and reproduces the anxiety in pre-war European culture; whereas this foreboding is, with the exception of Hardy,
absent from British pre-war poetry.'[3] War, before it broke out, was
seen as a cleansing, heroic, almost holiday-like interlude. The
deep anxiety in European culture at the start of the twentieth
century that Modernism tried to reflect was not so widely shared
by the largely traditional war poets who wrote in Britain.

After the War, as Silkin points out, there was a greater con-
gruence as all sides were brought face to face with the horror of
actual war. The Italian Futurists, in manifestos like that printed
for their famous exhibition of paintings in March 1912 at the
Sackville Gallery in London, wrote about war in purely aesthetic
terms as these points extracted from the 1912 manifesto show:

1.   We shall sing the love of danger, the habit of energy and
      boldness.
2.   The essential elements of our poetry shall be courage,
      daring and rebellion . . .
3.   . . . we shall extol aggressive movement . . .

4. We declare that the world's splendour has been enriched by a new beauty; the beauty of speed. A racing motor-car, its frame adorned with great pipes, like snakes with explosive breath . . . a roaring motor-car, which looks as though running on shrapnel, is more beautiful than the VICTORY OF SAMOTHRACE.

5. We shall sing of the man at the steering-wheel . . .

7. There is no more beauty except in strife. No masterpiece without aggressiveness. Poetry must be a violent onslaught upon the unknown forces, to command them to bow before man.

9. We wish to glorify War – the only health giver of the world – militarism, patriotism, the destructive arm of the Anarchist, the beautiful Ideas that kill, the contempt for woman [etc etc!].[4]

That glory of war and aggression (and the gratuitous misogyny which was widespread in the Futurist manifestos), seen as some kind of principle of avant-garde daring and revolutionary modernity, is absent from poems like Giuseppe Ungaretti's 'No More Crying Out'. And the German poets like Wilhelm Klemm and Anton Schnack in Silkin's anthology also wrote of the 'horror of war' with all the revulsion of the British trench poets.

One of the most useful of the many current anthologies is *The Winter of the World: Poems of the Great War*,[5] edited by Dominic Hibberd and John Onions, which arranges the poems in chronological order, year by year, enabling the reader to trace changing attitudes to the War and to be aware of when they were written and in what circumstances – where it is possible to be certain of these things. It also rectifies to some extent the poor representation of women in anthologies of war poetry, a lack addressed in Catherine Reilly's important and extremely popular volume *Scars upon My Heart: Women's Poetry and Verse of the First World War* (1981), which has gone through countless editions.

In her introduction to *Scars upon My Heart*, the poet Judith Kazantzis writes of these 'voices of despair and endurance and anger'[6] that quietly mount in a crescendo. She refers to 'the male agony of the trenches' that the well-known poets articulated, but adds, 'We know little in poetry of what that agony and its millions of deaths meant to the millions of English women who had to endure them – to learn to survive survival.' It needs only a moment of reflection to grasp how enormous was the impact of war on women, but women's poetry of the War is not just about grieving for lost menfolk. Women wrote as variously and covering as wide a range of themes as the male poets did. A poem like Vera Brittain's 'The Lament of the Demobilised' is as direct and colloquial as Sassoon's satires, and 'Perhaps', her lament for Roland Leighton her lover who died of wounds in France on 23 December 1915, made more poignant by the fact that she wrote it while serving in a London war hospital some time later, is moving, if conventional in form and metre. Her real originality was as a writer of prose, and in particular her *Testament of Youth* (1933) is a classic of First World War literature. Based on her own war diary, it was written, she said, 'to understand how the whole calamity had happened, to know why it had been possible for me and my contemporaries, through our own ignorance and others' ingenuity, to be used, hypnotised and slaughtered'.[7]

Inevitably (because poems are rooted in experiential truth) women wrote about the complexity of feelings and thoughts that centred on what it was like to be excluded from the horror of war. Rose Macaulay's poem 'Picnic' describes an English picnic in the summer of 1917 when the conflict seems far away:

We are shut about by guarding walls:
(We have built them lest we run
Mad from dreaming of naked fear
And of black things done.)

And in Harriet Monroe's 'On the Porch' there is a similar
expression of being screened from the horror while at the same
time being perfectly aware of it, lying on her porch in the
summer rain:

> As I lie roofed in, screened in,
> From the pattering rain,
> The summer rain –
> As I lie
> Snug and dry,
> And hear the birds complain.

Another fine poet was Charlotte Mew, whose poem 'The
Cenotaph' is widely anthologised. It has some of the subdued
bitterness of the best of the war poems of the combatants and
its opening lines, 'Nor yet will those measureless fields be green
again/ Where only yesterday the wild, sweet, blood of wonderful youth was shed', seem to contain an echo of Brooke's
'begloried' lines about the shedding of 'the red sweet wine of
youth'. She envisages the Cenotaph raised in a local market-
place and constituting a reproach to everyone about their daily
trades and huckstering, a reproach from 'the Face/Of God: and
some young, piteous, murdered face'.[8] No spirit of peaceful
post-war reconciliation in these lines.

The poet Ezra Pound, an American but resident in London
from before the War, and a potent influence on the Modernist
style, published in 1920 his poem *Hugh Selwyn Mauberley* which
responded to the same Horatian lines that Owen had glossed in
'Dulce et Decorum Est':

> Died some, pro patria,
>   non 'dulce' non 'et decor' . . .
> walked eye-deep in hell
> believing in old men's lies, then unbelieving

came home, home to a lie,
home to many deceits,
home to old lies and new infamy;
usury age-old and age-thick
and liars in public places.[9]

The poem goes on to say that many died 'For an old bitch gone in the teeth,/ For a botched civilization', and this (setting aside the bees in Pound's bonnet about usury) was clearly not an isolated reaction, post-war, to events – though one would have to place it in the context of a wider state of public opinion which may simply have been relieved that the War was over and anxious to blot out the memory. Lloyd George promised 'a fit country for heroes to live in', but unrest and industrial discord culminating in the 1926 General Strike meant that the post-war Paradise was postponed. An understandable bitterness at the waste of young lives, and a questioning of what the War's purposes had been, informed many of the war books that began to emerge – slowly, after the initial aftershock, the period of mental healing. Pound's Modernist hero, the sculptor Henri Gaudier-Brzeska, who died in the Belgian Army at Neuville-St Vaast on 5 June 1915, was 'the gravest individual loss which the arts have sustained during the war'.[10] Before his death, the sculptor had contributed an article to a special War number of *Blast*, the avant-garde journal of Vorticism edited by Wyndham Lewis, and it had all the bold, reckless assertiveness of Modernist polemic. 'I HAVE BEEN FIGHTING FOR TWO MONTHS and I can now gauge the intensity of life,'[11] his contribution – marked 'written from the trenches' – began. He continued:

WITH ALL THE DESTRUCTION that works around us
NOTHING IS CHANGED, EVEN SUPERFICIALLY.
LIFE IS THE SAME STRENGTH, THE MOVING

AGENT THAT PERMITS THE SMALL INDIVIDUAL
TO ASSERT HIMSELF.

THE BURSTING SHELLS, the volleys, wire entanglements, projectors, motors, the chaos of battle DO NOT
ALTER IN THE LEAST the outlines of the hill we are
besieging. A company of PARTRIDGES scuttle along before
our very trench.

IT WOULD BE FOLLY TO SEEK ARTISTIC EMO-
TION AMID THESE LITTLE WORKS OF OURS.

THIS PALTRY MECHANISM, WHICH SERVES AS A
PURGE TO OVER-NUMEROUS HUMANITY.

THIS WAR IS A GREAT REMEDY.

IN THE INDIVIDUAL IT KILLS ARROGANCE,
SELF-ESTEEM, PRIDE.

IT TAKES AWAY FROM THE MASSES NUMBERS
UPON NUMBERS OF UNIMPORTANT UNITS,
WHOSE ECONOMIC ACTIVITIES BECOME NOX-
IOUS AS THE RECENT TRADES CRISIS HAVE
SHOWN US.

MY VIEWS ON SCULPTURE REMAIN ABSO-
LUTELY THE SAME.

This extraordinary declaration could be dismissed as dotty
(or worse, the politics seeming to point in the rancid direction
muddlingly embarked upon by Pound), but it is a bracing cor-
rective to the view that the war was *aesthetically* momentous for
artists in general and poets in particular. 'Nothing is changed'
would certainly not be the message from the British poets of the
Western Front.

Wyndham Lewis himself, the founder of Vorticism, published in 1937 *Blasting and Bombardiering*, an autobiographical
account which described his war experiences and lambasted
'one of England's stupidest wars'.[12] It was one of many prose
accounts of the war (though it was much else besides) and it

appeared in the same year as Siegfried Sassoon's *The Complete Memoirs of George Sherston* which brought together all three of his memoirs, the first of which, *Memoirs of a Fox-hunting Man*, had appeared in 1928 and its sequel *Memoirs of an Infantry Officer* in 1930. In 1929 Robert Graves's *Goodbye to All That* and Richard Aldington's *Death of a Hero* were both published, the outlines of a literary view of the war now beginning to take shape.

Aldington had written a handful of war poems such as 'Trench Idyll' in the hard, dry, spare manner of Hulme, as befitted a prominent Imagist, but *Death of a Hero* is probably his most important contribution to the way the War was perceived. It was written in anger by an ex-combatant and it stressed the need to atone for the dead: 'It is the poison that makes us heartless and hopeless and lifeless – us the war generation, and the new generation too . . . Somehow we must atone, somehow we must free ourselves from the curse – the blood-guiltiness . . . the dead poison us and those who come after us.'[13] He was horrified to hear a man on a London bus during the war saying, 'What we need is a bit of blood-letting', but he argued, like Pound, that the War was in some sense a terrible cleansing of the old order: 'The long, unendurable nightmare had begun. And the reign of Cant, Delusion, and Delirium . . . It was the supreme and tragic climax of Victorian Cant, for after all the Victorians were still in full blast in 1914, and had pretty much control of everything.'[14] Through his alter ego George Winterbourne, Aldington conveys the full horror of the trench experience in a way that is unsparing and as shocking as anything in the corpus of war poetry. The year 1929 also saw the publication of Frederic Manning's *Her Privates We*, a more earthy account of ordinary soldiers at war that sounded a more cautionary note: 'To call [war] a crime against mankind is to miss at least half of its significance; it is also the punishment of a crime. That raises a moral question, the kind of problem with which the present age is disinclined to deal.'[15]

Other countries, too, had their war books and two which lived and have continued to live are Erich Maria Remarque's *All Quiet on the Western Front* (*Im Westen nichts Neues*, Berlin, 1929), which conveys in harrowing detail the reality of trench life for German soldiers, and Barbusse's *Under Fire* (*Le Feu*, Paris, 1916), the latter read by several of the British war poets while in the trenches and giving a French perspective on the years 1915 and 1916. And Ernest Hemingway's *A Farewell to Arms* (1929) was one of the most important American books from the War. Beyond these there have been the popular works of fiction of more recent years whose authors, writing not from experience but from imaginative projection back into that time, have tried to render the Great War. The debate continues about whether this helps us to understand the conflict, or whether it has become a myth with its own independent life regardless of historical truth, fulfilling other needs and purposes in British culture.

I began this book by describing, as it were at random, the war memorial in a small Welsh village where I once lived. One blustery November day in 1989 I was walking in the deserted main street when I saw coming towards me a little knot of retired residents – a teacher, a clergyman, and a librarian. Their scarves and coats streamed in the wind and, as they approached, they told me what they were doing. It was 11 November, seventy-one years after the Armistice, and on that day each year they would gather in one or other of their cottages to listen to Benjamin Britten's *War Requiem*, which makes use of some of the well-known poems of Wilfred Owen. I was moved by the quiet dignity of this little annual rite of remembrance, far-removed from the bitterness and anger, the noise and strife, the unrelenting horror, that have been recorded in this book. There have been subsequent wars and there will be more to come but the act of remembering, in its unostentatious way, endures, and the poets are among the principal enablers of that process.

A Military Chronology of the British War Poets

1914

August

War is declared on the 4th

Julian Grenfell (joined Royal Dragoons in 1910) is sent to France; awarded DSO

Charles Hamilton Sorley enlists; receives a commission in the 7th Battalion, the Suffolk Regiment

T. E. Hulme enlists as a private in the Honourable Artillery Company

Siegfried Sassoon joins the Sussex Yeomanry

Ivor Gurney attempts unsuccessfully to enlist

Edmund Blunden is commissioned as 2nd lieutenant in the Royal Sussex Regiment

Robert Graves is commissioned in the Royal Welch Fusiliers

September

Rupert Brooke obtains a commission in the Royal Naval Division (RNVR)

First Battle of the Marne halts German invasion in France

First trenches dug on Western Front

October

Rupert Brooke with Anson Battalion near Walmer, Kent, and for the rest of the month takes part in the Antwerp expedition

November

Charles Sorley promoted 1st lieutenant

December
Rupert Brooke drafted to Hood Battalion, 2nd Naval Brigade, Royal
    Naval Division at Blandford Camp, Dorset
T. E. Hulme arrives in France

1915

January
David Jones enlists in the 15th (London Welsh) Battalion of the Royal
    Welch Fusiliers
First Zeppelin raids on London

February
Ivor Gurney volunteers and is drafted into 2nd/5th Gloucester
    Regiment, B Company

March
Rupert Brooke's battalion embarks for the Dardanelles

April
Julian Grenfell writes 'Into Battle' during second Battle of Ypres
T. E. Hulme wounded and sent home to hospital
Robert Graves posted to France
Rupert Brooke dies at Skyros on the eve of the Gallipoli campaign

May
Siegfried Sassoon receives commission in the Royal Welch Fusiliers
Julian Grenfell wounded by shell splinter to the head; dies in military
    hospital in Boulogne
Charles Sorley's battalion arrives in France

July
Ivor Gurney in reserve at Aubers Ridge
Edward Thomas joins the Artists' Rifles

August
Charles Sorley is promoted captain

September
First use of gas by British in battle at Loos

October
Isaac Rosenberg enlists in the Bantam Battalion, 12th Suffolk Regiment, 40th Division

Charles Sorley is killed by a sniper in the Battle of Loos

Wilfred Owen joins up in the Artists' Rifles

November
Edward Thomas is sent to Hare Hall Camp, Gidea Park, Essex, working as a map instructor

Wilfred Owen also goes to Hare Hall, as a cadet in the Artists' Rifles

Siegfried Sassoon goes to France until August 1916

December
David Jones's battalion crosses to France; he has his first spell in the trenches after training

Sir Douglas Haig becomes commander of British Expeditionary Force

1916

January
Isaac Rosenberg goes to 12th South Lancashires training camp, Farnborough, then transfers to 11th Battalion, King's Own Royal Lancasters, at Blackdown Camp

Edmund Blunden sent to Flanders; wins Military Cross

February
Ivor Gurney trains at Tidworth, Salisbury Plain

Conscription comes into force in Britain

Battle of Verdun commences (lasts to December)

March
Isaac Rosenberg arrives in France

Wilfred Owen goes to Officers' School, Gidea Park, Essex

T. E. Hulme returns to France with commission as a temporary 2nd lieutenant in the Royal Marines Artillery

April
Canadians take Vimy Ridge

May
Ivor Gurney arrives with the Gloucesters at Le Havre and marches to
    Flanders in the Laventie–Fauquissart sector; then in trenches
    with the Welsh regiments at Riez Bailleul
Naval Battle of Jutland

June
Siegfried Sassoon receives Military Cross
Wilfred Owen reports to 5th (Reserve) Battalion, Manchester
    Regiment, Milford Camp, Surrey, and is commissioned into the
    Manchester Regiment

July
Somme offensive begins on the 1st and lasts until November
David Jones wounded in the attack on Mametz Wood
Wilfred Owen sent on a musketry course to 25th Battalion, Middlesex
    Regiment, Aldershot
Robert Graves wrongly reported dead after the Battle of the Somme

August
Siegfried Sassoon sent home from France with trench fever
Wilfred Owen goes to Mytchett Musketry Camp, Farnborough, in
    command of 5th Manchesters contingent

September
Edward Thomas begins training as an officer cadet with the Royal
    Garrison Artillery
Wilfred Owen, with the 5th Manchesters, moves to Oswestry

October
Ivor Gurney's battalion moves south to the Somme sector near Albert,
    then to the Somme front line
David Jones back in France from hospital
Wilfred Owen with the 5th Manchesters in Southport until 8 December

November
Edward Thomas commissioned as 2nd lieutenant

December
Edward Thomas volunteers for service overseas
Wilfred Owen goes to France and arrives at base camp at Étaples
Siegfried Sassoon reports to regimental depot at Litherland, Liverpool
David Lloyd George becomes Prime Minister

1917

January
Isaac Rosenberg back in the trenches with 4th Platoon, A Company, 11th King's Own Royal Lancasters
Ivor Gurney trains at Varennes
Edward Thomas embarks for France and serves with No. 244 Siege Battery
Wilfred Owen joins the 2nd Manchesters on the Somme near Beaumont Hamel and assumes command of 3 Platoon, A Company

February
Siegfried Sassoon returns to France from three months' sick leave
Robert Graves finishes active service

March
Wilfred Owen rejoins battalion near Fresnoy and is posted to B Company, then following concussion sent to military hospital at Nesle
Siegfried Sassoon joins 2nd Battalion Royal Welch Fusiliers on the Somme front

April
Sassoon wounded in the right shoulder
Wilfred Owen rejoins his battalion at Selency
Ivor Gurney wounded in the arm and in hospital at Rouen for six weeks
Edward Thomas is killed during the first hour of the Battle of Arras and buried in Agny military cemetery the following day

May

Wilfred Owen evacuated to 13th Casualty Clearing Station with shell-
shock

Ivor Gurney back with his regiment, transferred to machine-guns,
then to Arras front

Isaac Rosenberg reassigned to 229 Field Company Royal Engineers
attached to 11th Battalion, KORL

June

Wilfred Owen sent to the Welsh Hospital, Netley, Hampshire, then
to Craiglockhart Hospital

July

Siegfried Sassoon arrives at Craiglockhart after appearing before medical board in Liverpool; his statement of protest read out in the
House of Commons on the 30th

Wilfred Owen introduces himself to Sassoon at Craiglockhart

Ivor Gurney and the Gloucesters move north to Ypres as the offensive
begins

Third Battle of Ypres (Passchendaele), lasts until November

American Expeditionary Force arrives in France

September

Gurney in gas attack at St Julien near Passchendaele; gets 'blighty'
and is sent to Bangour War Hospital near Edinburgh

Isaac Rosenberg admitted to 51st General Hospital with influenza
until December

T. E. Hulme killed in action in Belgium

October

Wilfred Owen introduced by Sassoon to Robert Graves; appears
before medical board and is given three weeks' leave pending
return to unit

Ivor Gurney's *Severn and Somme* published

November

Gurney at Seaton Delaval, Northumberland, on a signalling course

Wilfred Owen joins 5th Manchesters at Scarborough

Siegfried Sassoon passed fit for general service

December

Sassoon reports back to Litherland

Wilfred Owen promoted lieutenant and posted back to France

1918

January

Siegfried Sassoon posted to Limerick

February

David Jones has severe attack of trench fever

Ivor Gurney in hospital in Newcastle suffering from effects of gas

Sassoon posted to Palestine with 25th Battalion, Royal Welch Fusiliers

March

Wilfred Owen posted to Northern Command Depot, Ripon

Germans launch 'spring offensive', the first of five major offensives

April

Isaac Rosenberg's 1st Battalion, KORL, moves to front line, Greenland Hill sector near Arras

Rosenberg fails to return from a wiring patrol; remains found later

German advance stopped near Amiens

May

Ivor Gurney in hospital at Warrington

Siegfried Sassoon's battalion arrives in France

Germans stopped on banks of Marne near Paris

June

Ivor Gurney has breakdown in hospital at Seaton Delaval

Wilfred Owen graded fit for general service again; rejoins 5th Manchesters at Scarborough

July

Ivor Gurney at Napsbury Hospital, St Albans

Siegfried Sassoon wounded in the head and sent to American Red Cross Hospital, Lancaster Gate, London

August

Wilfred Owen on embarkation leave; later reports to base camp, Étaples

Siegfried Sassoon to convalescent home at Lennel House, Coldstream, Berwickshire; then on indefinite sick leave

Counter-offensives on the Somme force Germans into retreat

September

Wilfred Owen in successful assault on Beaurevoir-Fonsomme line until 3 October; awarded MC

Allied forces break through German defences at Hindenburg Line

October

Ivor Gurney discharged with 'deferred shell-shock' and returns to Gloucester with army pension

Wilfred Owen at St Souplet joins line for the last time

November

Owen killed in the early morning on banks of Oise–Sambre Canal on the 4th

Armistice signed on the 11th

Notes

Prologue

1 *Women's Writing of the First World War: An Anthology* (2000), ed. Angela K. Smith, p. 1. She continues: 'Engrossing as the key texts are they actually constitute the experience of a distinct minority of the population. For a great many non-combatant men, and all women, this historical impression of the War is a misrepresentation of the experience of 1914–1918. What this majority actually did, how they actually felt, has for many years been obscured by the overriding horror of the life of the trench soldier.'

2 Ibid., p. 6

3 H.D., *Bid Me to Live* (1960), p. 37; 1984 Virago edn, edited and introduced by Helen McNeil, afterword by Perdita Schaffner

4 Philip Larkin, 'This be the Verse', *Collected Poems* (1988), p. 180

5 *The Collected Works of Isaac Rosenberg* (1984), ed. Ian Parsons, p. 227

6 *The Collected Writings of T. E. Hulme* (1994), ed. Karen Csengeri, p. 336

7 Ibid., p. 353

8 *The Letters of Rupert Brooke* (1968) chosen and ed. Geoffrey Keynes, p. 627

9 *Poems by Wilfred Owen* (1921), Introduction by Siegfried Sassoon, p. vi

10 Andrew Motion, Introduction to *First World War Poets* (2003)

11 The fateful glamour of the Western Front can make us sometimes forget that there was an Eastern Front and war at sea and in the air.

1 The West End Front

1   Richard Aldington, 'Preface' to *Some Imagist Poets* (1916).

2   Robert Graves, *In Broken Images: Selected Letters of Robert Graves 1914–1946* (1982), ed., with commentary, by Paul O'Prey, p. 30

3   William Watson, *Pencraft: A Plea for the Older Ways* (1916), cited in Myron Simon, *The Georgian Poetic* (1975), p. 50

4   *Letters from Edward Thomas to Gordon Bottomley* (1968), ed. and introduced by R. George Thomas, p. 233

5   H. D. *Bid Me to Live*, p. 7

6   C. K. Stead, *The New Poetic* (1964), p. 93

7   T. S. Eliot, Introduction to *Literary Essays of Ezra Pound* (1924), p. xiii

8   Andrew McNeillie (ed.), *The Essays of Virginia Woolf*, vol. III (1986), p. 421

9   Harold Monro, *Some Contemporary Poets* (1920), p. 18

10 Christopher Hassall, *Edward Marsh: Patron of the Arts. A Biography* (1959), pp. 189–90

11 Edward Marsh, *A Number of People: A Book of Reminiscences* (1939), p. 321

12 Frank Swinnerton, *Background With Chorus: A Footnote to Changes in English Literary Fashion between 1901 and 1917* (1956), p. 154

13 Cited in Joy Grant, *Harold Monro and the Poetry Bookshop* (1967), pp. 92–3

14 See Marsh, *A Number of People*, p. 326

15 Cited in Hassall, *Edward Marsh*, p. 194

16 Ibid., p. 208

17 Marsh, *A Number of People*, p. 322

18 Edward Marsh, Prefatory Note, *Georgian Poetry 1911–1912* (1912)

19 Edward Marsh, Prefatory Note, *Georgian Poetry 1913–1915* (1915)

20 Edward Marsh, Prefatory Note, *Georgian Poetry 1918–1919* (1919)

21 Edward Marsh, Prefatory Note, *Georgian Poetry 1920–1922* (1922)

22 C. Day Lewis, *A Hope for Poetry* (1944), p. 2

23 Harriet Monroe, *Poetry* (Chicago), 16 (May 1920), pp. 108–9

24 Peter Quennell, *The Sign of the Fish* (1960), p. 14

25 Stephen Spender, *The Making of a Poem* (1955), p. 14

26 Myron Simon, *The Georgian Poetic* (1975), pp. 11–12. See also Robert H. Ross, *The Georgian Revolt 1910–1922: Rise and Fall of a Poetic Ideal* (1965); and Timothy Rogers (ed.), *Georgian Poetry 1911–1922: The Critical Heritage* (1977)

27 Watson, *Pencraft*, p. 50

28 *Wilfred Owen: Selected Letters*, ed. John Bell (1985), p. 306

29 *Rhythm*, vol. 1, no. 1 (1911), Editorial by Frederick Goodyear

30 *Rhythm*, vol. 2, no. 5, June 1912

31 D. H. Lawrence, 'The Georgian Renaissance', *Rhythm Literary Supplement*, March 1913

32 *Imagist Poetry*, ed. Peter Jones (1972), Introduction, p. 19. See also Glenn Hughes, *Imagism and the Imagists: A Study in Modern Poetry* (1931)

33 Grant, *Harold Monro*, Chapter 3, 'The Poetry Bookshop'

34 For fuller accounts of this artistic and intellectual background see for example Hugh Kenner, *The Pound Era* (1972); Helen Carr, *The Verse Revolutionaries* (2009); and Christopher Butler, *Early Modernism: Literature, Music and Painting in Europe 1900–1916* (1994)

35 *The Egoist*, 1 April 1913, p. 27

36 Richard Aldington, 'Modern Poetry and the Imagists', *The Egoist*, 1 June 1914, p. 202

37 Both reproduced in full in *Imagist Poetry*, ed. Jones, pp. 129–34

38 Richard Aldington, 'Notes on the Present Situation', *The Egoist*, 1 September 1914, p. 326

39 Ross, *Georgian Revolt*, p. 142

40 Harold Monro, *Some Contemporary Poets* (1920), p. 26

41 *The Collected Letters of Charles Hamilton Sorley* (1990) edited by Jean Moorcroft Wilson, p. 210

42 Swinnerton, *Background*, p. 175

2 The First Phase, 1914 to the Somme: Rupert Brooke, Julian Grenfell, and Charles Hamilton Sorley

1 *The Letters of Rupert Brooke* (1968), chosen and ed. Geoffrey Keynes, p. 655.

2 *The Collected Letters of Charles Hamilton Sorley*, ed. Jean Moorcroft Wilson (1990) p. 236

3   Constantine Benckendorff, *Half a Life: The Reminiscences of a Russian Gentleman* (1954), Chapter V, 'The 1914 War', p. 150

4   See for example Peter Parker, *The Old Lie: The Great War and the Public-School Ethos* (1987)

5   Siegfried Sassoon, *Memoirs of a Fox-hunting Man* (1928), in *The Complete Memoirs of George Sherston* (1932), p. 219

6   Gary S. Messenger, *British Propaganda and the State in the First World War* (1992), p. 34

7   Florence Hardy, *The Life of Thomas Hardy* (1962), p. 366

8   Arnold Bennett, *The Journals of Arnold Bennett* (1933), pp. 524–35

9   Letter to *The Times*, 18 September 1914, p. 3

10 John Gould Fletcher, 'War Poetry', *The Egoist*, 2 November 1914, p. 410

11 John Gould Fletcher, 'More War Poetry', *The Egoist*, 16 November 1914, pp. 424–5

12 Herbert Blenheim, 'Song: in War-Time', *The Egoist*, 1 December 1914, p. 446

13 Rupert Brooke, *New Statesman*, 29 August 1914, p. 199

14 See Paul Delany, *The Neo-Pagans: Friendship and Love in the Rupert Brooke Circle* (1987)

15 Maurice Browne, *Recollections of Rupert Brooke* (1927), p. 16

16 *Letters of Rupert Brooke* (henceforward *Brooke Letters*), ed. Geoffrey Keynes, p. 601

17 *Brooke Letters*, p. 603; 18, p. 607; 19, p. 609; 20, p. 611; 21, p. 613; 22, p. 616, 23, p. 619

24 John Drinkwater, *Rupert Brooke: An Essay* (1916), p. 21

25 *Brooke Letters*, p. 621; 26, p. 622; 27, p. 622; 28, p. 624; 29, p. 624; 30, p. 625; 31, p. 627

32 Siegfried Sassoon, *The Complete Memoirs of George Sherston* (1932), p. 247, 'we were in clover compared to the men'

33 *Brooke Letters*, p. 630; 34, p. 631; 35, p. 632–3

36 Sassoon, *Complete Memoirs*, p. 230, 'the essential tragedy of the War, which, as everyone now agrees, was a crime against humanity'

37 *Brooke Letters*, p. 636; 38, p. 637; 39, p. 638; 40, p. 641; 41, p. 645; 42, p. 651; 43, p. 652; 44, p. 655; 45, p. 655

46 Browne, *Rupert Brooke*, p. 48

47 *Brooke Letters*, p. 659; 48, p. 660; 49, p. 661; 50, p. 662; 51, p. 664; 52, p. 665

53 John Masefield, *Gallipoli* (1916), p. 8

54 *Brooke Letters*, p. 666; 55, p. 667; 56, p. 669; 57, p. 669; 58, pp. 671–2; 59, p. 672; 60, p. 678; 61, p. 680

62 Cited by Nigel Jones, *Rupert Brooke: Life, Death and Myth* (1999), p. 423

63 Ibid., p. 423

64 Winston Churchill, *The Times*, 26 April 1915

65 Cited in Winston Churchill, *Rupert Brooke: Two Sonnets with a Memoir of Winston S. Churchill* (1945)

66 Browne, *Rupert Brooke*, p. 55

67 Drinkwater, *Rupert Brooke*, p. 5

68 *The Collected Works of Isaac Rosenberg* (1984), ed. Ian Parsons, p. 237

69 Gavin Ewart, Introduction to *Rupert Brooke: The Collected Poems* (1984), p. 3

70 *Collected Letters of Charles Hamilton Sorley*, ed. Wilson, pp. 218–19

71 Edward Shanks, *Second Essays on Literature* (1927), p. 109

72 Nicholas Mosley, *Julian Grenfell* (1999), p. 175; 73, p. 344; 74, p. 353; 75, p. 362; 76, p. 358; 77, p. 360; 78, p. 363; 79, p. 364; 80, p. 383

81 Introduction to *Collected Letters of Charles Hamilton Sorley* (henceforward *Sorley Letters*), ed. Wilson, p. 9: 'Sorley was unique among early First World War poets in his complete realism from the very beginning, long before the horrors of the Somme and other grim battles had destroyed the kind of untried idealism seen in Rupert Brooke and Julian Grenfell.'

82 Jean Moorcroft Wilson, *Charles Hamilton Sorley: A Biography* (1985), p. 204

83 Ibid., p. 205

84 Ibid., p. 209

85 Mrs W. R. Sorley, 'Biographical', in William Ritchie Sorley, *The Letters of Charles Sorley: With a Chapter of Biography* (1919), p. 1

86 *Sorley Letters*, ed. Wilson, p. 47; 87, p. 76; 88, p. 78; 89, p. 153; 90, p. 133; 91, p. 144; 92 p. 169; 93, p. 181

94 Mrs W. R. Sorley, in W. R. Sorley, *Letters of Charles Sorley*, p. 10

95 *Sorley Letters*, ed. Wilson, p. 181; 96, p. 184; 97, p. 188; 98, p. 190; 99, p. 191; 100, p. 193; 101, p. 200; 102, p. 210; 103, p. 211; 104, pp. 211–12; 105, p. 217; 106, p. 218; 107, p. 223; 108, p. 224; 109,

p. 225; 110, p. 228; 111, p. 236; 112, p. 236; 113, p. 242; 114, p. 243; 115, p. 254; 116, p. 258; 117, p. 260; 118, p. 261

119 W. R. Sorley, *Letters of Charles Sorley*, p. vii

120 All quotations from Sorley's poems from *The Collected Poems of Charles Hamilton Sorley* (1985), ed. Jean Moorcroft Wilson

121 Ibid., footnote, p. 70

3 The Somme and After: Siegfried Sassoon and the Poetry of Protest

1 Siegfried Sassoon, 'Sick Leave', *Collected Poems* (1961), p. 78

2 For an explanation of the spelling of 'Welch' see Robert Graves, *Goodbye to All That* (1929; Penguin edn, 1957), p. 75

3 'A close comparison of these books with his diaries shows that they are faithful records of his experiences, based on his contemporary descriptions, occasionally heightened but never distorted.' *Siegfried Sassoon: Diaries 1915–1918* (1983), ed. and introduced by Rupert Hart-Davis, p. 9

4 Imperial War Museum, Sassoon Papers SS4, Ms Notebook, 33pp. (1929–32)

5 Paul Fussell, *The Great War and Modern Memory* (1975; 2000 edn), Preface

6 Brian Bond, *The Unquiet Western Front: Britain's Role in Literature and History* (2002).

7 Desmond McCarthy, *Life and Letters* (1929), cited in Douglas Jerrold, *The Lie About the War*, p. 7

8 Jerrold, *The Lie*, p. 8

9 Ibid., pp. 44–6

10 Siegfried Sassoon, *Memoirs of a Fox-hunting Man* in *The Complete Memoirs of George Sherston* (1937), p. 280

11 Sassoon's words to Dame Felicitas Corrigan, quoted by Jean Moorcroft Wilson, *Siegfried Sassoon: The Making of a War Poet: A Biography (1886–1918)* (1998), p. 2

12 Max Egremont, *Siegfried Sassoon: A Life* (2005), p. 46

13 Hart-Davis, *Sassoon: Diaries*, p. 53

14 Wilson, *Siegfried Sassoon*: 'The outbreak of the First World War on 4 August 1914 came at exactly the right moment for Sassoon, who felt almost as if he had been waiting for it to happen', p. 179

15   Hart-Davis, *Sassoon: Diaries*, p. 21; 16, p. 21; 17, pp. 22–3; 18, p. 26; 19, p. 32; 20, p. 33; 21, p. 34; 22, p. 40; 23, p. 44; 24, p. 45; 25, p. 50

26   Sassoon, *Memoirs of a Fox-hunting Man*, p. 4

27   Hart-Davis, *Sassoon: Diaries*, p. 54; 28, p. 60; 29, p. 67; 30, p. 70; 31, p. 74; 32, pp. 83–4

33   Quoted in Michael Howard, *The First World War* (2002), p. 65

34   Sassoon, *Collected Poems* (1961), p. 20

35   Hart-Davis, *Sassoon: Diaries*, p. 87; 36, p. 88; 37, p. 93; 38, p. 93; 39, p. 94; 40, p. 96; 41, p. 100

42   Cited from *Ottoline at Garsington: Memoirs of Lady Ottoline Morrell 1915–18*, edited with an introduction by Robert Gathorne-Hardy (1974), in footnote to Hart-Davis, *Sassoon: Diaries*, p. 103

43   Siegfried Sassoon, *Siegfried's Journey: 1916–1920* (1945; 1982 edn), p. 5; 44, p. 12; 45, pp. 14–15; 46, p. 16; 47, p. 17; 48, p. 18; 49, p. 19

50   quoted in ibid., p. 20

51   Ibid., p. 20

52   Nicholas Murray, *Aldous Huxley: An English Intellectual* (2002), p. 92

53   Sassoon, *Siegfried's Journey*, p. 22; 54, p. 25; 55, p. 26; 56, p. 28; 57, p. 29

58   Jonathan Fryer, *Robbie Ross: Oscar Wilde's True Love* (2000), p. 244

59   Sassoon, *Siegfried's Journey*, p. 37; 60, p. 38; 61, p. 40

62   Hart-Davis, *Sassoon: Diaries*, p. 104; 63, p. 105; 64, p. 106; 65, p. 106; 66, p. 109; 67, p. 117; 68, p. 119; 69, p. 119; 70, p. 119; 71, p. 121

72   Sassoon, *Siegfried's Journey*, p. 46

73   Hart-Davis, *Sassoon: Diaries*, p. 132; 74, p. 133; 75, p. 134; 76, p. 142; 77, p. 151; 78, p. 156; 79, p. 162

80   Cited in ibid., p. 168

81   Ibid., p. 171

82   Sassoon, *Siegfried's Journey*, p. 50; 83, p. 52; 84, p. 55

85   Hart-Davis, *Sassoon: Diaries*, p. 175; 86, p. 177

87   Quoted in ibid., pp. 173–4

88   Egremont, *Siegfried Sassoon*, p. 145

89   Quoted in Hart-Davis, *Sassoon: Diaries*, p. 178

90   Also quoted in ibid., as are all the reactions quoted here, p. 178

91   Graves, *Goodbye to All That*, p. 215

92   Siegfried Sassoon, *Memoirs of an Infantry Officer* (1930), p. 223

93   *Ivor Gurney: Collected Letters* (1991), ed. R. K. R. Thornton, p. 370

94   Medical notes cited by Egremont, *Siegfried Sassoon*, p. 156

95   Hart-Davis, *Sassoon: Diaries*, p. 183

96   Imperial War Museum (herewith IWM), Sassoon Papers SS7 C, Rivers correspondence. Medical Case Sheet Army Form I.1237.

97   *Sherston's Progress* (1932) from Sassoon, *Complete Memoirs*, p. 521

98   IWM, Sassoon Papers SS7, Robbie Ross correspondence

99   IWM, Sassoon Papers SS4, Ms Notebook, 33pp. (1929–32). Scholars are not currently allowed to see the original notebook and are restricted to microfilm of pencilled notes, so some errors of transcription might have occurred.

100 Sassoon, *Complete Memoirs*, p. 541

101 Ibid.

102 Hart-Davis, *Sassoon: Diaries*, p. 190; 103, p. 192; 104, p. 197; 105, p. 198; 106, p. 219; 107, p. 225; 108, p. 242; 109, p. 258; 110, p. 271; 111, p. 274; 112, p. 275; 113, p. 276

114 Sassoon, *Siegfried's Journey*, p. 71

115 Ibid., p. 72

116 Hart-Davis, *Sassoon: Diaries*, p. 282

117 *The War Poems of Siegfried Sassoon* (1983), Introduction by Rupert Hart-Davis, p. 11

118 Ibid., p. 15

119 Ibid., p. 22

120 Ibid., pp. 46–7

121 Philip Hoare, entry in *Oxford Dictionary of National Biography*

122 Philip Hoare, *Serious Pleasures: The Life of Stephen Tennant* (Penguin, 1990) p. 132

123 Ibid.

124 Egremont, *Siegfried Sassoon*, p. 377

4 The Poetry and the Pity: Wilfred Owen and Robert Graves

1   *Wilfred Owen: Selected Letters* (hereafter *Owen: Letters*) (1985), ed. John Bell, p. 282

2   See Jon Stallworthy, *Wilfred Owen: A Biography* (1974), entry by Stallworthy in *Oxford Dictionary of National Biography* (2004–9) and Dominic Hibberd, *Wilfred Owen* (2002)

3   Dominic Hibberd, *Wilfred Owen: A New Biography* (2002), p. 27

4   *Owen: Letters*, p. 53; 5, p. 68; 6, p. 9; 7, p. 111; 8, p. 117; 9, p. 119; 10, p. 89; 11, p. 127; 12, p. 128; 13, p. 130; 14, p. 135; 15, p. 144; 16, p. 149; 17, p. 153; 18, p. 159; 19, p. 167; 20 p. 169; 21, p. 170; 22, p. 171; 23, p. 172; 24, p. 180; 25, p. 182; 26, p. 188; 27, p. 209; 28, p. 209; 29, p. 212; 30, p. 212; 31, pp. 213–14; 32, p. 216; 33, p. 216; 34, pp. 217–18

35 See an example reproduced in the invaluable World War One Digital Archive: http://www.oucs.ox.ac.uk/ww1lit/collections

36 *Dai Greatcoat: A Self-portrait of David Jones in His Letters* (1980), ed. René Hague, p. 245

37 *Owen: Letters*, p. 236; 38, p. 238; 39, p. 239; 40, pp. 246–7; 41, p. 254; 42, p. 257; 43, p. 258; 44, p. 266; 45, p. 266; 46, p. 268; 47, p. 269; 48, p. 270; 49, pp. 271–2; 50, p. 272

51 Sassoon, *Siegfried's Journey*, p. 58; 52, p. 59; 53, p. 60; 54, p. 61; 55, p. 63; 56, p. 64

57 Hart-Davis, *Sassoon: Diaries*, p. 191

58 *Owen: Letters*, p. 273; 59, p. 275; 60, pp. 277–8; 61, p. 282; 62, p. 283; 63, p. 284; 64, p. 283; 65, p. 304; 66, p. 283; 67, p. 287; 68, pp. 289–90; 69, p. 291; 70, p. 305; 71, p. 306; 72, p. 306

73 *Observer*, 12 July 2009, p. 7

74 *Owen: Letters*, p. 307; 75, p. 308; 76, p. 311; 77, p. 311; 78, p. 317; 79, p. 320; 80, p. 321; 81, p. 328; 82, p. 329; 83, p. 339; 84, p. 341; 85, p. 342; 86, p. 347; 87, p. 349; 88, p. 349; 89, p. 351; 90, p. 352; 91, p. 353; 92, p. 355; 93, p. 360; 94, p. 361; 95, p. 362

96 *Poems by Wilfred Owen*, ed. and with an Introduction by Siegfried Sassoon (1921), p. v

97 Graves, *Goodbye to All That*, p. 89

98 See Martin Seymour-Smith, *Robert Graves: His Life and Work* (1995); *Dictionary of National Biography* by Richard Perceval Graves.

99 *In Broken Images: Selected Letters of Robert Graves 1914–1946* (hereafter *Graves Letters*) (1982), ed. Paul O'Prey, pp. 29–30

100 *Graves Letters*, p. 31; 101, p. 32

102 Graves, *Goodbye to All That*, p. 146

103 *Graves Letters*, p. 39; 104, p. 43; 105, p. 44; 106, p. 46; 107, p. 51
108 Graves, *Goodbye to All That*, p. 181
109 *Graves Letters*, p. 62; 110, p. 67; 111, p. 68; 112, p. 69; 113, p. 72; 114, p. 77; 115, p. 79; 116, p. 80; 117, p. 83; 118, pp. 85–6; 119, p. 87; 120, p. 89; 121, p. 101
122 *The Winter of the World: Poems of the Great War* (2007), Dominic Hibberd and John Onions (eds), p. 58
123 Ibid., p. 101
124 Ibid.
125 Ibid., p. 102
126 Ibid., p. 148
127 Ibid., p. 243

5 Transcripts of the Battlefields: Isaac Rosenberg

1 *The Collected Works of Isaac Rosenberg* (1984), ed. Ian Parsons, p. 227
2 To read the original manuscript with Rosenberg's revisions see: http://www.oucs.ox.ac.uk/ww1lit
3 'In the Trenches', Parsons, *Collected Works*, p. 102
4 Ibid., pp. 103–4
5 Alec W. G. Randall, 'Poetry and Patriotism', *The Egoist*, 1 February 1916, p. 27
6 John Gould Fletcher, 'On Subject-matter and War Poetry', *The Egoist*, no. 12, vol. 3 (December 1916), p. 189
7 Jean Liddiard (ed.), *Poetry out of My Head and Heart*, p. 92
8 *Isaac Rosenberg: Soldier Poets: Songs of the Fighting Men* (1916), ed. Galloway Kyle, p. 7
9 *Poems Written During the Great War 1914–1918: An Anthology* (1918), ed. Bertram Lloyd
10 Parsons, *Collected Works*, p. 237
11 See Jean Moorcroft Wilson, *Isaac Rosenberg: The Making of a Great War Poet: A New Life* (2008); Jon Stallworthy, entry in online *Oxford Dictionary of National Biography* (2004–9); and *Isaac Rosenberg: Poetry out of My Head and Heart: Unpublished Letters and Poem Versions* (2007), ed. and introduced by Jean Liddiard
12 Parsons, *Collected Works*, p. 180; 13, p. 186; 14, p. 193
15 *Poems by Isaac Rosenberg* (1922), selected and ed. Gordon

Bottomley, with an introductory memoir by Laurence Binyon, p. 3

16 Liddiard (ed.), *Poetry out of my Head and Heart*, p. 63
17 Ibid., p. 64
18 Parsons, *Collected Works*, p. xvi; 19, p. 221
20 Bottomley, *Poems by Isaac Rosenberg*, p. 8
21 Parsons, *Collected Works*, p. 205; 22, p. 216; 23, p. 219; 24, p. 219; 25, p. 221; 26, p. 222; 27, p. 223; 28, p. 225; 29, p. 225; 30, p. 227; 31, p. 230; 32, p. 232; 33, p. 232; 34, p. 235; 35, p. 236
36 For an account of the poetic group to which Lascelles Abercrombie belonged see Sean Street's valuable *The Dymock Poets* (1994)
37 Parsons, *Collected Works*, p. 239; 38, p. 239; 39, p. 242; 40, p. 245; 41, p. 248
42 Liddiard (ed.), *Poetry out of My Head and Heart*, p. 66
43 Parsons, *Collected Works*, p. 250
44 Liddiard (ed.), *Poetry out of My Head and Heart*, p. 87
45 Ibid., p. 89
46 Parsons, *Collected Works*, p. 252; 47, p. 253; 48, p. 254; 49, p. 255; 50, p. 255; 51, p. 256; 52, p. 257; 53, p. 257; 54, p. 258; 55, p. 260; 56, p. 262; 57, pp. 264–5; 58, p. 267; 59, p. 267; 60, p. 268; 61, p. 268; 62, p. 269; 63, p. 272
64 Siegfried Sassoon, Foreword to *Collected Works*, p. ix
65 Liddiard (ed.), *Poetry out of My Head and Heart*, p. 50
66 Ibid., p. 73
67 Ibid., p. 95
68 *The Poems and Plays of Isaac Rosenberg* (2004), ed. Vivien Noakes, p. 120
69 Ibid., p. 356n
70 Ibid.

6 The English Line: Ivor Gurney, Edward Thomas, Edmund Blunden

1   George Orwell, *The Lion and the Unicorn: Socialism and the English Genius* (1982), ed. Bernard Crick, p. 42 (original edn 1941)
2   *Ivor Gurney: Collected Letters* (hereafter *Gurney Letters*) (1991), ed. R. K. R. Thornton, p. 125
3   Andrew Motion, *First World War Poets* (2003), Introduction

4   Ivor Gurney, *Collected Poems* (2004), ed. P. J. Kavanagh, p. 45

5   See Michael Hurd, *The Ordeal of Ivor Gurney* (1978), and his entry in the *Oxford Dictionary of National Biography*.

6   *Gurney Letters*, p. 11; 7, p. 12; 8, p. 13; 9, p. 14; 10, p. 15; 11, p. 17; 12, p. 17; 13, p. 19; 14, p. 21; 15, p. 29; 16, p. 42; 17, p. 43; 18, p. 52; 19, p. 60; 20, p. 64; 21, p. 70; 22, p. 71; 23, p. 77; 24, p. 81; 25, p. 82; 26, p. 87; 27 p. 88; 28, p. 89; 29, p. 91

30 Kavanagh (ed.), *Collected Poems*, p. 149. The second, shorter, version of the two poems with this title is the best.

31 *Gurney Letters*, p. 90; 32, p. 92; 33, p. 93; 34, p. 93; 35, p. 101; 36, p. 102; 37, p. 103; 38, p. 115; 39, p. 115; 40, p. 125; 41, p. 128; 42, p. 134; 43, p. 161; 44, p. 171; 45, p. 136; 46, p. 189; 47, p. 160; 48, p. 195; 49, p. 201; 50, p. 213; 51, p. 213; 52, p. 215; 53, p. 216; 54, p. 219; 55, p. 230; 56, p. 240; 57, p. 260; 58, p. 261; 59, p. 288; 60, p. 308; 61, p. 322; 62, p. 319; 63, p. 319; 64, p. 321; 65, p. 329; 66, p. 332; 67, p. 375; 68, p. 338; 69, p. 339; 70, p. 374; 71, p. 379; 72, p. 418; 73, p. 449; 74, p. 355

75 John Lucas, *Ivor Gurney* (2001), p. 3

76 Ivor Gurney, *Severn and Somme* (1917), p. 7

77 *Gurney Letters*, p. 375; 78, p. 382; 79, p. 292

80 Helen Thomas, *World Without End* (Faber, 1956), p. 108

81 Sir Ian MacAlister, cited in William Cooke, *Edward Thomas: A Critical Biography* (1970)

82 See R. G. Thomas, *Edward Thomas: A Portrait* (1985); Cooke, *Edward Thomas*; and Edna Longley, in *Oxford Dictionary of National Biography* entry.

83 Edward Thomas, *The Letters of Edward Thomas to Jesse Berridge* (1983), p. 76

84 R. G. Thomas, *Letters from Edward Thomas to Gordon Bottomley* (1968), p. 245

85 Ibid., p. 251

86 Edward Thomas, *Letters to America 1914–1917* (1989), pp. 12–13

87 Dominic Hibberd, *Wilfred Owen* (2003), p. 218

88 Edward Thomas, *Letters to America*, p. 22

89 R. G. Thomas, *Letters to Bottomley*, p. 270; 90, p. 277; 91, p. 278; 92, p. 279; 93, p. 280; 94, p. 282; 95, p. 284; 96, p. 283

97 Edna Longley's 'Introduction' to her *Edward Thomas: The Annotated Collected Poems* (2008) is an essential starting point for understanding Thomas and his critics.

98   Notebook entry cited in ibid., p. 263n

99   Eleanor Farjeon, *Edward Thomas: The Last Four Years* (1958),
     p. 154, cited in Longley, *Collected Poems*, p. 267n

100 Rupert Hart-Davis, *Edmund Blunden 1896–1974: An Address*
     (1974)

101 Edmund Blunden, *Undertones of War* (1928), p. viii

102 Hart-Davis, *Sassoon: Diaries*, p. 170

103 For more on Blunden's war service see his 'A Battalion History'
     in *Overtones of War*, ed. Martin Taylor (1996), Appendix,
     pp. 213–26, written in 1933.

104 Blunden, *Undertones*, p. 1; 105, p. 3

106 Edmund Blunden, *De Bello Germanico: A Fragment of Trench
     History Written in 1918 by the author of Undertones of War* (1930),
     p. 5

107 Blunden, *Undertones*, p. 13; 108, p. 14; 109, p. 24; 110, p. 73; 111,
     p. 76; 112, p. 76; 113, p. 100; 114, p. 134; 115, p. 198; 116, p. 196;
     117, p. 227; 118, p. 236

119 Blunden, *De Bello Germanico*, Introduction; 120, p. 7; 121, p. 8;
     122, p. 10; 123, p. 11; 124, p. 13; 125, p. 17; 126, p. 19; 127,
     p. 24; 128, p. 29; 129, p. 30; 130, p. 37; 131, p. 70; 132, p. 71;
     133, p. 78

134 Edmund Blunden, *The Mind's Eye* (1934), p. 15; 135, p. 17; 136,
     pp. 17–18; 137, p. 19; 138, p. 20; 139, p. 20; 140, p. 27; 141, p. 34;
     142, p. 36; 143, p. 37; 144, p. 38; 145, p. 39; 146, p. 43

147 Cited by Barry Webb in *Edmund Blunden: A Biography* (1990),
     p. 101

148 Blunden, *Overtones of War*

149 Edmund Blunden, *War Poets 1914–1918* (1958), p. 26

150 Both poems in Edmund Blunden, *Poems 1914–30* (1930),
     Hibberd and Onions (eds), pp. 151–2

7 Two Modernists: David Jones and T. E. Hulme

1   David Jones, *In Parenthesis* (1937), p. xiv

2   T. S. Eliot, *In Parenthesis* (1963), Note of Introduction, p. vii

3   Jones, *In Parenthesis*, p. ix; 4, p. x; 5, p. ix; 6, p. xiv; 7, p. x; 8,
     p. xi; 9, p. xii; 10, epigraph; 11, Part 4, pp. 86–7

12   *Dai Greatcoat: A Self-portrait of David Jones in His Letters* (1980),
     ed. René Hague, p. 23; 13, p. 195; 14, p. 26; 15, p. 26

16 See Colin Hughes, *David Jones: The Man Who Was on the Field: 'In Parenthesis' as Straight Reporting* (1979), p. 7

17 Hague, *Dai Greatcoat*, p. 254; 18, p. 6

19 Harman Grisewood (ed.), *The Dying Gaul and Other Writings* (1978), p. 28

20 Hague, *Dai Greatcoat*, p. 260; 21, p. 238; 22, p. 250

23 Grisewood, *Dying Gaul*, p. 28

24 Hague, *Dai Greatcoat*, p. 251; 25, p. 252; 26, p. 252; 27, p. 215

28 Grisewood, *Dying Gaul*, p. 29

29 Hague, *Dai Greatcoat*, p. 28; 30, p. 47; 31, p. 58; 32, p. 58; 33, p. 72; 34, p. 241; 35, p. 242; 36, p. 245; 37, p. 246; 38, p. 248; 39, p. 249; 40, p. 255; 41, p. 258; 42, p. 174

43 Quoted in Robert Ferguson, *The Short, Sharp Life of T. E. Hulme* (2002), p. 1

44 T. E. Hulme, *Speculations* (1960), p. 133

45 Ibid., p. 126

46 See Ferguson, *Short, Sharp*, and *Oxford Dictionary of National Biography* entry by Karen Csengeri

47 *The Collected Writings of T. E. Hulme* (1994), ed. Karen Csengeri, 'War Writings' (transcript of letters to family between Dec. 1914 and Apr. 1915; also reprinted in Ferguson, *Short, Sharp*, Chapter 11), p. 313

48 Csengeri, 'War Writings', in *Collected Writings*, p. 314; 49, p. 316; 50, p. 316; 51, p. 316; 52, p. 317; 53, p. 319; 54, p. 320; 55, p. 320; 56, p. 321; 57, p. 322; 58, p. 323; 59, p. 325; 60, p. 327; 61, p. 328

62 Hulme, *Speculations*, p. 236

63 Csengeri, 'War Notes', in *Collected Writings*, p. 331; 64, p. 332; 65, p. 334; 66, p. 340; 67, p. 345; 68, p. 362; 69, p. 375; 70, p. 377; 71, p. 392; 72, p. 395; 73, p. 415

74 Cited in Ferguson, *Short, Sharp*, p. 267

8 Other Voices

1 Vera Brittain, 'To My Brother', in *Scars upon My Heart: Women's Poetry and Verse of the First World War* (1981), ed. Catherine Reilly. The poem was written four days before Captain E. H. Brittain died in action, on 15 July 1918.

2 See for example the disturbingly prophetic 'Der Krieg' ('War') of 1911, in *Poems* (2004) by Georg Heym, ed. and trans. Antony Hasler, p. 142

3   Jon Silkin and David McDuff, *The Penguin Book of First World War Poetry* (1981), Note to the Second Edition, p. 12. Confusingly, the current Penguin anthology with the same title is actually a reissue of George Walter's *In Flander's Fields: Poetry of the First World War* (2004).

4   *Exhibition of Works by the Italian Futurist Painters* (catalogue, March 1912) at the Sackville Gallery. 'Initial Manifesto' signed by Umberto Boccioni, Carlo D. Carrà, Luigi Russolo, Giacomo Balla and Gino Severini.

5   *The Winter of the World: Poems of the Great War* (2007), ed. Dominic Hibberd and John Onions

6   Reilly (ed.), *Scars upon My Heart*, p. xv

7   Vera Brittain, *Testament of Youth* (1978) p. 471

8   Charlotte Mew, *Selected Poems* (2008), ed. and with an Introduction by Eavan Boland, p. 21

9   Ezra Pound, *Selected Poems* (1948 edn), p. 175

10 Ezra Pound, *A Memoir of Gaudier-Brzeska* (1970), p. 136

11 Cited in ibid., p. 27

12 Percy Wyndham Lewis, *Blasting and Bombardiering: An Autobiography (1914–1926)* (1937; 1982 edn), p. 107

13 Richard Aldington, *Death of a Hero* (1929; 1984 edn), p. 35

14 Ibid., p. 221

15 Frederic Manning, *Her Privates We* (1929; 1986 edn), Author's Prefatory Note

Bibliography

Abercrombie, Lascelles, and others. *New Numbers*. 1914.

Aldington, Richard. 'Modern Poetry and the Imagists'. *The Egoist*, 1914.

—— *Some Imagist Poets*. 1916.

—— *Death of a Hero*. 1929.

—— and others. *Imagist Anthology 1930*. 1930.

Aldritt, Keith. *David Jones: Writer and Artist*. Constable, 2003.

Beckett, Ian F. W. *The First World War: The Essential Guide to Sources in the UK National Archives*. 2002.

Beckett, Ian F. W., and Keith Simpson. *A Nation in Arms: A Social Study of the British Army in the First World War*. Manchester University Press, 1985.

Bell, John (ed.). *Wilfred Owen: Selected Letters*. 1985.

Benckendorff, Constantine. *Half a Life: The Reminiscences of a Russian Gentleman*. 1954.

Bennett, Arnold. *The Journals of Arnold Bennett*. 1933.

Bergonzi, Bernard. *Heroes' Twilight*. 1965.

Bishop, Major. *Winged Warfare*. 1918.

Blunden, Edmund. *Undertones of War*. 1937 (Penguin edn, 1928).

—— *Poems 1914–30*. 1930.

—— *De Bello Germanico: A Fragment of Trench History*. G. A. Blunden. 1930.

—— *The Mind's Eye*. 1934.

—— *War Poets 1914–1918*. 1958.

—— *Overtones of War: Poems of the First World War*, ed. Martin Taylor. Duckworth, 1996.

Boccioni, Umberto. Exhibition of Works by the Italian Futurist Painters, March 1912. Sackville Gallery, 1912.

Bolger, Dermot (ed.). *Francis Ledwidge: Selected Poems*. New Island Books, Dublin, 1992.

Bond, Brian. *The Unquiet Western Front*. 2002.

Booth, Allyson. *Postcards from the Trenches: Negotiating the Space between Modernism and the First World War*. Oxford University Press, 1996.

Bottomley, Gordon (ed.). *Poems by Isaac Rosenberg*. William Heinemann, 1922.

—— and Denys Harding (eds). *The Collected Works of Isaac Rosenberg: Poetry, Prose, Letters and Some Drawings*. Chatto, 1937.

Brittain, Vera. *Testament of Youth*. 1978.

Brooke, Rupert. *The Poetical Works of Rupert Brooke*. Geoffrey Keynes, 1946.

—— *The Prose of Rupert Brooke*. Christopher Hassall, 1956.

—— *Letters from Rupert Brooke to His Publisher 1911–1914*. Geoffrey Keynes, 1975.

—— *The Collected Poems of Rupert Brooke*. Macmillan, 1987.

Browne, Maurice. *Recollections of Rupert Brooke*. 1927.

Buitenhuis, Peter. *The Great War of Words: Literature as Propaganda in 1914–18 and After*. 1989.

Bushaway, Bob. 'Name upon Name: The Great War and Remembrance' in *Myths of the English*, ed. Roy Porter. Polity, 1992.

Butler, Christopher. *Early Modernism: Literature, Music and Painting in Europe 1900–1916*. Oxford University Press, 1994.

Carr, Helen. *The Verse Revolutionaries*. Jonathan Cape, 2009.

Casson, Stanley. *Rupert Brooke and Skyros*. 1921.

Cecil, Hugh. *The Flower of Battle: British Fiction Writers of the First World War*. Secker & Warburg, 1995.

Churchill, Winston. *Rupert Brooke: Two Sonnets with a Memoir of Winston S. Churchill*. 1945.

Clarke, Peter. *Hope and Glory: Britain 1900–1990*. Penguin, 1996.

Cohen, Joseph. *Journey to the Trenches: The Life of Isaac Rosenberg 1890–1918*. Robson Books, 1975.

Cooke, William. *Edward Thomas: A Critical Biography*. 1970.

Cross, Tim. *The Lost Voices of World War I*. 1988.

Csengeri, Karen (ed.). *The Collected Writings of T. E. Hulme*. Oxford University Press, 1994.

Curtayne, Alice (ed.). *The Complete Poems of Francis Ledwidge*. Martin Brian & O'Keeffe, 1974.

David, Albert Augustus. *Counting the Cost: A Sermon Preached in Rugby Chapel on Sunday, 9th May 1915*. 1915.

DeGroot, Gerald. *Blighty*. 1996.

De la Mare, Walter. *Rupert Brooke and the Intellectual Imagination*. 1919.

Delany, Paul. *The Neo-Pagans: Friendship and Love in the Rupert Brooke Circle*. 1987.

Drinkwater, John. *Rupert Brooke: An Essay*. 1916.

Ebbatson, Roger. *An Imaginary England: Nation, Landscape and Literature, 1840–1920*. 2005.

Egremont, Max. *Siegfried Sassoon: A Life*. Picador, 2005.

Eksteins, Modris. *Rites of Spring: The Great War and the Birth of the Modern Age*. 1989.

Eliot, T. S. (ed.). *Literary Essays of Ezra Pound*. Faber, 1924.

English Association. *Poems of To-day: An Anthology*. 1915.

Ewart, Gavin. (ed.) *Rupert Brooke: The Collected Poems*, Introduction. 1984.

Farjeon, Eleanor. *Edward Thomas: The Last Four Years*. 1958.

Ferguson, Robert. *The Short, Sharp Life of T. E. Hulme*. 2002.

Ferro, Marc. *The Great War 1914–1918*. Routledge, 1973.

Fletcher, John Gould. 'On Subject-matter and War Poetry'. *The Egoist*, December 1916.

Fryer, Jonathan. *Robbie Ross: Oscar Wilde's True Love*. 2000.

Fussell, Paul. *The Great War and Modern Memory*. 1975.

Garafola, Lynn, and Nancy Van Norman Baer (eds). *The Ballets Russes and Its World*. Yale, 1999.

Gibson, Wilfrid Wilson. *Battle*. Elkin Matthews, 1915.

Goodyear, Frederick. Editorial, *Rhythm*, vol. 1, no. 1 (1911).

Grant, Joy. *Harold Monro and the Poetry Bookshop*. 1967.

Graves, Robert. *Over the Brazier*. 1916.

—— *Fairies and Fusiliers*. 1917.

—— *Goliath and David*. 1917.

—— *Country Sentiment*. 1920.

—— *Goodbye to All That*. Penguin, Jonathan Cape edn, 1929.

—— *Collected Poems 1965*. Cassell, 1965.

—— *Poems about War*. Cassell, 1988.

Grisewood, Harman (ed.). *The Dying Gaul and Other Writings*. Faber, 1978.

Guest, Barbara. *Herself Defined: The Poet H.D. and Her World*. Collins, 1984.

Gurney, Ivor. *Severn and Somme.* Sidgwick & Jackson, 1917.

—— *Collected Poems of Ivor Gurney,* ed. P. J. Kavanagh. Oxford University Press, 1984.

—— *Ivor Gurney: Collected Letters,* ed. R. K. R. Thornton. Carcanet, 1991.

—— *Collected Poems,* ed. P. J. Kavanagh. Carcanet, 2004.

H.D. *Bid Me to Live.* Virago, 1984.

Hague, René (ed.). *Dai Greatcoat: A Self-portrait of David Jones in His Letters.* Faber, 1980.

Hardy, Florence. *The Life of Thomas Hardy.* 1962.

Hart-Davis, Rupert. *Edmund Blunden 1896–1974: An Address.* 1974.

—— (ed.). *The War Poems of Siegfried Sassoon.* Faber, 1983.

—— (ed.). *Siegfried Sassoon: Diaries 1915–1918.* Faber, 1983.

Hassall, Christopher. *Edward Marsh: Patron of the Arts.* 1959.

—— *Rupert Brooke: A Biography.* Faber, 1964.

Hemingway, Ernest. *A Farewell to Arms.* Jonathan Cape, 1929.

Heym, Georg. *Poems,* ed. and trans. Antony Hasler. 2004.

Hibberd, Dominic. *Wilfred Owen: A New Biography.* 2002.

—— and John Onions (eds). *The Winter of the World: Poems of the Great War.* Constable, 2007.

Higonnet, Margaret Randolph, et al. *Behind the Lines: Gender and the Two World Wars.* Yale, 1987.

Howard, Michael. *The First World War: A Very Short Introduction.* 2002.

Hueffer, Ford Madox. *Thus to Revisit: Some Reminiscences.* 1921.

Hughes, Colin. *David Jones: The Man Who Was on the Field. 'In Parenthesis' as Straight Reporting.* David Jones Society, 1979.

Hughes, Glenn. *Imagism and the Imagists: A Study in Modern Poetry.* 1931.

Hulme, T. E. *Speculations.* 1960.

Hurd, Michael. *The Ordeal of Ivor Gurney.* Oxford University Press, 1978.

Hynes, Samuel. *A War Imagined: The First World War and English Culture.* 1990.

Jerrold, Douglas. *The Lie about the War.* Faber, 1930.

Jones, David. *In Parenthesis.* Faber 2nd edn, 1961, with an introduction by T. S. Eliot.

Jones, Nigel. *Rupert Brooke: Life, Death and Myth.* Richard Cohen, 1999.

Jones, Peter (ed.). *Imagist Poetry.* Penguin, 1972.

Kendall, Tim. *Modern English War Poetry.* 2005.

—— *The Oxford Handbook of British and Irish War Poetry*. Oxford University Press, 2007.

Kenner, Hugh. *The Pound Era*. 1975 (Faber edn, 1972).

Keppel, Sonia. *Edwardian Daughter*. Hamish Hamilton, 1958.

Keynes, Geoffrey (ed.). *The Letters of Rupert Brooke*. Faber, 1968.

Klein, Holger. *The First World War in Fiction*. 1976.

Kyle, Galloway (ed.). *Soldier Poets: Songs of the Fighting Men*. Erskine MacDonald, 1916.

—— (ed.). *More Songs by the Fighting Men* (Soldier Poets: Second Series). Erskine MacDonald, 1917.

Larkin, Philip. *Collected Poems*. Faber, 1988.

Leed, Eric. *No Man's Land*. 1979.

Lehmann, John. *The English Poets of the First World War*. 1981.

Lewis, Cecil Day. *Sagittarius Rising*. Peter Davies, 1936.

—— *A Hope for Poetry*. 1944.

Lewis, Percy Wyndham. *Blasting and Bombardiering*. Calder & Boyars, 1967.

Liddiard, Jean. *Isaac Rosenberg: The Half Used Life*. Gollancz, 1975.

—— (ed.). *Isaac Rosenberg: Poetry Out of My Head and Heart: Unpublished Letters and Poem Versions*. Enitharmon, 2007.

Liddle, Peter H. *Voices of War: Front Line and Home Front*. Leo Cooper, 1988.

Lloyd, Bertram. *Poems Written During the Great War 1914–1918: An Anthology*. Bertram Lloyd, 1918.

Longley, Edna. *Poetry in the Wars*. Bloodaxe, 1986.

Lucas, John. *Ivor Gurney*. 2001.

Macaulay, Rose. *Told by an Idiot*. Collins, 1923.

McCarthy, Desmond. *Life and Letters*. 1929.

Manning, Frederic. *Her Privates We*. Chatto, 1929.

Marsh, Edward (ed.). *Georgian Poetry 1911–1912*, Prefatory Note. 1912.

—— *Georgian Poetry 1913–1915*, Prefatory Note. 1915.

—— *Georgian Poetry 1918–1919*, Prefatory Note. 1919.

—— *Georgian Poetry 1920–1922*, Prefatory Note. 1922.

—— *A Number of People: A Book of Reminiscences*. 1939.

Marsland, Elizabeth A. *The Nation's Cause: French, English and German Poetry of the First World War*. 1991.

Marwick, Arthur. *The Deluge*. 1995.

Masefield, John. *Gallipoli*. 1916.

Messenger, Gary S. *British Propaganda and the State in the First World War*. 1992.

Mew, Charlotte. *Selected Poems*. 2008.

Meynell, Viola. *Julian Grenfell*. 1918.

Mitchell, David. *Women on the Warpath: The Story of the Women of the First World War*. Jonathan Cape, 1966.

Monro, Harold. *Some Contemporary Poets*. 1920.

Monroe, Harriet. *Poetry*, 16. Chicago, May 1920.

Montague, C. E. *Disenchantment*. Chatto, 1922.

Mosley, Nicholas. *Julian Grenfell: His Life and the Times of His Death*. Persephone, 1999.

Motion, Andrew (ed.). *First World War Poets*. Faber, 2003.

Murray, Nicholas. *Aldous Huxley: An English Intellectual*. Little, Brown, 2002.

Murry, John Middleton. *Between Two Worlds: An Autobiography*. 1935.

Noakes, Vivien (ed.). *The Poems and Plays of Isaac Rosenberg*. 2004.

O'Prey, Paul (ed.). *In Broken Images: Selected Letters of Robert Graves 1914–1946*. Hutchinson, 1982.

Orwell, George. *The Lion and the Unicorn*, ed. Bernard Crick. Penguin, 1982.

Osborn, E. B. (ed.). *The Muse in Arms*. E. B. Osborn, 1917.

Owen, Harold. *Journey from Obscurity: Wilfred Owen 1893–1918*. 1963.

Owen, Wilfred. *Poems by Wilfred Owen*, ed. Siegfried Sassoon. Chatto, 1921.

—— *Wilfred Owen: War Poems and Others*, ed. Dominic Hibberd. Chatto, 1973.

Pankhurst, E. Sylvia. *The Home Front: A Mirror to Life in England during the World War*. Hutchinson, 1932.

Parfitt, George. *Fiction of the First World War: A Study*. Faber, 1988.

Parker, Peter. *The Old Lie: The Great War and the Public-School Ethos*. Constable, 1987.

Parsons, Ian (ed.). *The Collected Works of Isaac Rosenberg*. 1984.

Pound, Ezra. *Selected Poems*, ed. T. S. Eliot. Faber, 1948.

—— *A Memoir of Gaudier-Brzeska*. New Directions, 1970.

Pryor, Ruth (ed.). *David Jones: Letters to Vernon Watkins*. University of Wales Press, 1976.

Quennell, Peter. *The Sign of the Fish*. 1960.

Quinn, Patrick (ed.). *The Literature of the Great War Reconsidered: Beyond Modern Memory*. 2001.

Randall, Alec W. G. 'Poetry and Patriotism'. *The Egoist*, 1 February 1916.

Reeves, James (ed.). *Georgian Poetry*. Penguin, 1962.

Reilly, Catherine W. (ed.). *Scars upon My Heart: Women's Poetry and Verse of the First World War*. Virago, 1981.

Remarque, Erich Maria. *All Quiet on the Western Front*, trans. Brian Murdoch. Jonathan Cape, 1929.

Richards, Frank. *Old Soldiers Never Die*. Faber, 1933.

Roberts, David. *Minds at War: The Poetry and Experience of the First World War*. Saxon Books, 1996.

Roberts, John Stuart. *Siegfried Sassoon*. Richard Cohen, 1998.

Roberts, Michael. *T. E. Hulme*. Faber, 1938.

Rogers, Timothy (ed.). *Georgian Poetry 1911–1922: The Critical Heritage*. 1977.

Rose, Jonathan. *The Edwardian Temperament: 1895–1919*. Ohio University Press, 1986.

Ross, Robert H. *The Georgian Revolt 1910–1922: Rise and Fall of a Poetic Ideal*. 1965.

Russolo, Luigi. *The Art of Noise: Futurist Manifesto, 1913*. Something Else Press, NY, 1967.

Sassoon, Siegfried. *Memoirs of a Fox-hunting Man*. 1928.

—— *Memoirs of an Infantry Officer*. Faber, 1930.

—— *The Complete Memoirs of George Sherston*. Faber, 1932.

—— *Siegfried's Journey: 1916–1920*. Faber, 1945.

—— *Collected Poems*. Faber, 1961.

Seymour, Miranda. *Robert Graves: Life on the Edge*. Doubleday, 1995.

Seymour-Smith, Martin. *Robert Graves: His Life and Work*. Bloomsbury, 1995.

Shanks, Edward. *Second Essays on Literature*. 1927.

Sherry, Vincent (ed.). *The Cambridge Companion to the Literature of the First World War*. Cambridge, 2005.

Silkin, John. *The Penguin Book of First World War Poetry*. 1979.

Sillars, Stuart. *Art and Survival in First World War Britain*. 1987.

Simon, Myron. *The Georgian Poetic*. 1975.

Sitwell, Osbert. *Great Morning*. 1948.

Smith, Angela K. *Women's Writing of the First World War*. Manchester University Press, 2000.

Sorley, Charles Hamilton. *The Collected Poems of Charles Hamilton Sorley*, ed. Jean Moorcroft Wilson. Cecil Woolf, 1985.

—— *The Collected Letters of Charles Hamilton Sorley*, ed. Jean Moorcroft Wilson. 1990.

Sorley, William Ritchie. *The Letters of Charles Sorley: With a Chapter of Biography*. 1919.

Spender, Stephen. *The Making of a Poem*. 1955.

Stallworthy, Jon. *Wilfred Owen: A Biography*. Oxford, 1974.

—— *Poets of the First World War*. 1979.

—— *British Poets of the First World War*. 1988.

—— (ed.). *The War Poems of Wilfred Owen*. Chatto, 1994.

—— *Anthem for Doomed Youth: Twelve Soldier Poets of the First World War*. Constable, 2002.

Stead, C. K. *The New Poetic: Yeats to Eliot*. 1964.

Strachan, Hew. *The Outbreak of the First World War*. 2004.

Street, Sean. *The Dymock Poets*. Seren, 1994.

Swinnerton, Frank. *Background With Chorus: A Footnote to Changes in English Literary Fashion between 1901 and 1917*. 1956.

Thomas, Edward. *The Letters of Edward Thomas to Jesse Berridge*. 1983.

—— *Letters to America 1914–1917*. 1989.

—— *Edward Thomas: The Annotated Collected Poems*, ed. Edna Longley. Carcanet, 2008.

—— *The Annotated Collected Poems*, ed. Edna Longley. Bloodaxe, 2008.

Thomas, R. G. *Edward Thomas: A Portrait*. 1985.

Thomas, R. George (ed.). *Letters from Edward Thomas to Gordon Bottomley*. 1968.

Thornton, R. K. R., and George Walter. *Ivor Gurney: Towards a Bibliography*. University of Birmingham Press, 1996.

Tuchman, Barbara. *August 1914*. Constable, 1962.

Vansittart, Peter. *Voices from the Great War*. Jonathan Cape, 1981.

Walter, George (ed.). *The Penguin Book of First World War Poetry* (formerly *In Flanders Fields*). Penguin, 2006.

Watson, Janet S. K. *Fighting Different Wars: Experience, Memory, and the First World War in Britain*. 2004.

Watson, William. *Pencraft: A Plea for the Older Ways*. 1916.

Webb, Barry. *Edmund Blunden: A Biography*. 1990.

West, Arthur Graeme. *Diary of a Dead Officer*. Allen & Unwin, 1919.

Wilson, Jean Moorcroft. *Isaac Rosenberg Poet and Painter*. Cecil Woolf, 1975.

—— *Siegfried Sassoon: The Making of a War Poet, A Biography (1886–1918)*. Duckworth, 1998.

—— *Isaac Rosenberg: The Making of a Great War Poet: A New Life*. Weidenfeld & Nicolson, 2008.

Winter, Jay. *The Great War and the British People*. 1985.

Wohl, Robert. *The Generation of 1914*. 1980.

Woolf, Virginia. *The Captain's Death Bed and Other Essays*. 1950.

Acknowledgements

In writing this book I have been indebted to the excellent biographies that have appeared in recent years, greatly enhancing our knowledge and understanding of this remarkable constellation of poets. I have been helped particularly by the researches of Nigel Jones on Rupert Brooke; Nicholas Mosley on Julian Grenfell; Max Egremont, John Stuart Roberts, and Jean Moorcroft Wilson on Siegfried Sassoon; John Bell, Dominic Hibberd, and Jon Stallworthy on Wilfred Owen; Miranda Seymour and Martin Seymour-Smith on Robert Graves; Joseph Cohen, Jean Moorcroft Wilson, Jean Liddiard, and Vivien Noakes on Isaac Rosenberg; Michael Hurd on Ivor Gurney; William Cooke and Edna Longley on Edward Thomas; Barry Webb on Edmund Blunden; Keith Aldritt on David Jones; and Robert Ferguson on T. E. Hulme.

I am grateful to the Imperial War Museum for allowing me to consult the notebooks and letters of Siegfried Sassoon and to the Sassoon Estate for permission to quote from these and from the poet's poems. I am similarly grateful to the other owners of copyright for permissions where appropriate.

I should also like to acknowledge all those who offered advice and encouragement and insight, including my friends Tim Kendall, Professor of English at Exeter University, whose War Poetry blog is essential reading for anyone interested in the British poets of the Great War, Anthony Rudolf, and many others.

Finally, I should like to thank my wife, Susan Murray, for reading each chapter in draft and sharing trips to the military cemeteries of northern France, including a defiant visit to the grave of Isaac Rosenberg at Bailleul Road which the tourist office at Arras declared to be an impossibility *à pied*.

Index